*Key Issues*

# MILL AND RELIGION
Contemporary Responses to *Three Essays on Religion*

To D. O. Thomas
Scholarly philosopher, wise man, good friend

*Key Issues*

# MILL AND RELIGION

## Contemporary Responses to *Three Essays on Religion*

Edited and Introduced by
### ALAN P. F. SELL
ABERYSTWYTH AND LAMPETER UNIVERSITY
SCHOOL OF THEOLOGY

Series Editor
### ANDREW PYLE
University of Bristol

THOEMMES PRESS

© Thoemmes Press 1997

Published in 1997 by
Thoemmes Press
11 Great George Street
Bristol BS1 5RR, England

US office: Distribution and Marketing
22883 Quicksilver Drive
Dulles, Virginia 20166, USA

ISBN
Paper : 1 85506 542 8
Cloth : 1 85506 541 X

Mill and Religion
Key Issues No. 17

British Library Cataloguing-in-Publication Data
A catalogue record of this title is available
from the British Library

All rights reserved. No part of this publication may be reproduced, stored in a retrieval system, or transmitted in any way or by any means, electronic, mechanical, photocopying, recording or otherwise, without the written permission of the publisher.

Printed in Great Britain by Antony Rowe Ltd., Chippenham

## Contents

| | |
|---|---|
| *Introduction* | ix |
| *Select Bibliography* | l |
| *Acknowledgements* | lii |
| Alan P. F. Sell | |

1. [From] 'J. S. Mill's Essays on Religion' (1874) in *Criticisms on Contemporary Thought and Thinkers selected from the Spectator* (1894) pp. 193–203
Richard Holt Hutton    1

2. 'John Stuart Mill and Christianity' in *Baptist Quarterly* (Philadelphia) vol. 8 (1874), pp. 348–62
Cephas Bennett Crane    8

3. [From] *Job's Comforters: Scientific Sympathy* (1874), pp. 18–21, 24–32
Joseph Parker    19

4. [From] *The Jesus Christ of John Stuart Mill* (1875), pp. 3, 9, 15–16, 52–3, 64, 88
Antichrist    24

5. [From] *An Examination of Mr. Mill's Three Essays on Religion* (1875), pp. 3–6, 30–31, 38–42
William Josiah Irons    28

6. 'Mr. John Stuart Mill's Legacies' in *Evangelical Magazine and Missionary Chronicle*, vol. 6 ns (1874), pp. 715–18
James Baldwin Brown    37

7. [Review of] *Three Essays on Religion*
 in *Inquirer*, 28 November 1874, pp. 774–5
 Henry Shaen Solly    43

8. [From] *Science, Theism and Revelation, considered in relation to Mr. Mill's Essays on Nature, Religion, and Theism* (1875), pp. 74–9
 John T. Seccombe    50

9. [Review of] *Three Essays on Religion*
 in *British and Foreign Evangelical Review* vol. 24 (1875), pp. 172–6
 Anonymous    54

10. [Review of] *Three Essays on Religion*
 in *British Quarterly Review*, vol. 61 (1875), pp. 271–4
 Anonymous    60

11. 'John Stuart Mill as a Religious Philosopher'
 in *Dickinson's Theological Quarterly*, October 1875, pp. 492–507
 Noah Porter    65

12. [Review of] *Three Essays on Religion*
 in *Dublin Review*, vol. 24 (1875), p. 223
 Anonymous    82

13. [From review of] *Three Essays on Religion*
 in *Edinburgh Review*, vol. 141 (1875), pp. 8–31
 [Henry Reeve]    84

14. [Review of] *Three Essays on Religion*
 in *Leisure Hour*, vol. 24 (1875), pp. 117–19
 Anonymous    103

15. [From] 'Religious Opinions of J. Stuart Mill'
 in *Lutheran Quarterly*, vol. 5 (1875), pp. 279–80
 James Allen Brown    110

16. [From review of] *Three Essays on Religion*
 in *North American Review*, vol. 120 (1875)

pp. 465–9
James Elliott Cabot     111

17. [From] 'Theistic Reactions in Modern Speculation'
in *Presbyterian Quarterly and Princeton Review*
vol. 4 ns (1875), pp. 339–47
John William Mears     116

18. [From review of] *Three Essays on Religion*
in *Theological Review*, vol. 12 (1875)
pp. 127–45, 249–72
Charles Barnes Upton     124

19. [From review of] *Three Essays on Religion*
in *Westminster and Foreign Quarterly Review*, vol. 47 ns (1875), pp. 21–8
[Wathen Mark Wilks Call]     164

20. [From] *Leaving Us an Example: Is it Living – and Why?* (1876), pp. 7–8, 11–13, 229–36
Anonymous     173

21. [From] *Is Theism Immoral? An Examination of Mr. J. S. Mill's Arguments against Mansel's View of Religion* (1877), pp. 1–3, 22–3, 54–6
Anonymous     178

22. [From] 'Theism and Christianity'
in *Universalist Quarterly and General Review*
vol. 14 ns (1877), pp. 302–308
George Hill     186

23. 'John Stuart Mill and the Destruction of Theism'
in *Princeton Review*, vol. 54 ns (1878)
pp. 409–48
Daniel Seelye Gregory     192

24. [From] *The Hopes of the Human Race, Hereafter and Here: Essays on the Life after Death* (1880)
pp. 6, 20–22, 24–5, 35–8, 40, 44–5, 53
Frances Power Cobbe     198

25. [From] *John Stuart Mill. A Criticism: with Personal Recollections* (1882), pp. 133–40
    Alexander Bain                                                205

26. [From] *Movements of Religious Thought in Britain during the Nineteenth Century* (1885), pp. 234–46
    John Tulloch                                                  210

27. *What was Christ? A Reply to John Stuart Mill* (1887)
    George William Foote                                          219

28. [From] *Life of John Stuart Mill* (1889) pp. 165–73
    William Leonard Courtney                                      235

29. [From] 'John Stuart Mill and Christianity, II' in *Theological Monthly*, vol. 6 (1891) pp. 109–21
    James Orr                                                     241

30. [From] *John Stuart Mill. A Study of his Philosophy* (1895), pp. 267–74
    Charles Douglas                                               253

31. [From] *The English Utilitarans* (1900), vol. 3 pp. 444–52
    Leslie Stephen                                                257

32. [From] *The Philosophy of Religion in England and America* (1901), pp. 377–81
    Alfred Caldecott                                              264

# INTRODUCTION

## John Stuart Mill

John Stuart Mill was born on 20 May 1806 at Pentonville, London, the eldest son of the utilitarian philosopher, James Mill (1773–1836). He was educated by his father, a disaffected erstwhile ordinand, who ensured that although John's reading was wide, religion played no part – positively or negatively – in the formation of his son. A thirteen-month sojourn in France (1820–21) was followed by a period as tutor to his sisters, and student for the Bar. Forsaking the latter, Mill secured clerical work under his father at India House. He became active in journalism, contributing articles on a wide range of subjects to the periodicals of the day. In 1830 he met Mrs Harriet Taylor, finally marrying her after the death of her husband, in 1851.

Mill's first major philosophical work, *A System of Logic* appeared in 1843. While his indebtedness to Comte's positivism is clear, he insists that he had independently reached his conclusions on induction. There followed *On Liberty* (1859), *Representative Government* (1861), and *Utilitarianism* (1863). In addition, Mill conducted an extensive correspondence with many notables of the day, and in 1865 he was elected to Parliament where, with certain qualifications, he was a loyal supporter of Gladstone. On losing his seat in 1868, he returned to literary projects.

Consistently with the Benthamite utilitarianism in which he had been reared, which attempted to marry theory and practice, Mill was a social reformer as well as a philosopher. But it is with his ideas that we are here principally concerned. He stimulated the naturalistic thought of the age not only in Britain, but also in Europe and America; he upheld the value and prerogatives of the individual; he sought a just and humane society; and he imbibed the confidence of Turgot and

x  Introduction

Condorcet that the potential for the improvement of humanity's lot is unlimited. As John Morley wrote, 'his career, beside all else, was a protest of the simplest and loftiest kind against some of the most degrading features of our society'.[1] Mill died at Avignon on 8 May 1873.

## Mill and Religion

As far as religion – and especially Christianity – is concerned, Mill's attitude broadened significantly (however inconsistently) with the passage of the years. While he remained a sceptic – to him an intermediary position between belief on the one hand and agnosticism on the other – he became a more reluctant one as he grew older, and especially after the death of his wife in 1858. It is possible that Harriet's death did more than anything else to stimulate the imagination that, though by no means demonstrable, post-mortem reunion might not be an absolute impossibility.

Mill's course to this conclusion may briefly be charted. In his *Autobiography* (1873) he informs us that his father, who became appalled by the problem of reconciling the idea of a good and loving God with the world's suffering on the one hand, and by predestinarian Calvinism on the other, insulated him from religious teaching and practice, and also from hostile critiques of Christianity. Hence Mill became 'one of the very few examples, in this country, of one who has, not thrown off religious belief, but never had it'.[2] This did not,

---

[1] John Morley, *Critical Miscellanies* (London: Macmillan, 1898), vol. 3, p. 45. For Mill see *Dictionary of National Biography* (hereinafter, *DNB*), and works listed below and in the appended Bibliography. See also, Michael Laine, *A Bibliography of Works of John Stuart Mill* (University of Toronto Press, 1982).

[2] John Stuart Mill, *Autobiography* (London: Longmans, 1873), p. 43. Some of Mill's critics construed matters differently. For example, A. M. Fairbairn declares that Mill 'showed how little he understood either himself or his day or the Christian religion when he spoke of having been brought up outside it or in independence of it. That was impossible in his age and place....' See *Studies in Religion and Theology* (New York: Macmillan, 1910), p. 612. For Fairbairn (1838–1912), Congregational minister and first principal of Mansfield College, Oxford, see *DNB*; W. B. Selbie, *The Life of Andrew Martin Fairbairn* (London: Hodder and Stoughton, 1914); Alan P. F. Sell, *Dissenting Thought and the Life of the Churches. Studies*

however, prevent his commenting upon religion. In 1823 he sent five letters to the *Morning Chronicle*, of which three were published.³ In the first he advocated religious liberty over against a Church perceived as despotic; in the second he denied that morality required the sanction of Christianity; and in the third he argued that if Christianity were true, it would prevail over falsehood, and hence persecution was not necessary to its preservation. To some of these themes he returned in his paper on 'Civilisation' (1836).

Meanwhile in 1821 Mill had espoused Bentham's utilitarianism. This gave him a philosophical perspective, and an incentive to do what he could for the amelioration of society.⁴ However, by 1826 he found himself in a spiritual crisis of such proportions as to make Morley marvel that after such an analytical upbringing in which the affections had been stifled, Mill did not land in 'some of the extreme forms of transcendentalism'.⁵ Mill came to see that utilitarianism had given him only an 'outward purpose', and he felt overcome by a despair which, he thought, might have been alleviated had he been in love with someone in whom he could confide. He supposed that his desolation could be likened to the sense of conviction of sin felt by Methodist converts.

Mill determined to seek a 'balance among my faculties', and turned to poetry, art and music. He drew particular inspir-

*in an English Tradition* (Lewiston, NY: Edwin Mellen Press, 1990), chap. 19; Elaine Kaye, *Mansfield College Oxford, Its Origin, History and Significance* (London: Oxford University Press, 1996). From across the Atlantic, C. A. Stork reached a similar conclusion: 'that "the modern religion", as [Mill] calls it, had no more influence on his life than he affirms it to have had on his belief no one can credit.' See 'Mr. Mill's Autobiography as a contribution to Christian evidences', *Quarterly Review of the Evangelical Lutheran Church*, no. 4 (1874), p. 259. For Charles Augustus Stork (1838–83), Professor of Didactic Theology at Gettysburg Seminary, see Abdel Ross Wentz, *Gettysburg Lutheran Theological Seminary* (Harrisburg, Pa: The Evangelical Press, 1965), vol. 1, pp. 406–409. The Freethinker, G. W. Foote, declared that James Mill 'is the dominant figure of Mill's "Autobiography", and has about him a more august air than his son ever wore'. See his *Arrows of Free Thought* (London: H. A. Kemp, 1882), p. 98n.

³ On 28 January, and 8 and 12 February.
⁴ *Autobiography*, p. 133.
⁵ J. Morley, *Critical Miscellanies*, p. 57.

ation from the writings of Wordsworth, Coleridge and Goethe. Unpersuaded by Coleridge's philosophical underpinnings of Christianity, he nevertheless valued the poet's insistence that a stable society could be established only upon the basis of permanent, unquestioned foundations. But of what did such foundations consist? Which convictions had sustained society in the past? In order to find answers, Mill turned increasingly to the study of history and psychology, and as he did so, his adherence to Comte's positivism slackened, and he began to accord a greater place to imagination and hope. His concurrent devotion to Harriet Taylor, whose intellectual gifts many observers thought he greatly overestimated, was not the least important factor in kindling fresh insights into the human condition.[6]

We can trace something of Mill's intellectual pilgrimage if we read his *Three Essays on Religion* (1874) in succession. But before turning to these, and against any suggestion that Mill's inclination towards the poets, or his love affair, addled his brain, it must clearly be stated that at no time was Mill anything other than a sceptic (however reluctant), and that no one was less likely than he to succumb to fideism. This latter point is clearly exemplified by his critique of H. L. Mansel's

---

[6] The verdicts of others upon Mill's devotion and indebtedness to Harriet Taylor are delightfully contradictory. Thus C. A. Stork averred, 'Mr. Mill disdained to be a Christian or even a Theist; it looks very much as if instead of going higher, he had only taken a step lower and become an idolater'. See his 'Mr. Mill's Autobiography', *op. cit.*, p. 277. Mill's friend, the philosopher Alexander Bain, declared that Mill 'outraged all reasonable credibility in describing [Harriet's] matchless genius, without being able to supply any corroborating testimony'. See his *John Stuart Mill. A Criticism: with Personal Recollections* (London: Longmans, 1882; repr. Bristol: Thoemmes Press, 1993), p. 171. S. Parkes Cadman was as lofty as he was delicate: 'His introduction to the well-known Mrs. Taylor resulted in an intimacy which separated Mill from his highest self, and caused division in his family as well as anxiety to his friends. Despite continued remonstrance he persisted in this detrimental compact.' See his *Charles Darwin and Other English Thinkers. With Reference to their Religious and Ethical Value* (London: James Clarke, 1911), p. 104. More recently, Eugene August has written, 'Given James Mill's fatal harshness, John understandably resisted belief in an omnipotent deity addressed as "Our Father", but he exhibited imaginative skill in worshipping Harriet as Our lady, a sort of Virgin Mary in the Religion of Humanity'. See his *John Stuart Mill, A Mind at Large* (London: Vision, 1976), p. 245.

view that unavoidable epistemological agnosticism concerning the divine transcendence legitimates faith. Mill takes Mansel as broadly a disciple of Sir William Hamilton, and counters his view that the moral character of a religion's doctrines ought to be taken into account when deciding for or against that religion; for Mansel's stated conviction is that 'we cannot know the divine attributes in such a manner, as can entitle us to reject any statement respecting the Deity on the ground of its being inconsistent with his character'.[7] What Mill deems to be Mansel's semi-concession, namely, that since we are made in God's image our conception of such qualities as justice and goodness bears some resemblance to God's justice and goodness, far from rescuing him from the logical pitfall into which he has fallen, simply 'destroys the whole fabric of his argument'.[8] At the very least these are not the words of a thoroughgoing Romantic; they are the testimony of one whose deep-seated suspicion of intuitionism was quite easily provoked.

Against the background thus sketched we may now turn to the *Three Essays*.

## Three Essays on Religion

The essays are occasional pieces which were posthumously published together by Mill's stepdaughter, Helen Taylor. The first two were written between 1850 and 1858, the third between 1868 and 1870. Miss Taylor opines that they all – and especially the last – might have undergone revision, or even have been withheld from publication, had Mill lived.[9] She finds the essays fundamentally consistent – an opinion

---

[7] J. S. Mill, *An Examination of Sir William Hamilton's Philosophy* (1865), 4th ed. (London: Longmans, 1872), pp. 123–4. Mill here criticizes Mansel's Bampton Lectures of 1858, *The Limits of Religious Thought Examined*. Mansel replied to Mill in his *The Philosophy of the Unconditioned* (London: Alexander Strahan, 1866; repr. Bristol: Thoemmes Press, 1991). For Henry Longueville Mansel (1820–71) see *DNB*.

[8] *ibid.*, p. 133.

[9] H. Taylor, 'Introductory Notice', to J. S. Mill, *Three Essays on Religion*, 4th ed. (London: Longmans, 1885), pp. x–xi. I use this edition throughout.

with which a number of Mill's critics disagreed, as we shall see. If the respondents are to be understood, we must first review the contents of the essays – a task which, at the risk of bowdlerizing, I shall now attempt.[10]

'Nature'
Mill sets out from a lament over the ambiguities of 'nature'. He proceeds to analysis, contending that 'the Nature of a thing means...its entire capacity of exhibiting phenomena'. These phenomena may vary in different circumstances, but are always the same in the same circumstances. The general terms used to describe these phenomena 'are called the *laws* of the thing's nature'. The laws of nature are general propositions based upon direct observation of phenomena, or upon reasoning processes grounded in it.[11]

In another sense, 'nature' seems opposed to art, natural to artificial. However, 'even the volition which designs, the intelligence which contrives, and the muscular force whch executes these [creative] movements, are themselves powers of Nature'. Thus, 'in one sense, [nature] means all the powers existing in either the outer or inner world and everything which takes place by means of those powers. In another sense, it means, not everything which happens, but only what takes place without the agency, or without the voluntary and intentional agency, of man.'[12]

Historically, nature was widely understood as the foundation of morality, though Christianity, with its doctrine that human beings are by nature wicked, has provoked the deistic reaction which proclaims the divinity of nature and 'sets up its fancied dictates as an authoritative rule of action'.[13] Although few today attempt to decide rules of action from the

---

[10] I offer a fairly full account of the contents of the *Three Essays* in order to meet the needs of readers who do not have them conveniently to hand, and also to justify my pruning of the responses below, which would otherwise become repetitious, since many reviewers give a full account, sometimes with extensive quotations, of Mill's work.

[11] *Three Essays on Religion*, p. 5.

[12] *ibid.*, p. 8.

[13] *ibid.*, p. 10.

law of nature, an appeal to what nature enjoins still suffices to persuade people of the propriety of acting in a recommended way. Do ethics require a third sense of 'nature', namely, that which ought to be? No, because those who appeal to the law of nature do not mean that we ought to do what we ought to do. Rather, their appeal is to an external criterion of right action.

'Law' is likewise an ambiguous term, standing now for observed regularities in nature, now for the laws of the land, or of nations, or moral laws. Montesquieu is among those who have confused these senses – as if obedience to the physical laws of the universe were obligatory in the same sense and manner as obedience to moral laws.

In the first sense of 'nature' we see that to act in accordance with nature is the intelligent thing to do; but right action must mean more than this. Does it relate to the sense in which 'nature', distinguished from 'art', refers only to what takes place without human intervention? No, for 'while human action cannot help conforming to Nature in the one meaning of the term, the very aim and object of action is to alter and improve Nature in the other meaning'.[14] But to amend the created order is to imply its imperfection. Indeed, the idea that the order of nature was instituted by a just and benevolent God cannot be sustained in view of the fact that justice and benevolence call upon limited human beings to amend it. The truth is that 'nearly all the things which men are hanged or imprisoned for doing to one another, are nature's every day performances'.[15] If it be said that such occurrences are 'for wise and good ends', the retort is that even if this were so, it would not make it right for us to use nature as a model in ethical behaviour: 'either it is right that we should kill because nature kills; torture because nature tortures; ruin and devastate because nature does the like; or we ought not to consider at all what nature does, but what it is good to do.'[16]

If all things were in the hands of Providence, then all human

---

[14] ibid., p. 19.

[15] ibid., p. 28. The passage from which this sentence is drawn is Mill's most celebrated invective.

[16] ibid., p. 31.

attempts to modify the course of events – even by curing toothache or putting up an umbrella in the rain – would be impious acts; but this is not the case. We need not deny that good may come out of evil, or evil from well-intentioned acts; but normally good yields good and evil, evil. Even so, writers on natural theology have been slow to realize that 'if the maker of the world can all that he will, he wills misery, and there is no escape from the conclusion.... Not even on the most distorted and contracted theory of good which ever was framed by religious or philosophical fanaticism, can the government of Nature be made to resemble the work of a being at once good and omnipotent.'[17] Further, anyone who has 'the simplest notions of moral good and evil' cannot 'fail to believe, that if Nature and Man are both works of a Being of perfect goodness, that Being intended Nature as a scheme to be amended, not imitated, by Man'.[18] Despite all the difficulties, some continue to maintain that nature is designed for our moral instruction, though which features of it have this objective has never been established. Hence we are left to the predilections of individuals.

What, then, of the view that the active impulses of human and other animated beings constitute evidence of the creator's will? Surely God does not approve of all that is instinctively done – hence the retreat to the distinction between ourselves as made by God, and as fashioned by ourselves. In fact, 'nearly every respectable attribute of humanity is the result not of instinct, but of a victory over instinct'.[19] Human beings are no more instinctively brave than they are instinctively clean – such behaviours are learned. Similarly, on the social plane, while sympathy is natural, 'sympathetic characters, left uncultivated...are as selfish as others'.[20] Analogous difficulties arise with 'veracity' and 'natural justice', and the upshot is that 'the duty of man is the same in respect to his own nature as in respect to the nature of all other things, namely not to

[17] ibid., pp. 37–8.
[18] ibid., p. 41.
[19] ibid., p. 46.
[20] ibid., p. 49.

follow but to amend it'.[21] This is why 'there is a radical absurdity in all...attempts to discover, in detail, what are the designs of Providence, in order when they are discovered to help Providence in bringing them about'.[22]

'Conformity to nature, has no connection whatever with right and wrong. The idea can never be fitly introduced into ethical discussions at all, except, occasionally and partially, into the question of degrees of culpability.'[23] Any good which accrues to sentient beings from nature as a whole derives from our own attempts at 'bringing that part of [nature] over which we can exercise control, more nearly into conformity with a high standard of justice and goodness'.[24]

'Utility of Religion'
People have traditionally been more interested in the truth of religion than in its utility, but now that the truth of religion is questioned, the fact of its utility is increasingly urged. Although this is shaky ground, the sceptical position is not immune from difficulties, for 'when the only truth ascertainable is that nothing can be known, we do not, by this knowledge, gain any new fact by which to guide ourselves'.[25] It is conceivable that religion may be 'morally useful without being intellectually sustainable' – hence this enquiry.

Religious writers have not hesitated to advance the usefulness of religion, and they have been countered by those who have rehearsed the many disasters perpetrated in its name. But when considering whether or not the benefits of religion can be secured without it, we ought to view religion at its best. The questions are, 'what does religion do for society, and what for the individual?'[26]

Religion is said to have made many social improvements, but the authority, the belief and testimony of others, the

[21] *ibid.*, p. 54.
[22] *ibid.*, p. 55.
[23] *ibid.*, p. 62.
[24] *ibid.*, p. 65.
[25] *ibid.*, p. 73.
[26] *ibid.*, p. 77.

power of education and public opinion, have all been under the sway of religion, and the opinions of the majority have been governed by religion. Indeed, 'those great effects on human conduct, which are commonly ascribed to motives derived directly from religion, have mostly for their proximate cause the influence of human opinion. Religion has been powerful not by its intrinsic force, but because it has wielded that additional and more mighty power.'[27]

The sanctions of religion have little force, since in bad religions divine vengeance may be bought off; in better religions much is made of the divine mercy. Not that there are not depressive individuals for whom the prospect of religious punishment is powerful – indeed, 'what in sectarian phraseology, is called conversion' can ensue.[28] But those who have bravely undergone martyrdom have not been motivated by public opinion, nor yet by thoughts of rewards or punishments, but by 'a divine enthusiasm'.[29]

Even those who hold a more sophisticated view of religion may still regard it as a teacher of morality – which, historically, it has been. But the danger of attributing a supernatural origin to moral maxims is that 'that origin consecrates the whole of them, and protects them from being discussed or critic-ized'.[30] In fact, belief in the supernatural is no longer required on the part of those who wish to know what is right and wrong in social morality.

It is the 'craving for higher things' which causes human nature to require a religion.[31] But this need can be met without our travelling beyond the boundaries of this world. Love of country is strong; may not love of the world develop as ardently? Indeed, 'the essence of religion is the strong and earnest direction of the emotions and desires towards an ideal object, recognized as of the highest excellence, and as rightfully paramount over all selfish objects of desire. This condition is fulfilled by the Religion of Humanity in as

[27] ibid., p. 87.
[28] ibid., p. 93.
[29] ibid., p. 95.
[30] ibid., p. 99.
[31] ibid., p. 104.

eminent a degree, and in as high a sense, as by the supernatural religions even in their best manifestations, and far more so than in any of their others.'[32]

The Religion of Humanity is disinterested; it sets on one side the difficulty of reconciling the evil in the world with a supposedly perfect author and ruler of it; it bypasses such revealed moral difficulties and perversions as that the highest object of worship could make a hell for those predestined to it. No doubt supernatural religons have the advantage over the Religion of Humanity in that they offer the prospect of life after death. But 'if the Religion of Humanity were as sedulously cultivated as the supernatural religions are (and there is no difficulty in conceiving that it might be much more so), all who had received the customary amount of moral cultivation would up to the hour of death live ideally in the life of those who are to follow them.... It seems to me not only possible but probable, that in a higher, and, above all, a happier condition of human life, not annihilation but immortality may be the burdensome idea....'[33]

'Theism'
Despite the historical evidence that belief in gods is more natural to the human mind than belief in one author and ruler of nature, the general line of natural theology, namely that it concerns one God, will be followed here. The monotheistic conception is acquired either from early education, or by those of cultivated intellect. Theism has the general support of modern science insofar as 'every other theory of the government of the universe by supernatural beings, is inconsistent either with the carrying on of that government through a continual series of natural antecedents according to fixed laws, or with the interdependence of each of these series upon all the rest, which are the two most general results of science'.[34]

However, there are varieties of theism. The idea that God governs the world by acts of variable will is inconsistent with

---
[32] ibid., p. 109.
[33] ibid., pp. 119, 122.
[34] ibid, p. 133.

the most general deliverances of science; whereas the idea of a God who governs the world by invariable laws, is consistent with scientific truth. That nature is governed by a sovereign will cannot be disproved; but can it be proved? What is the nature and value of the evidence for the claim?

The a posteriori method of proof is by nature scientific; the a priori method is 'not only unscientific but condemned by science'.[35] Frequently, however, professedly a priori arguments assume a posteriori features, as in the first cause argument; 'for this has in truth a wide basis of experience in the universality of the relation of Cause and Effect among the phenomena of nature; while at the same time, theological philosophers have not been content to let it rest upon this basis, but have affirmed Causation as a truth of reason apprehended intuitively by its own light'.[36]

The following considerations may be brought against the first cause argument: is will an agency which, if not prior to force, is coeternal with it? No; because whatever will can do to create motion out of other forms of force can be done by chemical, electrical and other transforming agents. Hence it cannot be shown that physical nature was produced solely by a will; and insofar as theism rests on the necessity of a first cause, it is not supported by experience.

To those who claim by intuition that nothing can create mind but a greater and more powerful mind, the answer is that the creating mind needs a mind to be the source of its existence, and this is to embark upon an infinite regress. While it is self-evident that nothing can consciously produce mind but mind, we may not assume that there cannot be unconscious production, for this is the point to be proved.

The appeal to the general consent of humanity fails. The opinions of others comprise only second-hand evidence, which is of little weight. Such opinions are redundant if there are external – even if not completely conclusive – evidences to hand. If the claim is made that 'belief in the Deity is universal among barbarous tribes', the counter-claim is that 'the religious belief of savages is not belief in the God of

---

[35] ibid., p. 139.

[36] ibid., pp. 140–41.

Natural Theology'.[37] The latter belief is entertained by cultivated minds, and it turns upon rational arguments or the appearances in nature.

The argument from consciousness, set in motion by Descartes' appeal to his clear and distinct ideas, likewise fails; for it labours under the infirmity 'that one man cannot by proclaiming with ever so much confidence that *he* perceives an object, convince other people that they see it too'.[38]

To Kant, God was not an object of direct consciousness or a conclusion of reason, but a practically (though not a logically) necessary assumption 'imposed by the reality of the Moral Law'.[39] However, the feeling of obligation is known to those who have no positive belief in God, and hence the positing of God is not necessary to morality.

The genuinely scientific argument from marks of design in nature is much more important, though it cannot attain the security of direct induction, but remains at the inferior level of analogy. The most it can yield is probability. It concerns not only resemblances in nature to the works of human intelligence, but the special character of these resemblances. They are purposeful – as in the case of the parts of the eye, which together conduce to sight. In many cases such arguments are slight, but in others they are of considerable strength.

What attributes does nature suggest may appropriately be ascribed to God? Every indication of design in the universe constitutes evidence against the omnipotence of the designer. For 'who would have recourse to means if to attain his end his mere word was sufficient?'[40] The evidences of natural theology imply that the designer worked under limitations. If it be said that although the omnipotent designer did not need to employ contrivances, he nevertheless did so in order 'to leave traces by which man might recognize his creative hand',[41] God is, again, limited, for could not an omnipotent

---

[37] *ibid.*, p. 157.
[38] *ibid.*, p. 162.
[39] *ibid.*, p. 164.
[40] *ibid.*, p. 177.
[41] *ibid.*, pp. 178–9.

being have willed human beings to be aware of his omnipotence?

But if the fundamental principles of religion as deduced from natural religion negate God's omnipotence, it is otherwise with his omniscience. In reckoning with the limitation of God's power we neither contradict nor prove the limitation of his perfect knowledge and absolute wisdom.

If we confine ourselves to the principles of natural religion, the creator is less than almighty. We cannot rationally ascribe the limitation of his power to a devil or other evil agency, but rather to the intractability of the forces of nature, or to the creator's ignorance of the procedures appropriate to the achievement of his purposes. What indications does nature give of God's purposes? Most of nature's activities concern the requirements for the contrivance of phenomena, and serve no moral ends whatsoever. God, it seems, 'does not wish his works to perish as soon as created'.[42] There is thus some justification for concluding on grounds of natural theology that benevolence is an attribute of the creator; 'but to jump from this to the inference that his sole or chief purposes are those of benevolence, and that the single end and aim of Creation was the happiness of his creatures, is not only not justified by any evidence but is a conclusion in opposition to such evidence as we have'.[43]

Does nature afford any indications of the immortality of the soul and a future life? Some such indications are independent of any theory of the creator and his intentions; others depend upon an antecedent belief in God. Science offers no conclusive grounds for deducing, or for denying, the soul's immortality from its own nature. Most people are inclined to believe in immortality because of 'the disagreeableness of giving up existence', and because of 'the general traditions of mankind'.[44] As causes of belief these are powerful considerations, but 'as rational grounds of it they carry no weight at all'.[45]

[42] ibid., p. 190.
[43] ibid., p. 192.
[44] ibid., p. 203.
[45] ibid., p. 204.

What of the arguments for immortality which are grounded in theistic belief? We might suppose that it is not likely that a good God would 'ordain the annihilation of his noblest and richest work',[46] or doom our desire for immortality to disappointment. But, as we have seen, nature affords but faint indications that God probably exists, and even fainter that he is benevolent. Moreover, God will not or cannot grant all that we wish in this life, so why should we suppose that our desire for immortality is in any different case? 'To imagine that a miracle will be wrought at death by the act of God making perfect every one whom it is his will to include among his elect, might be justified by an express revelation duly authenticated, but is utterly opposed to every presumption that can be deduced from the light of Nature.'[47]

Slight though nature's indications of God are, they suffice to give revelation a starting point. The very imperfections of natural theology remove some of the objections to revelation, since the imperfections of nature are not conclusive against the God of limited power to whom nature points.

The evidences of revelation are said to be external (the testimony of the senses or of witnesses) and internal (revelation as self-authenticating). While the latter constitute grounds for rejecting a revelation, they cannot by themselves warrant acceptance of a revelation as divine. A revelation could be proved divine only by appeal to external, supernatural facts. Can this be done? From Hume we learn that testimony alone constitutes evidence of supernatural acts; but testimony may be intentionally or unintentionally false. Certainly the presumption against a miracle (*qua* act of God) is very much stronger than that against a merely new and surprising fact. The problem is that 'divine interposition is not certified by the direct evidence of perception, but is always a matter of inference, and more or less of speculative inference'.[48] Moreover, it is always possible that the alleged miracle may have had physical, but not apparent, causes. The upshot is that 'no extraordinary powers which have ever

---

[46] *ibid.*, p. 208.

[47] *ibid.*, p. 211.

[48] *ibid.*, p. 228.

been alleged to be exercises by any human being over nature, can be evidence of miraculous gifts to any one to whom the existence of a supernatural Being, and his interference in human affairs, is not already a *vera causa*'.[49] Nor should we overlook the fact that at the foundation of Christianity and of every other revealed religion we have 'the uncross-examined testimony of extremely ignorant people, credulous as such usually are...'.[50] Not even the testimony of Christ himself can be appealed to at this point, for he adduced no evidence of his mission except internal conviction, and the best men are always 'the readiest to ascribe any honourable peculiarity in themselves to that higher source, rather than to their own merits'.[51]

The general result is that 'the rational attitude of a thinking mind towards the supernatural, whether in natural or in revealed religion, is that of scepticism as distinguished from belief on the one hand, and from atheism on the other'.[52] Is it, then, irrational to maintain religious hope? Since human life needs the wider range of aspiration which the imagination provides, religious hope, provided that it does not run against the evidence, and that it goes hand in hand with the cultivation of 'severe reason', 'has no necessary tendency to pervert the judgement'.[53] Indeed, the benefit of an immortal hope is 'far from trifling'.[54] While it is possible to idealize our standard of excellence as a person even when the person is conceived as imaginary, our feelings on such matters are greatly strengthened when we have an 'undoubting belief in the real existence of a Being who realizes our own best ideas of perfection'.[55] However, this recourse is not open to those who take a rational view of the nature and amount of evidence for the existence and attributes of the creator. On

[49] *ibid.*, pp. 231–2.
[50] *ibid.*, p. 236.
[51] *ibid.*, p. 241.
[52] *ibid.*, p. 242.
[53] *ibid.*, p. 245.
[54] *ibid.*, p. 249.
[55] *ibid.*, p. 252.

the other hand, they are not encumbered with 'the moral contradictions which beset every form of religion which aims at justifying in a moral point of view the whole government of the world'.[56] This may fortify the Religion of Humanity, or Duty; though it would not be easy, 'even for an unbeliever, to find a better translation of the rule of virtue from the abstract into the concrete, than to endeavour so to live that Christ would approve our life'.[57] Although the Religion of Humanity will be the religion of the future, in the meantime, 'supernatural hopes, in the degree and kind in which what I have called rational scepticism does not refuse to sanction them, may still contribute not a little to give this religion its due ascendancy over the human mind'.[58]

*Respondents and Responses*

The numbering below follows the chronological order of the responses printed in the body of this book. Although a selection only of responses to the turn of the nineteenth century is reproduced below, it is believed that the most important ones, representative of a wide spectrum of philosophical and theological opinion, are included in this volume.

1. Richard Holt Hutton (1826–97), the son and grandson of Unitarian ministers, was educated at Manchester New College, London, under James Martineau and J. J. Tayler. A gold medalist in philosophy, he gained the BA and MA degrees of London University. Trained for the ministry, he

[56] *ibid.*

[57] *ibid.*, p. 255.

[58] *ibid.*, p. 257. An anonymous reviewer concluded that Mill's 'error was in supposing...that Christian belief might undergo, without fatal alteration, a metamorphosis into a vague Religion of Humanity with Man for its God'. See *The Quarterly Review*, no. 135 (1873), p. 201. Among those who practised the Religion of Humanity deriving from Comte were Richard Congreve, Edward Spencer Beesly and Frederic Harrison; hence the jibe that those who attended the Fetter Lane meetings worshipped 'three persons and no God'. See Robert Forman Horton, *An Autobiography* (London: Allen & Unwin, 1917), p. 31. Congreve (1818–99) and Harrison (1831–1923) are in *DNB*; for Beesly (1831–1915), sometime editor of *The Positivist Review*, see *Who Was Who*, vol. 1 (1897–1915).

received no pastoral call, but became Principal of Unitarian Hall, and revisionist (that is, in the line of Martineau rather than that of Priestley and Belsham) editor of *The Inquirer*, until a breakdown in health caused him to relinquish both posts in 1853. He went to Barbados for his health, but his wife died there of yellow fever. On returning to England he undertook several literary projects, and became Professor of Mathematics at Bedford College (1856–65). By now he had forsaken Unitarianism for the Church of England, and was influenced towards incarnational theology by F. W. Robertson and F. D. Maurice. In 1861 he became joint proprietor of *The Spectator*. His numerous writings include a memoir of J. H. Newman, and an edition of the works of Walter Bagehot, with whom he had earlier edited *The National Review*.[59]

Hutton regrets Mill's confusion of 'the moral evil involved in the rash actions of ignorant and finite beings' with 'the same when proceeding from utterly different motives in an omniscient Being'. Further, while granting that we cannot comprehend omnipotence in its absolute sense, he contends that Mill has 'signally failed in his attempt to prove that if God were both perfect morally and also omnipotent, the state of the world could not be what it is'.

2. The son of the Reverend Wheeler Ingalls Crane and his wife Almena Riddell, Cephas Bennett Crane (1833–1917), Baptist minister, was born at Marion, Wayne County, New York. He was a graduate of Rochester University and Theological Seminary. After pastorates in Hartford, Connecticut (1860–78), Boston (1878–84) and Concord, New Hampshire (1885–96), he was acting pastor at Woburn, Massachusetts for six years, also serving as minister-at-large. A trustee of Rochester Theological Seminary, and of the Newton, Massachusetts Theological Institution, he held numerous other ecclesiastical and public appointments. He favoured interdenominational cooperation and travelled widely. A great reader, he was said to be 'philosophical yet wholly unpedantic'.[60]

---

[59] For Hutton see *DNB*; Alan Ruston, *The Inquirer. A History and Other Reflections* (London: Inquirer Publishing Co., 1992).

[60] For Crane see William Carthcart, *The Baptist Encyclopaedia* (Philadelphia:

From internal evidence it is clear that Crane wrote his speech before the publication of Mill's *Three Essays*. It is equally clear that Mill could never have satisfied him. He argues that Mill has enormous influence, and must be answered on religion, lest, by default, many conclude that no answer is possible: 'Your barber will appeal to him while he holds your nose between his finger and thumb.' Where Christianity enjoins humility, Mill exalts humanity. He knows nothing of sin, or of the need for repentance; and by considering neither Christianity's texts nor its best representatives, Mill proceeds in an unscientific manner. Not surprisingly, he cannot see that 'given the facts of man's moral being and man's sin, together with a redemption unmistakenly accomplishing, the problem of evil seems always possible of a solution which will not involve a denial of the wisdom and goodness of God'; and he pays no heed to the best current apologetic.

3. Joseph Parker (1830–1902), the son of a Northumberland stonemason who became one of the most celebrated London ministers in the heyday of Nonconformity, was born at Hexham. Arriving in London, he was drilled in homiletics over a period of nine months by John Campbell (1794–1867) of Whitefield's Tabernacle, Moorfields, and also attended lectures at University College, London. In 1852 he was appointed as Campbell's assistant. He then served Congregational churches at Banbury (1853–8), Cavendish Chapel, Manchester (1858–69), and Poultry Chapel, London (1869–1901), which congregation removed to the newly-erected City Temple in 1874. A lively preacher, who regarded the reporting of sermons in the press as literary piracy, Parker was capable of reactions ranging from the blunt to the tender. He is one around whose head anecdotes have gathered.[61] He

---

Louis H. Everts, 1881); *The National Cyclopaedia of American Biography* vol. 16 (New York: James T. White, 1937); *Who Was Who in America*, vol. 1 (1897–1942).

[61] For example, having received a letter informing him that the writer proposed to visit the City Temple in order to subject the sermon to philosophical analysis, Parker, having announced this fact to the congregation, paused and then declared, 'I may add that my trepidation is somewhat mitigated by the fact that the gentleman spells philosophical with an "f"'.

pressed for free, compulsory and secular education, and was twice Chairman of the Congregational Union of England and Wales (1884, 1901). Among his many publications is *John Stuart Mill on Liberty: A Critique* (1865).[62]

In *Job's Comforters: Scientific Sympathy*, Parker is in teasing-cum-allegorical mood. His texts (which here are triggers rather than materials for detailed exposition) are Jeremiah 2:28, Judges 10:14 and Hosea 8:5. Job is presented as a follower of Christ upon whom numerous troubles descend. His three 'comforters' appear. Huxley tells him 'his disturbance is entirely molecular', Tyndall tells him that while his children have indeed gone to dust, they will 'contribute somewhat to the nourishment of animals and plants, and in this way... be of great use in the chemic economy of nature'.[63] Mill wonders why Job's children should live for ever. Far better to 'Reform the sanitary arrangements of the country, etc. etc.', so that people may have better lives now. The three chastise Job for the manner in which he faces the evils which have befallen him, and the extract below begins with 'Mill's' testimony on the matter.

4. On the title-page of *The Jesus Christ of John Stuart Mill* is found the text, 'he is Antichrist that denieth the Father and the Son, and confesses not that Jesus Christ is come in the flesh' – I John 2:22; 4:2-3; II John 7. Finding that these words describe his own position, the pseudonymous author takes the name 'Antichrist'. For good measure he altogether denies the existence of God and of an afterlife. He cannot understand why Mill should deem the idea of God a moral obliquity and

Quoted by Alexander Gammie, *Preachers I Have Heard* (London: Pickering and Inglis, n.d.), p. 39.

[62] For Parker see *DNB*; *The Congregational Year Book* (London: Congregational Union of England and Wales, 1903), p. 208 (b)-(e); *A Preacher's Life, An Autobiography and an Album* (London: Hodder and Stoughton, 1899); Albert Dawson, *Joseph Parker, D.D., His Life and Ministry* (London: S. W. Partridge, 1901); William Adamson, *The Life of the Rev. Joseph Parker* (Glasgow: Inglis, Ker, 1902).

[63] In addition to Mill, the 'comforters' are the agnostic (and coiner of the term) Thomas Henry Huxley (1825–95) and John Tyndall (1820–93), the Irish scientist who sought to apply scientific method to all aspects of life. For both see *DNB*; Andrew Pyle (ed.), *Agnosticism. Contemporary Responses to Spencer and Huxley* (Bristol: Thoemmes Press, 1995).

an intellectual contradiction and then proceed to designate Christ an ideal pattern. The Gospels are fabrications, Christ's precepts are a mockery, and his character leaves much to be desired.

5. William Josiah Irons (1812–83), son of the Independent minister Joseph Irons (1785–1852), was educated at Oxford and, having become an Anglican, he served at St Mary, Newington Butts, Surrey (1835–7), removing to Barkway, Hertfordshire (1838), Brompton, Middlesex (1840), Wadingham, Lincolnshire (1870), and St Mary Woolnoth with St Mary Woolchurch-Haw, London (1872). In 1840 he was made an honorary prebendary of St Paul's Cathedral, and in 1870 he delivered his Bampton Lectures, *Christianity as Taught by St. Paul*. He upheld church establishment, and advocated free and compulsory education.[64]

Mill's *Three Essays* have disappointed the author's friends and foes alike. Mill is quite confused. He speaks of a governor of the universe while denying will to the governor; he supposes that invariable law accounts for the created order, whereas Tyndall, Morley, and Huxley deny this; in defiance of his own principles, he takes an abstract idea – whether 'nature' or 'force' – for an individual being; and his utilization of the argument from design is unsuccessful. Accordingly, 'the baffled logic of Natural Theism can do nothing without Revelation. Revelation stands first.' Mill's volume is 'distressing, and to a logician even humiliating'. He finds no religion in 'nature', yet advocates a 'Religion of Humanity' – as if oblivious to the fact that he has already claimed that humanity is part of nature. The value of Mill's book is to make it clear that there can be no argument without an a priori. Believers can say, 'we know', only on the ground of revelation.

6. James Baldwin Brown, the younger (1820–84), was destined for the law, but after being one of the first recipients of a degree from London University, and having kept his terms at the Inner Temple, he proceeded to Highbury College to train for the Congregational ministry. He served at Derby

---

[64] For Irons see *DNB*.

(1843–6), and Claylands Chapel, Clapham Road, London (1846–70). In 1870 he and his congregation removed to the larger Brixton Road chapel, where he remained until his death. He shocked more theologically conservative Congregationalists by arguing for the annihilaton, rather than the eternal punishment, of the impenitent wicked. In 1878, while Brown was Chairman of the Congregational Union of England and Wales, a theological conference at Leicester resolved to reaffirm traditional doctrinal views over against Brown and his 'advanced' colleagues. A prolific writer, he was well known as a preacher, and as a champion of causes designed to promote justice for workers and Dissenters; and he stood by T. T. Lynch, a fellow minister, whose hymns published in *The Rivulet* (1855) were said by opponents to be theologically unsound and pantheistic. His critique of Mill is the more telling as coming from one on the liberal wing of his denomination.[65]

In Baldwin Brown's opinion, Mill's *Three Essays* are even sadder than his *Autobiography*. Feeling internally the need of 'some such enlargement and quickening as spiritual belief and aspiration ring to man', he found 'no certain ground on which to rest a conviction'. His reputation as a philosopher has, accordingly, suffered, though perhaps as a person he has come closer to the great mass of humanity, multitudes of whom have regarded him as 'a cold, hard, incarnate thinking-machine'. Time and again Mill breaks the bounds of 'his dark and sad philosophy'. The necessarian pleads for liberty, the sceptic praises the character of Christ. Mill has in fact demonstrated the poverty of a religionless life.

7. Henry Shaen Solly (1848–1925), son of the Unitarian minister Henry Solly, graduated from London University and trained for the ministry as Manchester New College, under James Martineau and James Drummond. Following a year of study in Berlin, and the award of his London MA, he held pastorates at Padiham, Lancashire (1873–8), Beaufort Street Domestic Mission, Liverpool (1878–81), Southampton (1881–7), Bridport (1887–1906), and Poole (1906–11). He

---

[65] For Baldwin Brown see *DNB*; Elizabeth Baldwin Brown, *In Memoriam James Baldwin Brown* (London: James Clarke, 1884).

translated Ewald's *Antiquities*, and his own major work was a *Life* of Henry Morley, his father-in-law. His great loves were geology and archaeology, and he belonged to a number of learned societies. In his last service he delivered 'a vigorous extempore sermon on the *Alcestis* of Euripides'.[66]

To Solly the publication of the *Three Essays* is 'another warning to the orthodox world to set its house in order, and to the sensational philosophy to look to its most fundamental principles, but to our own modern liberal theology it bears a message of the most inspiring encouragement'. Mill was made a sceptic by 'the obsolete and false phases of religion which we have abandoned', and kept one by 'the false [empiricist] philosophy which we have relinquished'. Thus he 'misses the real characteristic of his theme, and will not allow religion to consist essentially in that which helps us rise above the dictates of a self-regarding prudence'. Again, while the ideals of Mill's Religion of Humanity shine by their own light, it may be doubted how far they will be practised unless people draw strength from religion. It is regrettable that Mill rules out an internal authority (conscience/the voice of God) which consecrates the 'received maxims of morality'. If people heeded Mill's criticisms of theism they would learn the need of 'another faculty for the vision of spiritual things'.

8. John T. Seccombe, MD, MRCS, FRAS, was born in 1834, and was surgeon to the Lynn district of the Great Northern Railway. He published *Science, Theism, and Revelation, considered in relation to Mr. Mill's Essays on Nature, Religion, & Theism* in 1875.[67]

After detailed scrutiny of Mill's *Three Essays*, Seccombe concludes that a line of Christian apologetic may be drawn from Mill if the Gospel revelation of God's atoning love in Christ is brought to bear upon the difficulties (they are not objections) posed to Christianity to which Mill has so capably pointed.

9. To the anonymous reviewer in *The British and Foreign*

---

[66] For Solly see *The Inquirer*, 4 April 1925, p. 213.

[67] For Seccombe see J. F. Kirk, *A Supplement to Allibone's Critical Dictionary of English Literature* (Philadelphia: J. B. Lippincott, 1891).

*Evangelical Review* Mill's essay on 'Nature' is 'the best statement in modern times of Manichaeanism, untinged by Christianity', in which Mill makes no attempt to meet Butler's view of the supremacy of conscience. 'The utility of religion' is deficient as omitting immutability and the sense of the divine; and 'Theism' reveals Mill's prejudice that while we are required to judge human beings fairly, it is permissible to find God deficient by our own limited standards! Mill's lack of a sense of sin is regretted, as is his omission of the moral argument, which the reviewer feels is the strongest argument for the existence of God.

10. In delightful prose, the anonymous contributor to the *British Quarterly Review* contemplates the alarm of disbelievers at the lever, in the form of intimations of transcendence, which Mill's *Three Essays* have given to those they regard as ignorant and prejudiced Christians. Humanity's objective, says Mill, must be to thwart nature; he has no eye for God's plan in nature. It is agreed that 'the whole creation groans', but this prompts the quest of 'other and deeper revelations of the Supreme will'. Lacking the necessary insight, Mill's reflections upon immortality and theism cannot be other than restricted, and this makes his elevation of Christ the more poignant.

11. Noah Porter (1811–92) was born in Farmington, Connecticut where, for sixty years, his father was the Congregational minister. As an undergraduate at Yale he thrived on Coleridge. Following two years as Rector of Hopkins Grammar School, New Haven, Porter entered Yale Divinity School under Nathaniel W. Taylor, whose daughter he married in 1836. In the same year he became minister at New Milford, Connecticut, subsequently serving at the Second Congregational Church, Springfield, Massachusetts (1843–6). In the latter year he became Clark Professor of Moral Philosophy and Metaphysics at Yale College, succeeding to the Presidency in 1871. An indifferent teacher and a less than competent administrator, his attitudes in education and philosophy alike were conservative. His major work was *The Human Intellect* (1868). He opposed positivism, mater-

ialism and Unitarianism, and objected to a colleague's introducing Herbert Spencer's *Study of Sociology* as a text book for students. On the other hand, he was on cordial terms with the Unitarian Theodore Parker.[68]

Porter claims that although Mill has been eclipsed by Spencer, his religious philosophy is 'to say the least, a metaphysical curiosity'. The essay on 'Nature' is feeble, and its conclusions repulsive. Mill's understanding of nature is unduly restrictive, since he excludes both all reference to what nature is intended for, and any detailed analysis of human nature – traditionally so prominent in ethical discussion. Not surprisingly, therefore, Mill cannot explain whence came our concept of duty or sense of obligation. His conclusions, those of a 'narrow and splenetic dogmatist', could only be expected from one whose system combines associational psychology, empirical metaphysics, prudential ethics and necessitarian fatalism. The second essay reaches the lame and impotent conclusion that since human beings have outgrown the need of a supernatural religion, annihilation is their most likely end. Oddly, in 'Theism' Mill concludes that although outgrown, religion may yet serve as a source of ideals – a tribute to his human sensitivity if not to his philosophical consistency.

12. The curt and anonymous reviewer in *The Dublin Review* finds the *Three Essays* weak. By their idealizing of Christ, which runs counter to Mill's philosophical principles, they epitomize the height from which, as a thinker, he has fallen. They also show him to be a better man than many of 'his brother irreligionists'.

13. Henry Reeve (1813–95), a doctor's son from Norwich, completed his education in Geneva, and became acquainted with many British and European writers and men of affairs. He contributed to periodicals in Germany and Britain and, for fifty years from 1837, worked for the privy council. Concurrently, he was on the staff of *The Times* (1840–55) and editor of *The Edinburgh Review* (1855–95). The confidant of statesmen, highly regarded for his counsel, he

---

[68] For Porter see *DAB*.

received honours from England, France and Portugal.

Reeve challenges Mill's definition of nature as 'the sum of phenomena, together with the causes that produce them', on the ground that this assumes that nature includes its causes – but this is what must be proved. Mill's best reason for worshipping the gods is their capacity to inflict evil; his view of humanity is as gloomy as that of which he accuses most Christian denominations. Indeed, 'it is this strange absence of the sense of beauty, order, and rational powers which seems to us to be the characteristic of Mr. Mill's system'. Where Mill concludes from the presence of evil in the world that God is either not good or not omnipotent, the reviewer says that it is more consistent to suppose that Mill's faculties and philosophy are limited, than that God is. Again, 'the conscience of mankind' rejects Mill's view that the creator is either evil's author or slave. Where Mill declares that the balance of probability is in favour of creation by intelligence, the reviewer insists that creation is 'absolutely inconceivable without it'. Mill errs in annihilating the sovereignty of God in favour of his limited God; and in annihilating the sanction of the law by denying the system of retributive justice. Having done this he, like others, grants that religion is useful as a stimulus to humanity's nobler aspirations – thereby revealing the perversity of their systems. A 'dream of imagination, a thrill of emotion' is no substitute for the truth of the objects to which religious belief is directed.

14. The anonymous reviewer in *The Leisure Hour* accepts Mill's *Three Essays* as decisive evidence that 'by wisdom the world cannot find out God'. We know God first in his word, and then we see him in his works. Pure and undiluted theism has never existed, and can never exist. It either assumes shape in an historical religion, or it ends in pantheism or Manichaeism. For his part, Mill passed from 'the ice-house of materialism' to 'the hot-house of mysticism'. He is thus derided by his erstwhile Benthamite philosophical coadjutors, while Christians have the truth confirmed that human beings are made for God and eternity, and that the highest good alone will permanently satisfy.

15. James Allen Brown (1821–82), the son of Quaker parents, learned Greek as he followed the plough, and eventually enrolled at Gettysburg College in 1841. Here he was baptized, and became a member of the Presbyterian Church. On graduation he transferred to the Lutheran Church, and studied theology while teaching in private schools. He served at Luther Chapel, Baltimore (1845–8), and St Matthew's, Reading, Pennsylvania (1848–59). In 1859 he became Professor of Theology and Ancient Languages, and in 1860 President of Newberry College, South Carolina. A staunch unionist, he returned to York, Pennsylvania, as the Civil War was about to break out. He served as an army chaplain for one year, and as a hospital chaplain for two, before being called to the Chair of Didactic Theology at Gettysburg Seminary in 1864. His appointment caused a breach, with high confessional Lutherans withdrawing to found another seminary. He became ill in 1879, and resigned in 1881. He removed to Lancaster, Pennsylvania, where he died. A doughty opponent of Universalism, and an advocate of temperance, he was co-founder, and for nine years editor, of *The Lutheran Quarterly*.[69]

Regretting that Mill chose to refrain from publishing his religious views until after his death, and finding it unpleasant 'to carry on controversy over the grave', Brown quotes passages from the *Three Essays*, the mere presentation of which will, he thinks, serve to refute their author.

16. James Elliott Cabot was born in Boston in 1851 and educated at Harvard University. He wrote a two-volume *Memoir* of Emerson (1887).[70]

In stating his question, Mill empties it of all meaning, for 'if Nature is only a general name for our sensations, it is easy to see that it cannot serve as a guide, an ideal, or a rule of conduct'. Mill constantly adverts 'to facts which he cannot overlook, but which do not fit into his framework of thought'.

---

[69] For Brown see Abdel Ross Wentz, *Gettysburg Lutheran Theological Seminary*, vol. 1, pp. 396–400.

[70] For Cabot see S. Austin Allibone, *A Critical Dictionary of English Literature, and British and American Authors, Living and Deceased* (Philadelphia: Childs & Peterson 1859), vol. 1.

Indeed, 'there is something fairly comic in the conception of a probable God, of limited capacities, whom we may perhaps help out in his desperate task of governing the world'. Mill's philosophy really has no room either for God or for the self and will not permit us to go beyond our own sensations.

17. John William Mears (1825–81) was trained at Yale Divinity School and ordained to the Presbyterian ministry in 1852. He served at Camden, New Jersey (1852–3), Elkton, Maryland (1854–7) and Milford, Delaware (1857–60). From 1860 to 1865 he was an editor, and from 1865 to 1870 editor and publisher, of the 'new school' *American Presbyterian*. From 1871 until his death he was Albert Barnes Professor of Intellectual and Moral Philosophy at Hamilton College, Clinton, New York. An advocate of prohibition, he unsuccessfully stood for Congress in 1878, and for Governor of New York in 1879. An idealist devotee of Kant, he published books and papers on a variety of non-philosophical topics.[71]

Mears finds Mill's views in 'Nature' narrow and bigoted, and his treatment of the problem of evil 'crude, puerile and shallow'. This is an atheistic essay. On the other hand, 'Theism' is theistic; the two essays taken together are mutually contradictory. However, Mears is glad that Mill lived long enough to compose 'Theism', for 'it is a contribution, real, though slight, towards undoing the great mischiefs of his earlier writings, and of the general drift of his example during a long, able, and influential career'.

18. Charles Barnes Upton (1831–1920) trained for the Unitarian ministry at Manchester New College under John James Tayler and James Martineau, the latter of whom he assisted and then succeeded as Professor of Philosophy, following a pastorate at Toxteth (1867–75). He retired in 1903, having removed to Oxford with the College (now Harris Manchester College) in 1892. His Hibbert Lectures on *The Bases of Religious Belief* were published in 1894. A substantial section on Martineau's religious philosophy which he contributed to *The Life and Letters of James Martineau*

---

[71] For Mears see *DAB*.

(1902), which he compiled with James Drummond, was subsequently published separately. A strong advocate of religious liberty, a devoted Unitarian, a careful thinker, and an enthusiastic cultivator of fruit trees, Upton was a friend to colleagues and students alike.[72]

To Upton, Mill's *Three Essays* are the last gasp of deism. The last especially witnesses to 'the worth of the man and the worthlessness of his philosophy'. Upton has never held the view of omnipotence which Mill trounces, nor the view of religion whose utility Mill questions. As a necessarian experimentalist, Mill has no right to contrast his ideal of beauty and goodness with the moral character he believes nature displays, for he must, if he is consistent, believe that he owes these ideals to nature alone. Or, if he wishes to sever intuitive truth and moral freedom from the natural in order to criticize nature's blemishes, he must not forbid the appeal of others to the same intuitions in the cause of solving the appearances of evil in creation. Since our faith does not originate in nature (though nature's signs of intelligence and benevolence confirm our faith), the partial absence of such signs, though able to perplex faith can never wholly destroy it.

The essay on 'The utility of religion' is marred by Mill's understanding of religion as other-worldliness shored up by a revealed system of rewards and punishment, and guaranteed by miracles. 'Theism', however, with its rejection of the evidential value of miracles and its kinder attitude towards religious hope, has Mill sounding at times like a liberal Christian of the kind approved by Upton – a change attributed by Upton to the death of Mill's wife. But still Mill's 'theory of the human mind closes for him that avenue of internal evidence' on which Christians depend. Hence only the teleological argument can save him from scepticism. Sadly, both dogmatic science and dogmatic religion have connived to produce 'extreme dulness of spiritual apprehension' in many. From this point of view Mill's upbringing and that of many restless Christians raised on orthodox confessionalism mirror one another. But for the 'shackles of

---

[72] For Upton see *The Inquirer*, 27 November 1920, p. 596 and 30 June 1923, pp. 419–20.

early intellectual habit' Mill could have been a Christian apologist himself.

19. Wathen Mark Wilks Call (1817–90) was educated at St John's College, Cambridge. A man of letters, he served as deacon and priest in the Church of England from 1843 to 1856, during which period he translated the hymns of Prudentius. His views having become positivist, he resigned from the Church on conscientious grounds, and continued to write both poetry and prose.

Call finds that Mill really recognizes only constructive, not creative, power, and leaves us with but a probable, limited God. Clearly, Mill has not saved natural theology. He has attempted the impossible task of demonstrating the existence of God from finite considerations, and his limited deity is the result. While, to Mill, the possibility of revelation is not absolutely incredible, miracles do not constitute evidence that an alleged revelation is genuine. He recognizes that in a suffering world people need consolation, and claims that this need can be met by the imagination which proposes hypotheses which cannot be known to be false. The reviewer, however, is not persuaded that groundless hopes can withstand scepticism. He opts for identification with the race in action, science and the con-templation of the lovely in nature, life, and the arts; and he predicts that while for the moment 'the despairing champions of orthodoxy' will turn Mill's concessions to their own advantage, (humanistic) truth will out.[73]

20. The author of *Leaving Us an Example* (of which four editions appeared) is greatly impressed by the fact that authors as diverse as Renan and Mill testify to the continuing power of Christ's example, and to his superiority over all other human beings. His case is that these effects derive from their cause, namely, that the Religion of Humanity's ideal is made actual in Christianity. Moreover, the former's lack of a

---

[73] For Call see F. Boase, *Modern English Biography*, 6 vols. (Truro: Netherton & Worth, 1892–1921); J. F. Kirk, *A Supplement*; L. C. Sanders, *Celebrities of the Century* (London: Cassell, 1887); J. M. Wheeler, *A Biographical Dictionary of Freethinkers* (London: Progressive Publishing Co., 1889).

motivating force is supplied in Christianity, for while 'in offering to men His yoke Christ appeals to self-interest; ...the yoke which they are thus led to take upon themselves is the yoke of love...'. At this point the nineteenth-century's gospel of self-interest meets the Gospel of the first century.

21. The author of *Is Theism Immoral?* sets out to correct Mill's misrepresentation of Mansel's view of religion, and to show that Mill's attempted refutation of Mansel's argument against rationalism fails. Mansel's case is unanswerable. He is right to say that we cannot worship God as absolute and infinite, for we do not thus know him; and German rationalists who have made the attempt land in pantheistic contradictions. Contra Mill, we know God only as revealed in nature, the Scriptures and Christ – that is, as he exists relatively to us.

22. In 'Theism and Christianity', George Hill sets out from two poles: on the one hand we have supernaturalist conservative religion, on the other, naturalism in the forms of rationalism, theism and atheism. The truth lies between, in a combination of the natural with the supernatural – as liberal Christians seek to prove. Theism may contain subjectively all the essentials of religion, but it is defective in lacking the spiritual power of 'Christ as a teacher sent from God'. Mill speaks as if nature were a completed system, and does not allow that God may be completing his work, using human beings as his agents. Mill grants that human intelligence is the complement of physical nature, but will not consider the possibility that the religion of Jesus Christ is 'the complement of man's defective nature'. Christianity completes theism, and Hill cannot understand how theists and naturalists can deny Christ when they are so deeply indebted to him for the correct understanding of themselves and the world.

23. Daniel Seelye Gregory (1832–1915) graduated from Princeton Theological Seminary in 1860, and was ordained a Presbyterian minister. He served at Galena, Illinois (1860–63); Troy, New York (1863–6); New Haven, Connecticut (1866–9), and South Salem, New York (1869–71). From 1871 to 1878 he taught at Wooster College,

Ohio, and in the latter year he was elected president of Lake Forest University. He removed to Morgan, Minnesota, as pastor in 1886, and from 1889 he was engaged in literary and editorial work.[74]

In his provocatively-entitled paper, 'John Stuart Mill and the Destruction of Theism', Gregory pulls no punches. Fastening upon the criticism of Mill passed by the logician W. Stanley Jevons, namely, that Mill's mind was 'essentially illogical', Gregory feels that Jevons may overestimate Mill's candour and the goodness of his motives. He argues at some length that it is the mixture of sophistry and confusion with candour and fairness which makes the *Three Essays* so dangerous. He concludes by declaring that far from contentment at the demise of the traditional theistic proofs, modern theologians would do well to present them clearly, and to expose the sophistries of atheism and anti-theism.

24. Frances Power Cobbe (1822–1904), born into a Dublin family connected with two archbishops and five bishops, became a Unitarian. She read widely and published on numerous subjects. She edited the *Works* of Theodore Parker. Influenced by her friend Mary Carpenter, she worked at the Red Lodge reformatory, and in ragged schools in Bristol, and became a benefactress of orphanages. She advocated women's rights and opposed vivisection. She attended the services of James Martineau, and herself occasionally preached in Unitarian chapels. She did much to wean Unitarianism from supernaturalism.[75]

Miss Cobbe takes issue with Mill's presupposition that people in all ages have 'constructed a God by the method of the inductive philosophy'. On the contrary, the idea of God has developed along with the progressive moral development of humanity. Now, however, some seek corroboration of their intuitive faith from nature, while others painfully balance the two revelations. Reliance upon nature's ambiguous theistic testimony can lead us only to Mill's relatively

---

[74] For Gregory see *DAB*.

[75] For F. P. Cobbe see *DNB*; and the *Life of F. P. Cobbe by Herself* (1894), reprinted London: The British Library, 1987.

powerless, though well-intentioned, God. Her hope is in the increasing development of the social sentiment in human beings. Indeed, the very development of this sentiment explains the serious scepticism of the day.

Theodore Parker is an exemplar of hope in God in face of the problem of evil. Certainly God is not as weak, or his contrivances so clumsy, as Mill suggests; for this would mean that God had made a being more clever than himself, for we recognize the deficiencies in his handiwork. The ugliness in a beautiful world, and the evil in a good world demand a solution other than that of a God limited in power. The problem of evil is 'a vast, but not an immense exception, in a rule of Good'. Mill, lacking 'that spiritual organ whereby man obtains direct perception of the living God', could not see this. On this subject, and as compared with 'the tinker of Bedford' (that is, John Bunyan), Mill works as a blind man. Mill's religiously limited upbringing actually confirms the importance of spiritual insight.

Miss Cobbe throws down the gauntlet to the empiricists, who leave out of account the greatest of all the facts of nature – the human being possessed of noble ideas of justice and duty. Yet there is no reason why empirical philosophy may not endorse the knowledge of God derived from spiritual insight; for if it is prepared to allow that God has a moral nature, he must be altogether good.

Faulting Mill for overlooking hope in 'The Utility of Religion' whilst encouraging it – even in an imaginary being – in 'Theism', Miss Cobbe declares that Mill's religious blindness prompts him to overlook the desire for perfect communion with the divine love, which is the ground of faith in immort-ality.

25. Alexander Bain (1818–1903) was Professor of Logic and English Literature in the University of Aberdeen (1860–80), and Lord Rector of the University (1881–7). His Christian orthodoxy being suspected, he was unable to secure a Scottish Chair until he was in his forties, by which time he had published a number of works, among them, *The Senses and the Intellect* (1855), and *The Emotions and the Will* (1859). In addition to *John Stuart Mill. A Criticism: with Personal*

*Recollections* (1882) there followed *Mental and Moral Science* (1868), *Logic, Deductive and Inductive* (1870), and *James Mill. A Biography* (1882). His posthumous *Autobiography* (ed. W. L. Davidson) appeared in 1904. He also published works on English grammar, composition and rhetoric. A pioneer of modern psychology, Bain drew on the tradition flowing down from Hobbes, Locke, and James Mill, rather than upon that of Reid, Stewart and the German idealists. He was an associationist in psychology, a materialist in philosophy, and a utilitarian in ethics. He was the inspiration and the first financial backer of *Mind* (1876).[76]

Bain criticizes Mill from the standpoint of a traditional empiricist with strong psychological interests. He regards Mill's analysis of the causes of evil deficient in that he does not take sufficient account of 'the inadequacy of man's intellectual force to cope with the obscurities of nature', or of human inability 'to counteract known causes of mischief'. As for immortality, Mill does not do justice to the natural difficulties of reproducing human existence after death for an eternal duration, whilst casting doubts on 'the omnipotence of the Power that is to perform the miracle'. While Mill's 'Theism' is compatible with his 'warm human sympathies', it ill accords with his stated philosophy. Moreover, his last, kindlier feelings towards religion in no way detract from his negative opinion of the creed of Christendom.

26. John Tulloch (1823–86) studied at St Andrews University and in Edinburgh and Germany, and was minister of Kettins, Forfarshire (1849–54), before becoming Principal and Primarius Professor of Theology at St Mary's College, St Andrews (1854–86). He served as chief clerk and as moderator of the General Assembly of the Church of Scotland, staunchly opposing disestablishment. He was unperturbed by differences of doctrinal emphasis within the Church, and welcomed the contribution of the new historical and comparative methodologies to biblical and theological studies. In addition to *Movements of Religious Thought in Britain during the Nineteenth Century* (1885), his works

---

[76] For Bain see *DNB*.

include *Rational Theology and Christian Philosophy in England in the Seventeenth Century* (1872) and *Modern Theories in Philosophy and Religion* (1884).[77]

Tulloch contends that all true morality and religion imply in human beings a breach of Mill's law of natural causation, and he finds Mill inconsistent in constructing a theistic theory on the basis of the imperfections of the world which, on his view, should be deemed natural only, and of no moral significance. Even his reduced theism implies a metaphysic – an intelligent will at work behind experience – yet his philosophy prohibits this *ab initio*. Mill has, however, rendered assistance in reshaping our thought on such topics as order, miracle and free will; in making plain the choice between the divinity or materiality of humanity; and in vindicating the moral side of religion.

27. George William Foote, writer and orator, was born in 1850. He was 'converted' to Chrisianity as a youth, but became a Freethinker. Arriving in London in 1868, he joined the Young Men's Secular Association. He taught in the Hall of Science Sunday School, and became secretary of the Republican League. With G. J. Holyoake he founded *The Secularist* in 1876. In 1881 he founded *The Freethinker*. From 1881 to 1883 he was editor of *Progress*. In the latter year, on being sentenced to a year in prison by Judge North for publishing 'A Comic Life of Christ', he said, 'I thank you, my lord; your sentence is worthy of your creed'. The author of numerous works, Foote was President of the London Secular Federation and a vice-president of the National Secular Society.[78]

Mill's concessions to theism are incompatible with his philosophical position, and are to be explained by his devotion to Mrs Taylor, who 'disturbed his judgement in life and perverted it in death'. Mill's gifts were not those of a literary critic or an historian, yet such gifts are essential in those who would probe Christianity's origins. Further, Mill lacked basic

---

[77] For Tulloch see *DNB*; Mrs Oliphant, *A Memoir of the Life of John Tulloch, D.D., LL.D.* (Edinburgh: Blackwood, 1889).

[78] For Foote see J. M. Wheeler, *A Biographical Dictionary of Freethinkers.*

knowledge both of theological and of sceptical literature. He selected from the New Testament the Christ he desired, but there are many others there, and some of them are distasteful. In his *Essay on Liberty* Mill had wisely 'shown the evil of taking Christ, or any other man, as "the ideal representative and guide of humanity"'. But now his guard slips. In any case, Christ is not the hero he has been made out to be. His death was not so much a martyrdom as a sought-after suicide. As for his teaching, it can be replicated in numerous other sources.

28. William Leonard Courtney (1850–1928) was educated at University College, Oxford, and became a Fellow of Merton College (1872–5), and of New College (1876–90). He was Headmaster of his old school, Somersetshire College, Bath (1873–6), and for thirty-eight years he worked on Fleet Street, becoming literary editor of the *Daily Telegraph*, and editor of the *Fortnightly Review*. In addition to his *Life of John Stuart Mill* (1889), he published *Studies in Philosophy* (1882) and *Constructive Ethics* (1886).[79]

Courtney argues that Mill's understanding of nature requires correction now that Darwin and Spencer have shown that human beings, far from having the control over nature which Mill thought they had, are themselves natural, and 'swept along the current of natural forces'. Mill's substitution of what he deems to be the scientifically defensible religion of social duty for traditional religion cannot, being earthbound, accommodate the concept of other worlds than ours – yet this latter belief has hitherto been regarded as part of the essence of religion. Mill's surmise that 'religion may be morally useful without being intellectually sustainable' is the remark not of an iconoclast, but of a person whose intellectual destination has not yet been reached.

29. James Orr (1844–1913) studied under Edward Caird at Glasgow University, proceeding thence to the United Presbyterian Divinity Hall, Edinburgh. Following a period as

---

[79] For Courtney see *DNB*; Janet Courtney, *The Making of an Editor: W. L. Courtney 1850–1928* (London: Macmillan, 1930).

*locum tenens* at Trinity Church, Irvine, he served at East Bank United Presbyterian Church, Hawick. In 1891 he assumed the Chair of Church History at the Divinity Hall, Edinburgh, and, consequent upon the inauguration of the United Free Church, that of Apologetics and Systematic Theology at the Glasgow UF College (1900–1913). His most significant of many publications is *The Christian View of God and the World* (1893). Theologically conservative, Orr advocated church union, was open to biblical criticism, but stoutly opposed those who proposed the excision of the supernatural from Christianity.[80]

Orr faults Mill's logic at a number of points. For example, Mill's understanding of matter and force as self-existent entities is one for which, strictly, his sensationalist philosophy has no room. Again, how can Mill legitimately put himself into a position to pass adverse judgements upon the creator on the ground of physical suffering? How can he be so sure of 'the not uncertain final victory of Good' whilst holding that nature betrays no evidence of moral government? How can we account for the complexities of matter and force apart from the assumption of a presiding mind? As for revelation, either Mill's limited deity must be surrendered, or Christ's revelation be rejected as untrue. Christ is more than a moral teacher; he is a saviour – a fact which Mill misses because of 'his weak hold on the idea of sin'.

30. Charles MacKinnon Douglas (1865–1924), an Edinburgh doctor's son, was educated at the universities of Edinburgh and Freiburg. He became Lecturer in Moral Philosophy at the University of Edinburgh, where he wrote both his introduction to Mill's philosophy and edited *The Ethics of John Stuart Mill* (1897). A local magistrate, he served as MP for N.W. Lanarkshire from 1899 to 1906.[81]

---

[80] For Orr see *DNB*; Alan P. F. Sell, *Defending and Declaring the Faith. Some Scottish Examples 1860–1920* (Exeter: Paternoster Press and Colorado Springs: Helmers & Howard, 1987); Glen G. Scorgie, *A Call for Continuity: The Theological Contribution of James Orr* (Macon, GA: Mercer University Press, 1988).

[81] For Douglas see Andrew Pyle's Introduction to the reprint of C. Douglas, *John Stuart Mill. A Study of his Philosophy* (Bristol: Thoemmes Press, 1994).

Douglas finds in Mill an 'essentially religious conception of the moral life of man'. However, this 'can hardly be reconciled with the individualistic Deism which is expressed in Mill's natural theology'. His own view is that 'the inclusion of man in nature is fatal to that perverse cleavage of reality which makes the world independent of God'. Because Mill's topic is human life, 'the bonds of Deism cannot wholly restrain him from the attempt to interpret the world in terms of self-conscious reason'.

31. Leslie Stephen (1832–1904), philosopher and man of letters, was the first editor of the *Dictionary of National Biography*. After suffering indifferent health, and a number of false starts in education, he read mathematics at Cambridge. He was appointed Goodbehere Fellow at Trinity Hall and, his health having markedly improved, he became an athlete, mountaineer and rowing coach of some note. Raised in an orthodox Anglican home (his mother's father was the evangelical rector of Clapham, John Venn), he was himself ordained. However, in 1862, having read the arguments of Mill, Comte and Kant, he rejected the historical evidences of Christianity, and in 1870 renounced his orders. Meanwhile in 1864 he had removed to London, where he took up literary work, especially with the reviews of the day. There followed his *History of English Thought in the Eighteenth Century* (2 vols., 1876), and *The English Utilitarians* (3 vols., 1900).[82]

It is said that when Mill's *Three Essays* appeared, Stephen 'paced his study in angry surprise', his wife not very helpfully remarking, 'I always told you John Mill was orthodox'.[83] Stephen's verdict is that Mill's 'desire for a religious and even supernatural belief is a proof of dissatisfaction with his own position. He felt here, as elsewhere, that something was wanting in his philosophy.'

32. Alfred Caldecott (1850–1936), an ordained Anglican, was educated at Edinburgh and Cambridge Universities. He

---

[82] For Stephen see *DNB*.

[83] See S. Parkes Cadman, *Charles Darwin and Other English Thinkers*, pp. 130–31.

*Introduction* xlvii

served as Fellow and Dean of St John's College, Cambridge (1889–95); Principal of Codrington College, Barbados (1884–6); Professor of Logic and Mental Philosophy at King's College, London (1892–1917); Prebendary of St Paul's Cathedral (1915–35); Rector of Great Oakley, Harwich (1917–25). In addition to *The Philosophy of Religion in England and America* (1901), he published *Selections from the Philosophy of Theism* (with H. R. Mackintosh) (1904), and *English Colonialism and Empire* (1890).[84]

Caldecott notes a number of inconsistencies in the *Three Essays*, and adjudicates thus: on the one hand Mill finally permits a partial removal of the case for theism from the 'closed court of logical estimation of evidence', and, against atheism and agnosticism, sees evidence for a creative mind. On the other hand, the creative power is limited, matter and force are habitually given precedence over mind, and, where imagination and feeling are concerned, Mill is unfortunately content with 'a world-view in which humanity is the highest object of regard, the highest goal of effort'.

*Concluding Reflections*

Taken together, the responses to Mill's *Three Essays* show that even if some writers felt that Mill's views were unsatisfactory – either because they were inconsistent with, or indicated a betrayal of, his philosophical position; or because his arguments were riddled with logical inconsistencies; or because he did not take the force of Christianity as a religion of salvation from sin; or because he played down the mental and spiritual aspects of humanity (whilst relying upon them to judge what should have been, for him, self-sufficient nature); or because he had failed to realize that Christianity was entirely fraudulent – they were united in thinking that Mill's religious writings called for a response.

As we have seen, responses flowed from both sides of the Atlantic; from the theologically conservative Baptist, Crane;

---

[84] For Caldecott see *Who Was Who 1929–1940*.

Lutheran, Brown; and Presbyterians, Mears, Gregory and Orr; from the liberal Congregationalist, Baldwin Brown, the conservative Congregationalist, Porter, and the multifaceted Congregationalist, Parker; from the Unitarians Solly, Hill, Miss Cobbe, and Upton; from Tulloch, the 'Broad Church' Presbyterian; from the professional philosophers, Bain, Courtney, Douglas and Caldecott; from the 'professional' secularist, Foote, and the (eventual) agnostic, Stephen; from the thoughtful medical Englishman, Seccombe, and the American writer James E. Cabot; and from a number of anonymous authors and reviewers, some Christian, some humanist. In style the responses range from Parker's whimsicality, via Upton's sobriety, to 'Antichrist's' idiosyncracy.

That Mill managed to cause a fluttering in so many and varied dovecotes is not the least testimony to his perceived importance. Nor did the flow of responses dry up following the twenty-five years with which we have been concerned. Reference is made to Mill's religious views in all of the books in the Bibliography to follow, though some twentieth-century commentators on Mill have not found it necessary to treat this aspect of his thought.[85]

The overriding impression left by Mill's humanist respondents is that in the *Three Essays* he, by a sad lapse, allowed sentiment to encroach upon philosophical principles which he has previously so staunchly defended. Some wished he had been faithful to his empiricism, others that he had yielded to philosophical idealism. The general verdict (expressed by some more theologically than by others) of his confessionally disparate Christian respondents may be articulated by the Unitarian Henry Ireson. Of any new positivist religion, 'so far as it is not a matter of mere words and sentiment, as it evidently was to some extent with Mr Mill, it may be regarded as an attempt to bind under the yoke of phenomenal law, and for mundane ends, the most unmanageable of human feelings, the feeling of religion, the powerful protest of universal

---

[85] For example, the terms 'God', 'theism', 'religion', 'natural theology', 'hope', and 'immortality' are absent from the index to John Skorupski's substantial study, *John Stuart Mill* (London: Routledge, 1991).

experience against the earth-bound limitations of the experience-philosophy, – making a tram-road for the chariot of the sun'.[86]

Alan P. F. Sell
*Aberystwyth and Lampeter*
*University School of Theology, 1997*

---

[86] Henry Ireson, 'The Religious Views of John Stuart Mill', *Unitarian Review and Religious Magazine*, vol. 1, no. 2 (April 1874), pp. 105–106. For Ireson (1819–92) see *The Inquirer*, 3 September 1892, pp. 573–4; *ibid.*, 10 September 1892, pp. 591–2. Considering the reiteration of the adjective 'sad' by Christian respondents to the *Three Essays*, Wilfrid Ward's assertion that the religious press was jubliant, the utilitarians dismayed, is an exaggeration. See W. Ward, 'John Stuart Mill', *Quarterly Review* (1910), p. 289.

# SELECT BIBLIOGRAPHY

*The following works include discussions of Mill on religion, and are not mentioned elsewhere in this volume.*

Britton, Karl, *John Stuart Mill* (Harmondsworth: Penguin, 1953).

Britton, Karl, 'John Stuart Mill on Christianity', in John M. Robson and Michael Laine (eds.), *James and John Stuart Mill. Papers of the Centenary Conference* (University of Toronto Press, 1976), pp. 21–34.

Carr, Robert, 'The Religious Thought of John Stuart Mill: A Study in Reluctant Scepticism', *Journal of the History of Ideas*, no. 21 (1962), pp. 475–95.

Cockshut, A. O. J., *The Unbelievers. English Agnostic Thought 1840–1890* (London: Collins, 1964).

Flew, A. G. N., 'Divine Omnipotence and Human Freedom', in Antony Flew and Alasdair MacIntyre (eds.), *New Essays in Philosophical Theology* (London: SCM Press, 1955), pp. 144–69.

Harley, Clifford, 'Swedenborg and J. S. Mill', *The New-Church Magazine*, no. 41 (September–October 1921), pp. 209–18.

Harris, Robert T., 'Nature: Emerson and Mill', *The Western Humanities Review*, no. 6 (1952), pp. 1–13.

Hick, John, *Evil and the God of Love* (London: Macmillan, 1966).

Krook, Dorothea, *Three Traditions of Moral Thought* (Cambridge University Press, 1959).

McCloskey, H. J., *John Stuart Mill: A Critical Study* (New York: Macmillan, 1971).

Ryan, Alan, *J. S. Mill* (London: Routledge & Kegan Paul, 1974).

Taylor, Richard (ed.), *John Stuart Mill. Theism* (Indianapolis: Bobbs-Merrill, 1957).

Turk, Christopher, *Coleridge and Mill. A Study of Influence* (Aldershot: Avebury, 1988).

Willey, Basil, *Nineteenth Century Studies. Coleridge to Matthew Arnold* (London: Chatto & Windus, 1949).

Woods, Thomas, *Poetry and Philosophy. A Study in the Thought of John Stuart Mill* (London: Hutchinson, 1961).

# ACKNOWLEDGEMENTS

I am most grateful to the following, who have supplied elusive texts and/or biographical material:

The Reverend Joseph Alden Bassett, First Church in Chestnut Hill, Massachusetts; The Reverend William O. Harris, Princeton Theological Seminary Library; Dr Philip Hefner and Karen Scherer, Lutheran School of Theology, Chicago; Mark Herring and Billy Royal, Oklahoma Baptist University Library; The Reverend Andrew Hill, Secretary, Unitarian Historical Society; Professor Michael Laine, Victoria College, University of Toronto; Sara Mummert, Lutheran Theological Seminary, Gettysburg, Pennsylvania; Kenneth J. Ross, The Presbyterian Historical Society, Philadelphia, Pennsylvania; Margaret Sarosi, The Library, Harris Manchester College, Oxford; Howard W. Turner of The New Church Centre, London.

The staff of the following libraries:

The British Library, London; Dr Williams's Library, London; Hugh Owen Library, University of Wales, Aberystwyth; The National Library of Wales, Aberystwyth; The United Theological College, Aberystwyth.

Special thanks are due to Jane Williamson and Kate Docker at Thoemmes Press for their prompt and careful work on this project.

Alan P. F. Sell

# [FROM] J. S. MILL'S ESSAYS ON RELIGION
## Richard Holt Hutton

It is a little hard on Mr. John Stuart Mill[1] that the school which once treated him as an oracle, now turns round on him, because he has in many respects transgressed its very narrow limits, and speaks of him as little better than a crack-brained fanatic. As far as his wordly repute is concerned, he would have done much better to abide in those tents of Kedar in which he was brought up. The wider and wider flights which he indulged in round the centre of his hereditary philosophy, – a philosophy never really deserted, though he circled so far beyond its customary boundaries that his brethren in the craft almost looked upon him as a renegade and an adventurer, – never had the effect of convincing any fresh class of minds that he was of their kith and kin, though these excursions had the effect of exciting suspicion, jealousy, and contempt amongst his colleagues of the empirical school. And the result is that he has to some extent fallen between the two stools. The Millites of fifteen years ago know him no more. The believers in an Ethics that are something more than utility in disguise, and in a Religion which is something beyond a naked induction from the facts of human life, are disposed to claim him rather as an instance of a mind too great for the philosophy on which he was nourished, than as one great enough to throw off the trammels of its origin and grasp at the higher truth beyond. And no doubt this is the natural reward of Mr. Mill's candour, and of that expansion of his intellectual apprehensions which his candour betrayed. His step-daughter tells us, in the preface to these essays, that 'whatever discrepancies may seem to remain after a really careful comparison between different passages' cannot properly be held to be really fundamental, since he himself was intending to publish the first essay, – that on

---

[1] *Nature, the Utility of Religion, and Theism.* By John Stuart Mill. London: Longmans.

## 2  Mill and Religion

'Nature,' – in the year 1873, after he had already completed the last of the three, and that which is most religious in tone, namely, that on 'Theism.' But in truth, by far the most striking discrepancy in view in these essays is not one between anything in the first essay and the third, but one between a passage in the second essay and the third, – *i.e.*, between the essay on the 'Utility of Religion' and that on 'Theism.' In the former of these, Mr. Mill expressly declares that an ideal religion, – *i.e.*, a religion without any personal *object*, which consists solely in the cultivation of a particular class of ideal admirations and hopes in relation to humanity, is not only capable of fulfilling 'every important function of religion, but would fulfil them better than any form whatever of supernaturalism. It is not only entitled to be called a religion, it is a better religion than any of those which are ordinarily called by that title.' It is true that even in the course of the same essay, he makes a great exception to this assertion. He admits that to give up the hope of reunion in another world with those who have gone before us in this, is a loss 'neither to be denied nor extenuated. In many cases, it is beyond the reach of comparison or estimate.' But there Mr. Mill is speaking of a loss to the human heart, more than of one to the religious affections properly so called. In the final essay on 'Theism,' he goes far beyond this, and deals a blow at the relative influence of mere religious idealisms of all kinds, as compared with that of religious supernaturalism properly so called. 'It cannot be questioned,' he says, 'that the undoubting belief of the real existence of a Being who realises our own best ideas of perfection, and of our being in the hands of that Being as the ruler of the universe, gives an increase of power to these feelings [aspirations towards goodness] beyond what they can receive from reference to a merely ideal conception.' That seems to me in direct contradiction of the assertion that the idealisation of human life is not only a religion, but a better religion than any which supernaturalism is capable of affording us. In fact, it is evident that this progress of his mind from religious idealism towards religious realism, no less than its progress from something like pure indifference to Christianity to a genuine enthusiasm for Christ, shows Mr. Mill to have been unconsciously working his way out of the philosophical system in which he was *cast*, and so earning for himself the agreeable reputation of presenting to the world fruit 'sour and cankered with a worm at its wasted core.' For my own part, Mr. Mill's progress from a narrow and barren set of word-bound notions into a true religion of what he himself calls 'hope,' – though it was nothing more, – seems to show that he had a nature far richer than his intellect, and even an intellect capable of discerning in what direction the growth of his life was breaking down the barrier of his preconceived thoughts.

Still, though these essays contain ample evidence of a growing mind, it would be impossible to say that the great subjects treated in them are treated with the fulness and care exhibited in Mr. Mill's earlier works. They are rather outlines than dissertations, outlines which require filling up to produce their full effect on the reader. There are writers, as there are artists, with whom the rough sketch is even more than the finished work, – whose first designs are more fruitful of impression and suggestion than the elaborately executed picture. But Mr. Mill was never one of that class. Execution and elaboration were his forte; he exerted half his influence through the fidelity of his detail, and essays like these, which are mere rough outlines, do not produce the characteristic effect of painstaking exhaustiveness which we find in his *Logic*, or his *Examination of Sir William Hamilton*. Consider, for instance, how exceedingly faint and imperfect is his exposition here of the most remarkable and characteristic idea of this work. That idea I take to be that the existence of pain, and evil, and even of contrivance and design, in the Universe, is in itself ample evidence that the Creator of it, if there be a Creator, is either greatly limited in power, or morally imperfect, or both. This is the idea running through all the essays. To Mr. Mill, the Creator, if there be one, must be the Demiurgus of the Gnostics, hampered by the Omnipotent being of Christian theology....

Mr. Mill has assumed that Omnipotence is a perfectly intelligible conception to finite minds, the absence of which, or else the absence of perfect goodness, it is perfectly possible for us to prove, by merely producing evidence of pain or evil, and reasoning that if God were both perfectly good in the human sense, and could have removed such pain or evil, he must have done so; – therefore, either he is not omnipotent, or he is not perfectly good. But this seems to me to be mere groping in the dark. No doubt, goodness must mean, in an infinite being, the same *quality* which it means in a finite one, or it can mean nothing at all to us. But it does not in the least follow that because it must mean the same quality, it must involve, to an omniscient Creator, the same actions. When we, who never have any but the most strictly conditioned and minute power, come to lay down the laws regulating the exercise of his power by a being of infinite power, we are wholly out of our depth. Is, for instance, Omnipotence, or infinitude of power, better shown by the producton of an infinitude of grades, and scales, and modes of moral being, or by the production of only one, – the perfect mode? Is it more an evidence of Omnipotence to exhibit a world of power and joy growing within the very heart of weakness and suffering, or to limit itself to the creation of beings in whom there are no paradoxes? Are a number of true gaps, – of really dark lines, – in the moral spectrum of existence, greater proofs of power than the discovery that within these dark lines themselves there are a host of previously unsuspected bright lines, the light of which is only the brighter and tenderer by the contrast with the darkness? The truth is, that we no sooner come to try the idea of Omnipotence, than we see how utterly impossible it is for such a creature as man to say what is, and what is not, consistent with Omnipotence. Mr. Mill lays it down very peremptorily that an Omnipotent Being who permits the existence of a moral imperfection or a sensitive pain, cannot be a perfect Being. But what if the very idea of the maximum of moral being, positively includes, as it well may, the existence of relations between moral perfection and moral progression (which last implies, of course, moral imperfection)? What if a universe consisting exclusively of perfect beings would be a smaller and poorer moral universe than one consisting both of perfect and of imperfect beings, with a real relation between the two? What if the world of pain, as treated by God, includes secrets of moral glory and beauty, of which a world without pain would be incapable? Mr. Mill would apparently reply, – 'That only means that God is not Omnipotent. If he were, he could do as much without pain, which is in itself an evil, as with it. And if he cannot, he works under conditions which exclude Omnipotence.' ...

But this kind of reasoning seems to me purely verbal. Even Mr. Mill can hardly include in his idea of Omnipotence the power to make a thing both *be* and *not be* at the same time. All we *can* mean by Omnipotence is the power to do anything not self-contradictory. Now the power *both* to create the joy appropriate to the heart of pain, – what Mr. Arnold calls 'the secret of Jesus,' – *and* to keep all pain itself out of existence, is a power to reconcile contradictions. Mr. Mill might have said, perhaps, that in a strict sense, Omnipotence would imply the power to prevent any association between joy and pain, to keep all the highest joys pure and independent of self-abnegation or sorrow of any kind. Possibly. But as we really cannot conceive Omnipotence, and yet can compare together two different degrees of power, is it not the more instructive for us to compare the power which brings a divine joy out of pain and self-surrender, with the power which keeps joy quite aloof from pain; and if we do so, will not the former exercise of power seem much the greater of the two? The truth is, Mr. Mill evidently never gave himself the trouble to compare relative degrees of power, or he would have seen at once that a universe containing absolute perfection in an infinite variety of relations with imperfection is a universe which would at once impress us as one of larger scope and power, than one containing only the former. And this is really all man can do towards judging of Omnipotence. We are utterly unable to conceive the absolute attribute. But we are able to say whether a power that has created, and is always creating, all shades and degrees and varieties of progressive life, as well as perfect life, is greater or less than one which produces and sustains perfection only. It seems to me perfectly obvious that though moral goodness in man and in God must be of the same kind, it is childish to say that *actions* which are wicked in man, in whom they imply one kind of motive, must be evil in God, who sees the whole scope of what he is doing, and in whom they may imply a totally different kind of motive. You might much more reasonably identify capital punishment with murder, than identify, as Mr. Mill does, the infliction of death by the imposition of natural laws, with murder. Yet this confusion between the moral evil involved in the rash actions of ignorant and finite beings, and the same when proceeding from utterly different motives in an omniscient Being, pervades the whole of Mr. Mill's essay on 'Nature.'

Such is a characteristic specimen of the feebleness of thought and execution visible in these Essays. It will be replied, no doubt, that even if Mr. Mill were hazy in conceiving, or rather, in his disinclination to test his own power of conceiving, what is meant by Divine Omnipotence, he was not bound to attempt to apprehend an idea which is purely abstract to man, and one over the positive contents of which, as I have always admitted, man can have no command. If we cannot approximate to the meaning of Omnipotence, what business has such a notion in Religion at all, whether Natural or Revealed? To this I can only reply that the idealising faculty, of which even Mr. Mill thinks so highly as the foundation of a religion which is purely aspiration, blends itself so inevitably with the conviction that there is some *real* Power in communication with man, and one infinitely superior to him in knowledge, goodness, might, and life generally, that it becomes an effort, and an exceedingly unnatural effort, to disentangle the two lines of thought, and maintain that while our ideal faculty leads us to *imagine* One infinite in knowledge, goodness, and power, and our actual experience to *believe in* One infinitely above ourselves in all these qualities, the two modes of thought have no right to coalesce and blend into an actual faith in a God infinite in wisdom, power, and goodness. That such an effort of discrimination is conceivable enough, no one can deny. But I must say I think Mr. Mill has signally failed in his attempt to prove that if God were both perfect morally and also omnipotent, the state of the world could not be what it is. Were the fragment of the universe we see all, his case might be better; for it will be found that his implicit assumption throughout is, that the world of which we are cognisant is, morally speaking, the whole, instead of (probably) an infinitely small part. Now, it is quite beyond us to affirm that infinite goodness and power must at once annihilate moral evil and misery in all portions of the universe, when we know, as a matter of fact, that the highest pinnacles of goodness and power of which we have any personal knowledge are reached in the struggle with moral evil and misery, and that the absolute exclusion of such evil and misery would have involved the absolute exclusion also of the brightest summits of divine love. On the whole, Mr. Mill's chief endeavour, – his attempt to prove that God, if he exists, – which, as I understand him (though his language wavers), Mr. Mill thought more probable than not, – is either a being of considerable, but very limited power, or not a good being, appears to collapse utterly. But Mr. Mill was precluded by his philosophy from taking note at all of the attestation of God's goodness by the human conscience, and on this side also his essays seem to me deplorably defective for the purpose to which he intended them to contribute.

# JOHN STUART MILL AND CHRISTIANITY[1]
## Cephas Bennett Crane

Mr. Taine, on a certain occasion, said to a bright young Englishman: 'You lack philosophy. I mean what the Germans call metaphysics. You have learned men, but you have no thinkers. Your God impedes you. He is the supreme cause, and you dare not reason on causes out of respect for him. He is the most important personage in England. Yet this high rank has the inconvenience of all official positions; it produces a cant, prejudices, intolerance and courtiers.'

'I assure you,' was the reply, 'that there are thinkers amongst us. We have, not to speak of others, John Stuart Mill, a political writer, a logician, a man who has reached a grand conception of the universe, a man who has an individual and complete idea of nature and the mind.'

Our bright young Englishman lauded his hero extravagantly. Whatever John Stuart Mill did, there was one thing which he failed to do; he failed, as we shall soon discover, to 'reach a grand conception of the universe,' to 'gain an individual and complete idea of nature and the mind.'

But he was, undoubtedly, in the judgement of both colloquists, a thinker whom God did not impede. For, in his autobiography, equally interesting and mournful, he has declared himself a man without a religion and without a God.

Christian apologists will act unwisely if they allow this man to go unanswered. He is too great, too confident, too plausible, too fascinating, to remain unchallenged. It will not do to say – here I introduce a new rhetorical figure – that he did not ordinarily use a Damascus blade, well-tempered and elaborately wrought. But it may be successfully shown that, in his negligent and supercilious conflict with Christianity, his sword, though displaying a metallic lustre, had all the fragility of lath.

---

[1] The rhetorical cast of this paper is due to the fact that it was prepared and delivered as an address to the Alumui of the Rochester Theological Seminary at its late Commencement.

Let humble men venture to enter the lists against this doughty knight. He is, from almost every point of view, immeasurably their superior, but it should be remembered that Homer sometimes nods, that Socrates has his superstitions, that Plato has his fancies. Philosophers sometimes blunder, and the blunder may be detected and exposed by very common men.

I assure you that Mr. Mill, because of a premature disparagement and contempt of Christianity, went out against it in armor and with weapons which were not of proof. He thought that he had scattered an ambuscade, when he let off his small artillery as he passed; he did not know that the great guns of an impregnable fortress were not provoked to reply. Christianity is not to be demolished by metaphysicians and logicians, who turn aside with such purpose from their main path. It demands with firm stubborness the honor of at least one direct and vigorous campaign before it will consent to yield. It insists on suffering nothing less than a *glorious* defeat.

Mr. Mill should be answered, for the reason that the impression will obtain that he is as mighty in his infidel polemics as he is in logic and political economy. Men will say one to another, 'The repudiation of Christianity by the foremost mind of England raises a prodigious presumption against Christianity.' And if no answer is returned, they will go about boasting that no answer can be returned. You shall hear the note of triumph from superficial and conceited youths who everywhere abound – youths who know no more of Mr. Mill than that he is acknowledged great; youths who have never read so much as the title pages of his books. Your barber will appeal to him while he holds your nose between his finger and thumb. Your tailor will prattle of him while he takes your measure for a waistcoat. Your college student will pause, in his unsuccessful scanning of Horace, to laud him.

Why is it not wise to show these youths who are flying their little flags and beating their little drums that Mr. Mill, strong in almost everything else, has in infinite weakness ventured an assault upon Christianity?

But before taking up for careful consideration the method of his assault, we may legitimately bestow a little attention upon Mr. Mill himself. Who and what is this man who, sheathing his unbloody sword, is claiming a triumph? Possibly we shall discover that the man himself, apart from his reasonings, affords a sufficient explanation of his religious position and attitude; that between the character of the man and the spirit of Christianity there is a radical dissonance.

It is fashion in many quarters to disparage the intellectual ability and the scientific achievements of Mr. Mill. This is not the part of wisdom. Undoubtedly this man was not a genius, he was not possessed of creative power; he was not an originator; he was not a seer; he did not belong in the same class with Shakspeare and Goethe, with Kant and Descartes. He was not born; he was made. He was the product of culture, and that was not the best. He was his father's son; but he was even more his father's manufacture. James Mill is the explanation of John Stuart Mill.

Nevertheless, only a mind of extraordinary vigor and fertility could endure the remorseless drill to which this man was subjected, retain the form into which it was moulded, multiply applications of principles which it had been taught, advance from its inherited premises to conclusions hitherto unsuspected. The marble was good, else the statue would not have been so firm and so fair.

Nor should the scientific achievements of Mr. Mill be underrated. They are partial and imperfect; but they are real. Many are the fine truths which he has evolved, truths which abler men will turn to account. For *he* certainly did not turn them to the best account; he did not use them well. They were distorted in false processes, pilloried in false conclusions. It is noticeable that keen men, men whose natures have obtained catholic and harmonious development, men like the sagacious President of Yale College, pronounce upon him the verdict of *inconclusiveness*. Inconclusive, because he refused, in obedience to the canons of positive philosophy, to go forward to ultimate results; because in his singular blindness to Christianity, which informs everything of modern civilization, he failed to discern the entire contents of any subject which he handled; because his intellectual machinery lacked power and right inward adjustment. His book on Liberty, which he acknowledged to be in many respects his *chef d'oeuvre*, which, in the reduction of the authority of civil society to the minimum, lays undue emphasis on socialistic notions, can hardly be accepted by men of balanced faculties and accurate thought. In his logic, misled by a false philosophy and a false conception of the nature of the syllogism, he forbids you to affirm, even to seek for evidence, that in distant parts of the stellar regions there is the uniformity in the succession of events, otherwise called the law of causation, which obtains within the narrow limits of your terrestrial observation and experience. And this in the very teeth of spectrum analysis, all of whose suggestions point in exactly the contrary direction; and in the very teeth of the finest astronomical discoveries. He was unwilling to find in creation traces of a *plan*, lest he should be compelled to acknowledge a Creator. Refusing thus to the universe even the consistency of chaos, it cannot be justly said of him that he reached 'a grand conception of the universe,' that he gained 'an individual and complete idea of nature and the mind.' The 'universe' is a conundrum that he gave up; 'nature and the mind' he refused on principle to explore to their depths.

It cannot be denied that Mr. Mill disappointed even those who, at the outset of his career, welcomed him most hopefully. He has not a following. He equally fails as a philosophical and a parliamentary leader. The obituary notices of him, under an ostentatious show of respect and deference, contain a hostile criticism.

I think that his exchange of a servile homage paid to his father for an infatuated devotion paid to the woman who subsequently became his wife, will take its place among the chief curiosities of literature. Undoubtedly a keen psychologist will be able to show that the severe constraint which was imposed upon his earlier life accounts for the pitiable extravagances of his later career. It is probable also that an acute philosophical historian of literature will be able to discern in his writings traces of this remarkable inward revolution.

I know of no man deserving to be called great whom it is so difficult fairly to estimate. A product of culture, rather than of nature; incisive, rather than comprehensive; cold, yet capable of torrid heats; a vassal to persons, yet a depiser of the public; a discoverer, but not an inventor; analytic, but not synthetic; a slave to prejudice, yet inquisitive and innovating; refined, yet often coarse; self-controlled, yet erratic; challenging admiration, yet disappointing admiration; kindling enthusiasm, yet quenching enthusiasm; scientific, yet unscientific; a builder, yet not a founder; a Uhlan, but not a general; a gatherer of material, but not an organizer of material; it is easy to overestimate him, equally easy to under-estimate him.

But I must not occupy myself with generalities. The point to be taken is this: Know Mr. Mill well, know Christianity well; and, whether Mr. Mill be perfect or imperfect, whether Christianity be true or false, it will appear the most natural thing in the world that the religion is rejected by the man.

Christianity enjoins humility, because it professes to reveal a God. Mr. Mill knows no God save the ideal of human imagination which human endeavor may realize; he attributes supremacy to man; he is himself a man; why shall he go down upon his face? Proud toward God – his philosophy warrants this. But does he not contradict his philosophy when he flaunts his contempt of the people? Ought he not to cry: 'A man's a man for a' that?' This is the voice of Christianity: 'He that humbleth himself shall be exalted.' Mr. Mill would echo the sentiment of Emerson: 'Humility is the virtue of the whipped dog.' Christianity requires repentance for sin; Mr. Mill is ignorant of the vocabulary of repentance. Christianity offers a divine Saviour; Mr. Mill does not confess a need of salvation.

Gentlemen, here, on the one hand, is your man, proud, self-righteous, self-sufficient; here, on the other hand, is Christianity, teaching humility, penitence, faith in God. Which is the more admirable, the spirit of the man, or the spirit of the religion? It is natural, it is inevitable, that the man, being what he is, should reject the religion, being what it is. There is natural incompatibility here, and the two must be tried on their merits. This man's rejection of Christianity cannot be claimed to raise so much as a presumption against Christianity. For I, with equal reason, may reply that it raises a presumption against *him*.

But if we advance a step in our comparison of the two, the religion will seem to gain an advantage over the man. I discover that to the conjugal sanctities which are disclosed in the sacred Scriptures, the enlightened moral sense of the world pays the profoundest homage. But I also discover that Mr. Mill did not respect those sanctities. Far be it from me to hint that he was not scrupulously chaste; for, like a distinguished man of our own country, whom many-tongued rumor has cruelly assailed, there was that about him, that indescribable effluence and aroma of character, which rebuts the otherwise probable testimony of the most suspicious circumstances. But, my brother, even you, with all your meekness, would fiercely forbid such an intimacy with your wife as this man maintained with the woman whose husband he disrespectfully praised while living, and contemptuously eulogized when dead, and whom (I mean the woman of course) he afterwards married, and finally apotheosized. Behold here the identity of the requirements of Christianity and of the enlightened moral sense. Mr. Mill flaunted those requirements. Do you wonder that he rejected Christianity? Nay, do you not see that he sanctified Christianity by his rejection of it, and at the same time condemned himself?

Undoubtedly the denial of Christianity may often be accounted for by the character of him who denies it; just as the discovery of universal poltroonery is explained by the fact that the discoverer is himself a poltron. Unbelief thrives, not by what a man *proves*, but by what he *is*.

I may as well say here – for I can think of no place where it may appropriately be said – that what Mr. Mill knowingly rejected was not the genuine Christianity, but that wretched travesty of it, that horrible hyper-Calvinism, that ghastly skeleton, which his grim father had lighted upon in some dismal theological crypt. And while, right royally indignant, he was battering this monstrous chimera with his metaphysical bludgeon, the sweetly reasonable Christianity sent in from afar a certified *alibi*. Nevertheless, such were his avowed principles and manifest personal qualities, that it is certain that the sweetly reasonable Christianity would also have been rejected. . . .

Given the facts of man's moral being and man's sin, together with a redemption unmistakably accomplishing, the problem of evil seems always possible of a solution which will not involve a denial of the wisdom and goodness of God. This old Boethius, fourteen hundred years ago, clearly apprehended and generously acknowledged.

Meanwhile, it is observable – and this is a most significant fact – that as men approach a realization of the divine ideal of human integrity, they are more and more impressed by the mingled justice and mercy of God; and though surrounded by and suffering evil, they cry, 'Bless the Lord, O my soul, and all that is within me bless his holy name.'

In view of what has now been said, it may safely be affirmed that the rejection of Christianity because of the difficulties which it presents, even because of the portentous and awful fact of evil which it does not presume to deny, is wholly unwarrantable. The difficulties are closely connected with circumstances which suggest the method of their resolution – a resolution which will vindicate, rather than disprove, the wisdom and goodness of God.

It remains to be considered that, while the perplexities which beset Christianity, as they beset everything else, half explain themselves by their own manifest constitution and relations, and even throw a dim light on the rectitude of the divine government, Christianity offers in its own behalf positive evidences which no one who claims the scientific spirit can rightly neglect. Not negative evidence against, but positive evidence for, is proof of the highest kind; and the latter infinitely outweighs the former. Positiveness is mightier than negativeness. A single syllable of positive testimony refutes a whole volume of collected and classified difficulties and perplexities on the contrary side. Bishop Butler, in one of his Durham charges, set forth this principle as follows: 'A man may be fully convinced of the truth of a matter, and upon the strongest reasons, and yet not be able to answer all the difficulties which may be raised upon it.' A sound principle, which no one will have the temerity to question.

Now Christianity offers for itself 'the strongest reasons.' It confronts every phase of unbelief with appropriate evidence. It has provided a many volumed apologetic literature, which can justly challenge the admiration of the most gifted souls.

But Mr. Mill, so far as appears, never condescended to read a page of it. One ought not be surprised by this; for it is questionable whether he ever read the original records of Christianity. If he had been a critical, even though an unbelieving student of the Bible, the fact would have been revealed somewhere and somehow in his writings.

Indeed, his principal objection against Christianity is one which you may hear urged any day by ignorant striplings about whose chins the brown beard has not yet began to curl.

Ah, the *coterie* life of this man! How did it shut him out from the great world! Moses and Isaiah, John and Paul, did not cross his narrow firmament. And the supernal light which flushed it, he did not suspect of proceeding from the Sun of Righteousness.

It is difficult to suppress one's indignation against this superb Alcibiades, who treated Christianity with a neglect so horribly unscientific and contemptuous. Indeed, it would appear from the tone of some of his essays, that, like Walter Savage Landor, he was theoretically a pagan.

If the apologists for religion had failed to meet the men of modern science on their own ground, if they had failed to offer them evidence which their own distinctive principles would not forbid them to consider, the superciliousness of Mr. Mill might claim for itself a shadow of excuse. But there has been no such failure. The champions of religion have not been slow to learn that what was the principal and most credible evidence yesterday, is not the principal and most credible evidence to-day. They frankly confess that, for the so-called positive philosopher, miracles, instead of proving Christianity, render Christianity more difficult to be proved; and that the ontological argument, once so convincing, hangs covered with rust in the remotest corner of the arsenal.

They have even modified their definition of Christianity, bringing out conspicuously the three following elements: First, a Christ who gave the religion, and was, in a very profound sense, himself the religion; second, moral precepts for the moral enlightenment of men; third, moral forces for the moral transformation of men. From these three elements of the definition of Christianity they have drawn out three lines of evidence in support of it.

I briefly indicate the first line. The conception of Christ in literature can only be accounted for by his existence in history. Certain Galilean peasants, eighteen centuries ago, introduced him into literature. Is anyone so infatuated as to affirm that they created him? Or shall we say that he was the product either of Jewish, or of Roman, or of Greek thought? But Christ is not a Jew, nor yet a Roman, nor yet a Greek. He is a *man*, at home in every clime, under every sky, in the midst of every civilization; and a man whose mysterious atmosphere is suggestive of the immensity and exaltation of heaven.

He appeared in human literature, not to say human history, when Caesar ruled the world; he is to-day the recognized ideal of humanity. Think what advance has been made, since his first appearance, in philosophy, in morals, in all the sweet and gracious amenities of life. Still he holds his place; the world has not outgrown him; poets and moralists, and all profound thinkers stand in awe and adoration before the original august conception of him. The story of Christ is of itself the demonstration of his historic existence.

The moral teachings of Christianity are offered next in the way of evidence. They are given in a book which is eighteen hundred years old. Since that book was written, Paley and Butler, Wayland and Alexander, Mill and Lecky, have prosecuted their investigations in the splendid field of moral science. They have developed their theories of ethical philosophy, the intuitional and the inductive. But not one moral precept of Christ or of his apostles have they refuted or improved upon. A Unitarian minister, Charles Carroll Everett, in the book entitled 'Christianity and Modern Thought,' boldly affirms that 'the moral teaching of Christ is absolutely true – true as his thought of God.' And Dr. Bellows declares more generally, 'Christ's statements, Christ's character, Christ's words, do not become antiquated.' We are not called upon to explain away, as superstitions of the time, any of the certain words he said, or thoughts he had, or commandments he left. When we get, as we certainly do get in hundreds of cases, at Christ's own words; when we really see the true person and bearing and spirit of Jesus, we behold, we recognize, we know a Being who, transferred to this age, and placed in the centre of the choicest circle of saints and sages whom culture and science and wisdom could collect, would bear just the same exalted relation of superiority to them that he did to the fishermen and publicans and kings and high-priests and noble women and learned rabbi of his own day. We should not hesitate, any more than they did, to call him Master and Lord; to say: 'To whom else shall we go? Thou hast the words of eternal life.'

Francis William Newman has objected to the ethical teachings of Christianity – that they are impracticable. May we not accept the words of Benjamin Jowett as a sufficient answer to the objection? 'Our Saviour taught a lesson absolutely free from all the influences of a surrounding world. He made the last perfect revelation of God to man – a revelation not indeed immediately applicable to the state of society or the world, but in its truth and purity, inexhaustible by the after generations of men; and of the first application of the truth which he taught, as a counsel of perfection, to the actual circumstances of mankind, we have the example in the epistles.'

How shall we account for the incomparable ethical teachings of Christianity? How else than by the admission that Christianity came from God in heaven, the embodiment of eternal truth, and spake as never man spake?

The third positive evidence for Christianity is its manifold possession of moral forces for the transformation of human character.

On the 20th of May, 1806, a boy was born in London. He was educated by his scholarly father into hatred and contempt of Christianity. Before he reached his twelfth year he had learned more from books than most young men have learned when they are graduated from college. He devoted himself to severe intellectual labors, and by his achievements in philosophy he gained an illustrious name.

But he knew no God, consequently his character lacked a divine quality. He knew no Christ, consequently his character lacked a sweet humility. He knew no immortality, consequently his thought and life were stinted. He pleaded for tolerance of opinion, but whosoever contradicted him was banished from his presence. He clamored for free discussion, but his arrows were cruelly barbed. He was the champion of the people, but he counselled superior men to go down to the people in a full consciousness of their superiority. He dethroned Jehovah, but he enthroned in his place a woman. He ended his life, not triumphantly at the gates of the New Jerusalem, but despairingly beside the sepulchre of his best beloved, whose personal being had become extinct.

On a certain unknown day, in a certain unknown year, more than eighteen centuries ago, a boy was born in Tarsus, a city of Cilicia. He, too, was carefully taught and trained; he zealously perfected himself in a religion which was not a religion. He dressed himself in a righteousness which he himself had wrought, and many times in the day appeared before Jehovah for approval. He companied with the elect, and shunned the multitude, whom ignorance had bewildered and sin had brutalized. He was the defender of orthodoxy, and breathed out threatenings and slaughter against those who were innocently delighting themselves with what was unspeakably better than orthodoxy.

Jesus of Nazareth met him, enlightened him, transformed him. His pride, his bigotry, his cruelty, vanished. He became a servant of servants; he named himself the chief of sinners; he claimed the lowest place among the apostles; he risked his life for degraded men whom he never had seen; he took the world on his heart; he believed that the earth would become a new earth; he believed that the human race would live the life of God; by his intercourse with invisible and eternal realities his being was every day enlarged and exalted; when his arms became weak by age, he committed his sacred trust to youths of assured fidelity; when he died, his face was toward the glory about to be revealed.

Look upon the men whom I have contrasted. Then tell me whether or no Christianity is possessed of moral forces for the transformation of human character.

In Paul, in Augustine, in John Bunyan – why shall I lengthen the lustrous catalogue? – we behold the realization of the spiritual and divine morality which Christ enjoined. These individual transformations have brought about the transformation of society; and lo, the Christian civilization which exhibits the glory of the Son of God!

Now I affirm that there is not a single principle of positive philosophy which can justly require of those who maintain it, that they reject as irrelevant the three-fold evidence for Christianity which I have been indicating.

But we have not the slightest reason to believe that John Stuart Mill ever gave a moment's thought to this evidence which is so exactly suited to his ease.

Yet in the twenty-fifth chapter of his logic, entitled, 'Of the Grounds of Disbelief,' he admits the relevancy of precisely this kind of evidence; implying that if Christianity could offer it, it would attain to no inconsiderable success in the demonstration, not only of the truth of its doctrine, but also of the credibility of its miracles. Christianity does offer this evidence, but Mr. Mill refused to consider it.

All that this man did was to stand before Christianity, and say to it impudently: 'Thou art false.' An *ipse dixit*, only an *ipse dixit*.

John Stuart Mill has passed on into the solemn eternities; Christianity remains with us. In vain will you seek on the face of it a single scratch from the sword of lath so weakly and wildly brandished.

# [FROM] JOB'S COMFORTERS: SCIENTIFIC SYMPATHY
## Joseph Parker

... Then answered John Stuart the Millite, with unusual warmth: 'I, too, have been in trouble, but I needed no sackcloth, nor scattered any ashes on my head. I took a philosophic course. I mounted a philosophic steed, and sped away from my trouble. If Job will hear me, he shall know how to keep distress under his feet, and to defy the threatening storm. What time I am afraid I flee to metaphysics, and when conscience threatens to get the upper hand of me I consider the functions and the logical value of the Syllogism. When my father, who would never *allow* me to have any convictions about religion different from his own, melted into the infinite azure of the past, I comforted myself under such melting by testing Berthollet's curious law, that two soluble salts mutually decompose one another whenever the new combinations which result produce an insoluble compound, or one less soluble than the two former; and the comforting effect of the experiments was remarkable, – so much so that in an ecstasy of scientific surprise and delight I almost wished that he had melted sooner, that I might had longer possession of this prize. O that Job would do something of the same kind! He would forget the past in a trice, and be as happy as I am. Let me put you in possession of a secret, if by doing so I can rally the dejected Job. When I die there will be found in my desk the manuscript of my Autobiography, and so sustained was I by philosophic reflection during its composition, that never once in its pages have I mentioned my mother! Nobody could know from my Autobiography that I ever had a mother! That is what I call self-control! Other people talk of their mothers, and their mothers' influence, and their mothers' prayers, and their mothers' example, but I never own the relationship; I keep on the airy highlands of philosophy, and avoid the close and relaxing valleys of sentiment. Once, indeed, I was about to give way to the common folly, but I recovered my self-restraint by showing the fallacious reasoning which has been founded on the law of inertia and the first law of motion, and I never lost my balance again. If Job would take some such course, his grief would be for ever dissipated.'

And to the same effect, Huxley the Moleculite, who had insensibly increased his distance from Job: 'I have often steadied myself under a stunning blow by remembering that protoplasm, simple or nucleated, is the formal basis of all life. This has been a great comfort to me in many distresses. When death has invaded the household of any of my friends, I have always proved to them that all living powers are cognate, and that all living forms are fundamentally of one character, and they have invariably thanked me for my sympathetic and consolatory expressions. One dear old friend of mine, who suddenly lost all his income in a railway crash, would, I believe, have died of a broken heart had I not asked him to compare in his imagination the microscopic fungus – a mere infinitesimal ovoid particle – with the gigantic pine of California, towering to the dimensions of a cathedral spire; and my friend no sooner complied with my request than in a wave of victory, as Tyndall the Sadducee would call it, he was lifted far beyond rolling stocks and permanent ways with their fickle dividends and their treacherous attractions....

Then Job cried aloud, 'Though He slay me, yet will I trust in Him! He hath been with me in six troubles, and in seven He will not cast me off. Shall not the Judge of all the earth do right? Miserable comforters are ye all, though ye are the men, and wisdom will die with you! When you have exhausted your pretty science what have you told me that can touch the agony of my heart or bring back the light of my house? If *your* theory be right why should I suffer all this misery when in a moment I can end all my distress? If this chastening be for no higher good, why should I not interrupt it by the instant destruction of my consciousness? You mock me, but you have no satisfaction for my heart. You throw hard words at me, but you have no balm for my healing. Ye are as a bowing wall and a tottering fence: I will not lean upon you. The Lord is my light and my salvation. I had fainted unless I had believed to see the goodness of the Lord in the land of the living. O Lord, Thou hast brought up my soul from the grave; Thou hast kept me alive that I should not go down to the pit. Thine anger endureth but a moment; weeping may endure for a night, but joy cometh in the morning! I said in my haste, I am cut off from before Thine eyes; nevertheless Thou heardest the voice of my supplications when I cried unto Thee. Lord open the eyes of these men that they may see my defence as Thou seest it!'

And the Lord opened the eyes of the leaders of science, and they saw, and behold the mountain was full of horses and chariots of fire round about Job, and the Lord opened their ears so that they heard voices other than of men, saying: 'The chariots of God are twenty thousand, even thousands of angels: the angels of the Lord encampeth round about them that fear Him, and delivereth them: He shall give His angels charge over thee to keep thee in all thy ways. The Lord of hosts is with thee, the God of Jacob is thy refuge.'

And the heart of Job was lifted up in praise, and through the sob of his woe there came forth alleluias unto the Lord. Yea he magnified his God, and praised Him with many psalms: 'Bless the Lord, O my soul, and all that is within me bless His holy name. He healeth the broken in heart, and bindeth up their wounds; He is the God which fed me all my life long unto this day, the Angel which redeemed me from all evil. I know that my Redeemer liveth, and that my loved ones are standing before Him, glad in His light and beautiful in His holiness. Praise the Lord!'

And it came to pass that Job's three comforters – Huxley the Moleculite, Stuart the Millite, and Tyndall the Sadducee – gathered together their inaugural addresses at the British Association, their lectures at the School of Mines and the Royal Institution, their dissertations upon the ballot and the higher education of women, and returned with them to their several places. And it came to pass as they journeyed that they came near to a beautiful stream, spanned by a suspension bridge, nigh unto which there nestled the thatched cottage of a ranger in the woods.

'That,' said Stuart the Millite, 'seems to be an ideal house though so simple and unpretending. How clean the place is and sweet-looking, and how these tangled flowers on the front brighten it and give it quite a jewelled appearance; and a beautiful peep of the river must be caught from that western window.'

And it came to pass as they drew near to the house that the ranger in the woods leaned himself against an aged tree, and seemed as if he did so in heaviness of heart. And it was even so, for lifting up his eyes and seeing three men bearing many books, he said unto them:

'Be ye learned men who can tell us what to do when we are dizzy and senseless?'

'Perhaps indeed we can help you a little,' said Huxley the Moleculite; 'at any rate we are quite willing to try.'

'Come with me then and see what is in the house. I lost her mother but a twelvemonth since, and now she's slipping away.'

But Huxley the Moleculite and Stuart the Millite and Tyndall the Sadducee shrank from the man, and in remembrance of the sufferer they had left they dared not to speak of the sympathy of science.

'But mayhap you will pray with the child, and not pass by her on the other side. In such books as yours there must be something for broken hearts like mine. It is but a step or two to the girl's bedside. Come!'

'It would be but wasted time, my friend,' said Stuart the Millite, 'for we have no power over the laws of nature.'

'But cannot you speak comfortably to the child? for she says the river is very cold, and, bless her, her feet are very young.'

'You are not so very near the river, my friend,' said Stuart the Millite. Whereupon the man turned away, and answered with a great sob.

And it came to pass as the leaders of science had gotten away to the height of a distant hill that they laid down their books and rested a while. And presently Tyndall the Sadducee opened his mouth and said: 'We have been out of our depth to-day, and perhaps we had no business along this road at all. These books of ours are invaluable in their places, and very likely they are indispensable to the higher education of the world, but there are two men along this road who somehow need something that we have not got to give them. It is no use concealing the fact, or making it look less important than it is. I wish a great poet would arise who can sing these woes to sleep and charm us out of our ill-fortunes.'

And it came to pass that the Lord turned the captivity of Job and made him glad with new joy, yea he crushed for him the finest of the grapes and gave him wine with his own hand, and upon his wheatfields and orchards he sent the benediction of sun and shower until their abundance returned and was multiplied. And Job rebuilt his altar and bowed down before

God with all reverence and love, and sang the praise of the Most High with a loud voice, and made a joyful noise unto the Rock of his Salvation. And in the day of his prosperity, Job sent for the books of Huxley the Moleculite, John Stuart the Millite, and Tyndall the Sadducee and read them all with an attentive eye. Then he rose up and said: 'O wise yet foolish men! your books are full of knowledge and instruction, and mighty men are ye in the fields of learning. But have ye forgotten that there is a spirit in man, and that the inspiration of the Almighty gives him understanding? Know ye the way into the heart when it is in ruins? or can ye lift up those who are pressed down by the hand of God? Keep your learning in its proper place and it will help the progress of the world; but attempt not with it to heal the wounds of the heart. Not to your wisdom but to your simplicity will God reveal Himself: "He hath hidden Himself from the wise and prudent and shown forth His beauty unto babes: even so Father, for so it seemed good in Thy sight."'

And the woodman's little girl? Was the river so very cold when her young feet touched it? We cannot follow far along that drear road, nor see far into that great darkness. But there was no splash in the water; there was a quivering in the arch which spanned it, from which the ranger knew that his child had been taken, not through the river but over the bridge to the mountains of myrrh and the hills of frankincense.

# [FROM] THE JESUS CHRIST OF JOHN STUART MILL
Antichrist

According to our title-page we deny the Father and the Son, and we do not believe that Jesus Christ ever existed. As for the father, we may see from the epistle of John, that many in the time of the apostles, and who were Christians, said that the God of the Old Testament was not the father of Jesus Christ; and this was the idea of the Gnostics.

Nor was the Christ of the gospels the Son of God, the Messiah or Christ they expected. The word never had been incarnate. The Jesus Christ of the gospels never had existed . . .

Mill says of one God, it is a moral obliquity and an intellectual contradiction, and instead would make Christ an ideal pattern. For ourselves, we cannot see a greater moral obliquity and intellectual contradiction than in Christ, and brought more home to us. There is humanity – the God-man; and as the best specimen of humanity, Mill says, we are to follow him, when we think him the worst. We are not of any isms, not knowism, but noism; not Gnosticism, or the knowledge of God, or the mind of his Son, as Paul said, but we do agree with it in the non-existence of Christ and also with the Docetics from saying Christ was an opinion or fancy. We are heretics; that is, we have an opinion of our own, which is the meaning of the word, and which Christians have never allowed to each other, though claiming it for themselves.

We do not believe in the existence of a God, Christ, or future state; but we admire the Bible, and after reading the works of infidels, we think there is as much in Job, Proverbs, Eccles., Ecclus, Esdras, against a God and a future state, Atheism or Pantheism, the nowhere or everywhere, which is the same thing. And we find the same Pantheism or Atheism even in Christ, Paul, and John. Christians say it is all the word of God, and must be all received; but they choose what they like, and we do what we like. . . .

Mr. Mill . . . makes three statements as to Christ in the most solemn manner: that Christ assuredly did not think human nature was bad; that Christ never taught that it was necessary to believe in him or his mission in order to be saved, and that if you did not you would be damned; and Christ never said he was God, or made any pretensions to be God.

There are many other statements in these Essays which in the course of these pages we shall notice, as we think them all equally wrong and unfounded, in opinion and in evidence, – especially that Christ was not an invention; that his morality was the most perfect ever given to mankind; he himself was a pattern for humanity; if not God, one sent from God; a possibility of being either, and affording us the further possibility and prospect of a future state, or living after death.

Now, with regard to the first, Mr. Mill allows that almost all Christians have thought nature and human nature was bad. Certainly *they* are some authority in interpreting the language of Christ. Was Christ, or is the founder of a religion, in no way responsible for the creeds of his followers? Do not they and all the dogmas, in some measure, have their source in his words? Or else this profound genius of Mr. Mill, who had so deep an insight into human nature, was the most foolish and unfortunate of all teachers upon record, making men believe the contrary of his doctrines and intentions, and what was most injurious to their interests. Mr. Mill gives no reason for this or any other of his assertions. We are to take his 'assuredly' for it – 'Verily, verily, I say unto you;' and to this word he treats us more than once; that is his *ipse dixit*, or begging the question. . . .

Christ prefaced the directions he gave to his disciples by saying the harvest was plenteous. We are very soon and very often told how this harvest will be plenteous in hell, and by what means it will be accomplished.

There was never anything more atrocious uttered in the proclamation of a great reformer, and who pretended to be the Saviour of mankind, than in these two chapters of Matt. x. and xi., and the effects of them are considerably heightened in Luke. Matt. x. 15, he says of any city that does not receive them: – 'Verily I say unto you, it shall be more tolerable for the land of Sodom and Gomorrha in the day of judgement than for that city.' And the state of society produced (v. 21): – 'And the brother shall deliver up the brother to death, and the father the child: and the children shall rise up against their parents, and cause them to be put to death.' (x. 34–39): – 'Think not that I am come to send peace on earth: I came not to send peace, but a sword. For I am come to set a man at variance against his father, and the daughter against her mother, and the daughter-in-law against her mother-in-law. And a man's foes shall be they of his own household. He that loveth father or mother more than me is not worthy of me: and he that loveth son or daughter more than *me* is not worthy of *me*. And he that taketh not his cross, and followeth after me, is not worthy of me. He that findeth his life shall lose it: and he that loseth his life for my sake shall find it.'

He repeats here what he had said before, what would happen from his precepts, and in xi. 20–24, when he preaches to the cities, he says the same of them he had said to his disciples.

And throughout x. it is that he will send people to hell as in the sermon on the Mount, if they do not believe in him, contrary to Mill.

It is extraordinary and melancholy to think Mr. Mill should recommend a man as a pattern who made such a sad exhibition of himself, in the sermon on the Mount, but much more in his directions to his disciples, in his own preaching to the cities, and everywhere to the end of his life. Mr. Mill said he would rather go to hell than to the God of Mansel and the Christians in heaven, that is he would rather speak his mind of the immorality of God than flatter him, and say he was good when he was bad, though he should be sent to hell. But much more one would have thought Mill would not have wished to be in heaven with such a man as Christ, or would flatter him on earth, the exact counterpart of his father in heaven. Instead of which Mill holds up Christ as a pattern, in what he says and does, extols him with the greatest servility, and thinks we should aim at his approval, which is as much as to say he would like his company, and agrees with him, and yet, according to everything which Christ said, he would not have liked Mr. Mill, – he wanted babes and children without a particle of sense or understanding, and no wise or prudent men, no scribe among his followers, such as a Mill. . . .

We are astonished how Mr. Mill, the great preacher, if not the founder of the doctrine of utility, could find in the mission of Christ a 'precious gift,' which has not a particle of utility in it, and which, if the hopes were realized from it which Mr.

Mill says are possible, would in the kingdom of heaven upon earth, bring nothing but idleness; and if they were in another world, would in heaven bring on such a condition of ennui or boredom that a man would not wish to endure it for a moment, much less for eternity, and would end his existence immediately rather than have the horror of such everlasting punishment, as Achilles is made to say in the Odyssey. And the only hope for the unhappy subject of such felicity would be that he might escape to hell, and there have exercise and employment for his wits and hands in contending with the flames as a member of a fire brigade in the United States. . . .

The remainder of the history of Christ disproves all the statements of Mr. Mill regarding him, if we refer only to Matthew, or the Synoptics, excluding the 'poor stuff' of John, the opinion of Mr. Mill, the speaking for righteousness, and ultimate appeal of Mr. Matthew Arnold. The precepts, conduct, and character of Christ, raised to such an unprecedented elevation by Mr. Mill, and extolled for unparalleled excellence by Matthew Arnold, Greg, even Morley, and the author of 'Supernatural Religion,' and others, – are not only contrary to all the maxims, terms, and practice in which the moralities and duties of life have usually been conveyed; but the Christ with the attributes assigned to him, and under the circumstances, would argue not a real but an ideal or imaginary being.

The 'Quarterly' and 'Edinburgh' Reviews, Gleig in 'Blackwood,' the Rev. L. Davies in the 'Contemporary' of January, 1875, declare that Mr. Mill, in his essay on 'Theism,' supports supernaturalism and a God; a Christ, a divinely-sent person, therefore a God; and miracles, in making Christ a miracle. All these reviewers, in the same words, say the greatest of miracles was the appearance on earth of such a man, especially the man of Mr. Mill. Such a Christ would be a miracle; therefore, we think it is the greatest proof that, as there are no miracles, there never was such a miracle or man. The miracle is, as Hume said, in those who believe in one. Such a man, therefore, as Christ – never known to any one at the time, no evidence for him and every evidence against him in the nature of things, and in the records related of him, dependent only on the assertions of numerous miraculous, therefore mythical, narratives, mixed with mystical elements and speculations, – could never have existed, and must have been invented.

# [FROM] AN EXAMINATION OF MR. MILL'S THREE ESSAYS ON RELIGION
William Josiah Irons

1. Every one was anxious to know the real opinions of Mr. Mill on the primary subjects of Religious thought.

At the time of the election for Westminster, some ten years since, the charge of Atheism was freely brought against Mr. Mill – some said unjustly – as constituting a serious disqualification for the task of legislator in a country still professedly Christian. It was remembered that a judge in open court had refused evidence offered by a witness who avowed unbelief in God. Deism being thus regarded as the least amount of creed expected in a public man, Mr. Mill, when suspected and questioned, refused to satisfy the inquirer on this point, urging that no one had any right to demand a confession of the religious opinions of another. He said, too – and the evasive saying dazzled a few – that he thought it a duty to vindicate entire liberty of thought as belonging to men in Parliament as well as out of Parliament.

They, then, who had looked for a warm and instant repudiation of the 'charge' against Mr. Mill were certainly disappointed, and took refuge in admiring his courage. It was said, 'If he would admit nothing, he would deny nothing': he simply, 'on principle, would not be cross-examined.' It was found to be useless even for those who yet were importunately asked to elect him as their 'representative,' to urge that they had a right to know his principal opinions, and that that knowledge might touch the principal opinions of some, at least, of the electors; and also that frankness between electors and elected was but fair. No; Mr. Mill maintained his position, and was supported in it by persons of eminence in Church and State, who preferred to allege that there was no *arriere pensee*, and at all events resolutely subscribed to promote his return to Parliament.

2. There can be no doubt, too, that the desire to know Mr.

Mill's views was not mere curiosity. Many hoped for a grand thoughtful book. Then he was regarded even by the popular mind as what, in the language of the day, is called a 'thinker'; a logician, of even terrible exactness. (The vulgar, indeed, commonly suppose a logician to be pre-eminently a thinker, not knowing that his science, as such, is primarily engaged with the technicalities and modes, rather than with subjects, materials, or even grounds, of thought.) The announcement, then, that some 'Essays on RELIGION' had been found among Mr. Mill's papers after his death, was not unwelcome to the world. It was painful to observe, however, the tone which soon began to prevail both with the non-religious and with some of the religious portions of the community; the former anticipating, the latter dreading, the expected 'searching analysis' (p. 4) of all the grounds of Theism.

3. Another source of interest in the subject was doubtless found among those who had observed the Theistic controversy from a higher ground. The more recent, and too evidently feeble, surrender in some quarters of the *a priori* defence of 'first truths,' (and therefore of the Religious first truths), raised among many the anticipation of a great dialectical display – (some sort of attempt perhaps like that of Professor Clifford and others to resolve into simpler elements the axioms and postulates of Euclid): or, again, it was surmised that Mr. Mill could not help dealing with the *a posteriori* as Mr. Herbert Spencer had done, or might possibly be found working very near to Professor Huxley's protoplasm, or to Professor Tyndall's molecules. – The result, however, of the publication of Mr. Mill's book has been the disappointment probably of all classes. They who long persisted in saying that the candidate for Westminster might be a believer in God, have found that they were mistaken. They who were hoping for some new force of argument to support unbelief were not prepared for so halting a champion. They who expected a really scientific manipulation of these solemn subjects may justly have a sense of surprise, if not humiliation. The collapse was unprecedented in literature. The editorial Preface, with natural partiality perhaps, expresses an opinion that these Essays are 'exhaustive.' The editor of the *Fortnightly Review* is scarcely of that opinion. Indeed it should be added, in justice to Mr. Mill's kind panegyrist, that it is acknowledged also, in her Preface,

that the Essays are not a 'connected body of thought.' (*See Preface.*)

4. We find ourselves of course under a kind of necessity, in examining a book on such a subject, to compare it as we go on with principles we ourselves vindicate. It must be remembered, however, that we are not writing a treatise, but examining one which comes from an assumed master on his side of the questions raised. And we shall insist on good reasoning at all events.   The titles of the Three Essays are 'Nature,' 'Utility of Religion,' and 'Theism,' – an arrangement, we would observe, somewhat illogical, leading to a certain overlapping of the subjects, and not providing for the entire discussion. This is an inconvenience to begin with. – Lord Bacon, for example, in the *De Augmentis Scientiarum*, having to deal with the same matter, fitly divides the objects of Philosophy as 'God, Nature, Man,' the three comprehending the universe of thought, yet each being so far distinct ideally as to be capable of treatment *per se*. We feel at every turn, that many confusions, assumptions, and ambiguities, some anticipations which ought to have been proved and apparent concessions which have often virtually to be recalled, might have been spared had Mr. Mill's arrangement been more logical. Unhappily he begins with no precise premisses. Having to treat of 'Religion,' he felt obliged to look to 'Nature,' for he denied the Supernatural. He had Religion as an existing *fact* to deal with; and so also to consider common arguments for God; and the teaching of Christ.

Comparing the book with the writer as known to us by his own Biography, there may indeed be recognized a kind of order in his course of thought. Born and brought up with no Religion, his father having relinquished even Presbyterian Calvinism, he seems to have been 'left to Nature' by no fault of his own, while yet we see him feeling in thought for Religion of some kind, as his life wears on. Quite naturally, it may be, in such a position he scarcely came across Christianity as an Historical Revelation: it stood on one side. The discarded Presbyterianism of his father seems to have brought to a previous close any real Christian examination. Mr. Mill began where his father left off, and never seriously turned back. Yet he found he could not but think of Religion, and write about it in some way. It seemed as if he were not able to help it. It was the subjacent thought of his books, even when not expressed. Was a 'Religion' to be found by him, then, in

'Nature'? And could he trust Nature? – He thinks not, but he will say 'why.' Might Religion, however, since it existed on every side, be a delusion of some 'Utility' even if untrue? – He doubts that; but he will see. But, to try yet again, – Is there a God at all? What are the logical arguments for it? But was not the Christian Founder a marvellous fact of the past, influencing a vast moral future? – He would consider yet again. . . .

### § 3. – THEISM

42. The Third Essay is entitled 'THEISM.' The subject is so laid out in a kind of syllabus as to seem at first sight to cover the ground of the usual controversies. This prospect is delusive; and what has been already said as to the præ-phenomenal, in examining the former essays, supplies almost all that is needed for the reply to this. We must, however, go over the course, though it is unnecessary to tarry long on any part of it, as there is but little that is new in point of thinking though the tone is somewhat different.

We detect a worthy consciousness of the responsibility of making a final decision on some of the issues in this Essay. While not owning it in terms, the writer seems to feel that it is he himself, and not a 'reasoning machine,' as some had called him, who was making his conclusion. For this is free agency in action – the putting forth the awful inner power of saying 'Yes' or 'No' to truth and goodness. There is something overawing, too, in the reflection that this inner power at times, and perhaps not unfrequently, exhausts its freshness in some one effort or act; so that a choice really made for evil or for good, leaves the agent not exactly what he was before.

The motions of a mind like Mr. Mill's are worth watching for their own sake; and his conclusions of avowed – even if reluctant – Atheism, or non-Theism, are not common utterances. They have a harmony, too, far more than Strauss's, with the spirit of our times. If they reach Strauss's conclusions, it is not by the same way. Strauss once professed Christianity; Mr. Mill, we believe, had not done so. The 'unique' majesty of Christ Himself had a charm for Mr. Mill; Strauss, at length, seemed blind to it.

There is a painful account, if we remember rightly, in the Letters of Byron, or in the notes, about Shelley's having had the conviction that, to get rid of the alleged ineradicable tendency of man to Theism, it would be desirable to form an artificial community from which the very name and thought of God should be rigorously shut out, and the children be brought up entirely without the tradition of a Deity in any form. It is said that Shelley purchased an island in the Ægean, with a view of carrying out this barbarous project. It might, by excluding all literature, have been possible, in this unnatural way of determining our nature, (as Coleridge would say), to 'hunt men out of their humanity'; but the plan was abortive through the unhappy poet's death. The vessel in which he put forth to go to his island foundered, and he was lost. We had thought the theory had been lost too.

In truth, such idea of excluding the thought of God from the nature and mind of man resembles that of the king in Herodotus, who shut up a child in order to ascertain, by excluding him from definite knowledge of human speech, what would be the first sounds he might produce, – as if he might so determine what were the aboriginal elements of 'natural' language. Such treatment might possibly produce imbecility, if attempted on any child, or elicit entirely unhealthy development even in the strong.

43. But we can hardly help being thus reminded of Mr. Mill's own training, excluded from the ways of men. It may explain so much of his apparent inability to deal with the natural, and his misapprehension of tradition, and especially also of the *a priori*. Shut out too much from common homes and habits, he seemed scarcely one of his kind. There is a gentle self-contemplation in his life which touches the reader at times profoundly, as it gives us glimpses of what he might have been. Our feeling concerning him is deepened by the fact that he really wrestled with the ruinous predestinarian philosophy, and only succumbed to it as a materialist for want of the *a priori*, which had withered in him from his earliest hours. It was with him, then, no mere theory to be 'without God.' ...

55 (v.) The argument from '*Marks of Design in Nature*' stands for consideration last in order. This, Mr. Mill says, is an 'argument of a really scientific character,' but certainly he does not shine in it. We should have been glad if this popular and applauded argument had been of any use in leading Mr. Mill to Theism. But it seems to have failed; nor are we surprised. Mr. Mill simply opposes to it Mr. Darwin's hypothesis of the 'Survival of the fittest.' If wisely stated, full of subsidiary

interest indeed in Theology is the 'Argument from Design,' – it is like a Bible, if in the hands of the Church; but as standing alone it is bare, and liable as a mere argument, (as Lord Bacon implied,) to much perversion – as an *a posteriori* without *a priori*. We cannot but think, too, that it is most unhappily expounded, (*e.g.*, in a passage of Paley's *Natural Theology*, in which his hypothesis represents some creation as almost beneath the Supreme, or as if committed to a Demiurge,) whenever it is wrested from its true position, as St. Paul used it in conjuction with the *a priori*. The argument from Design is even painfully pressed against us by some writers, who take advantage of its ambiguity.

56. Quoting from Paley, Mr. Morley gives us this: – 'God prescribes limits to His power that He may let in the exercise, and thereby exhibit demonstrations of His wisdom.... It is as though one being should have fixed certain rules, and, if we may so speak, provided certain materials; and afterwards have committed to another being, out of those materials and in subordination to those rules, the task of drawing forth a creation; a supposition which evidently leaves room and induces, indeed, a necessity for *contrivance*. Nay, there may be many such agents, and many ranks of these. We do not advance this as a doctrine, either of philosophy or of religion, but we say, the subject may be safely represented under this view, because the Deity, acting Himself by general laws, will have the same consequences, upon our reasoning, *as if He had presented those laws to another.* It has been said that the problem of CREATION was, attraction and matter being given, to make a world out of them, &c.'

We feel bound to say – '*Non tali auxilio.*' It may be old Gnosticism in modern phrase. We hope the 'Argument from Design' does not mean this. A better ontology than Paley's would have saved it. Mr. Morley's difficulty, if briefly put, is this – Would not the Highest Agent attain His end, without that kind of incubation, which a rough statement of 'contrivance,' or design, would imply? He rightly thinks that a sort of contrivance which derogates from the Divine perfection and absoluteness can never be admitted. The 'fitness of things' is the best ultimate form of the *a posteriori* argument: and to this the philosopher or man of science has no certain or comprehensive reply, so far as we can see. The argument has a *pro tanto* value then, and is not exposed to the danger latent in all analogies. (*See further, the 'Whole Doctrine of Final Causes,' &c.*)

57. We feel that we have no further need to prolong our examination of Mr. Mill. His view of the 'Attributes of the Supreme' or, as we have said, Præ-phenomenal Being, has already been replied to as inconsistent with philosophy. (*Secs. 22, 23.*) We may be spared the necessity of watching him while, balancing the 'probabilities' of Immortality, – that possibility the very thought of which might hereafter, he supposes, be a burden to us! The fact, *a priori*, of our Nature having the hope in us, as truly as it has 'a reaching out after God,' remains, and will remain.

This book is one that has a kind of sobering influence, as we draw to a close. We had made a higher estimate of the writer – formed from his *Essay on Liberty*, his best achievement by far.

But he seems feeblest here, as a logician without an *a priori*. We are not untouched by his qualified decisions, therefore, on the ultimate problems of being, approached by him, (as by some others), from only one side. The failure seems as if it struck Mr. Mill himself – a failure, always certain beforehand, of every attempt from that side, to bear down the truth of God. Here it really is conspicuous, and good may come of it. Mr. Mill, as the supposed best spokesman of his school, had to bring out his forces for the battle, and the result is equivalent to a total discomfiture of Atheism in the field it had chosen; and yet nothing else in mere Nature is left for the reasoner to fall back on. The baffled logic of Natural Theism can do nothing without Revelation. Revelation stands first.

Yes; God has revealed Himself. The *a priori* is God's Revelation of His image in our nature. The *a posteriori* brings His Phenomenal Revelation at length in the Incarnate.

The deep foundations of our Religion are in the 'unseen and eternal.' It rises out of the Præ-phenomenal, and is 'ever-true.' God first shines out of darkness, and then gives us the knowledge of Himself, 'in the face of Jesus Christ.'

58. It is with no feeling but that of forbearance or of hope that we take leave of this distressing, and to a logician even humiliating, volume. Any other spirit would be unbefitting in the contemplation of this last work of such a man as Mr. Mill. Had he lived longer, the possibilities which he began to see of God and Christ, and immortal Life, might have ripened for

him into realities, though not arguments. In reading some almost relenting words of his, we are as if standing by the couch of the departed, while his final echo dies away, – incoherently indeed at last, and yet very solemnly listened to. – Was he indeed then 'feeling after God, if haply he might find Him'? There are, none can deny it, sentences here and there to make us hope this. – Was he really fascinated by the unique form and beauty of Christ our Lord, – the only Personage in all man's past history that holds now for Himself, after eighteen centuries, the earnest love of countless human hearts? – Yes, Mr. Mill spoke of Christ as, to his mind, 'unique'; and in one place he did so, as if there strangely stirred within him even the love of the Son of Man. – Was this long homeless spirit beginning to be led to 'the Father,' in that last closing sentence, when he dimly wrote of 'Supernatural hopes' as not impossible yet? – Might it mean, 'LORD, shew us the Father, and it sufficeth us'?

Certainly, though there is no strong reasoning in this book – for there could not be, with the first link missing – there is here and there this softened tone, even though it be too often a voice of deepest abandonment as to an inexorable fate, or even but –

'the gurgling cry
'of some strong swimmer in his agony.'

59. In watching, as we have now done, the downward struggle from 'Nature' to 'Theism,' from Theism to Atheism, and seen the individual loneliness and helplessness that remain – a despair as to existence itself – we have pursued the course of Mr. Mill's book. We have seen that he refuses to 'follow Nature,' finding no certain 'Religion' there; yet he hints a 'Religion of Humanity' for those who may wish it, as unconcernedly as if he had not just before considered 'Humanity' a part of Nature. We see him, then, sitting in judgment on Nature, of which he had called himself a necessary part; thus revealing how the *a priori* in his whole intelligent being was yet feeling for higher truth than mere argument could reach. Yet he goes on to deny political 'Utility,' and social advantage, to 'Religion,' or even to a 'belief in God,' and so gives us at the close of his work an entire and acknowledged blank, – on the surface of which, nevertheless, is projected the sacred form of Jesus Christ, dimly attracting his mind and heart!

Here we must leave both the author and his work. Our task with them is done. As a logician, or even as an analyst, Mr. Mill has no place. But what is more important by far in the controversy is, that his *method* is convicted of every fallacy. It may discover, perhaps, to some that a thorough inquiry as to the *a priori* is the need of the logic of the future, since an attempted 'argument' without an *a priori* is but a wrangle without a beginning, conducting to no clear rational end.

60. Mr. Spencer, for example, might reason more subtly than Mr. Mill, but he really has nothing else to say. He argues in better form, and with closer analysis. His admissions are more full and distinct; his sentiment and feeling being more refined do not so mislead him as to interfere with his logic. He sees that while he keeps to the phenomenal he is, however wrong, controversially safe. His position can only be approached from higher ground; and he is clearly aware of it. Could he not answer his own arguments?

The battle of 'Atheism' – (may we not add the battle of Revelation entirely?) must be fought out, with unbeliever or with misbeliever, on the field of the *a priori*, as occupied *de facto*, and as received historically, by the Reason and Faith of Human Nature itself, in every department of its knowledge.

The possessor of Revealed Truth may take no lower ground than – 'we know.' It may be expressed in better words than ours: – 'That which may be known of God (το γνωστον) is plain in men's very selves (φανερον εν αυτοις). God made it plain. His unseen things (ἀορατα), His Potentiality and Deity,' (the præ-phenomenal), 'are so seen of the mind as to leave men without excuse if, with knowledge so possessed, they become weakly entangled by their arguments (διαλογισμοις), and calling themselves philosophers lose their common understanding in total darkness.' (Rom. i. 19–23) – It is a solemn picture drawn by an apostle's hand.

# MR. JOHN STUART MILL'S LEGACIES
James Baldwin Brown

The profoundly sad book which Mr. John Stuart Mill left for publication, under the form of an autobiography, has been followed by a volume of essays which develop his matured views on the loftiest subjects of human speculation – on Nature, Theism, and the Utility of Religion. It is not too much to say that they are still more profoundly sad than his Autobiography. They reveal to us a mind keen and penetrative, rather than vigorous and masterful in its grasp of great themes, but intensely honest and earnest, searching painfully for the springs of comfort and inspiration, of the need of which it was intensely conscious; eager for certainty in all the realms of knowledge with which its restless activity impelled it to be conversant, yet compelled to content itself with a feeble and dreary 'perhaps' with regard to the subjects which man in all ages, and under all conditions, holds to be of the most vital importance, and on which he has nothing but a confession of nescience to offer to his fellow-men. And the pathetic sadness of the confession lies in the manifest, though to him half-conscious, straining of his spirit after certainty, after that 'widening of vision,' and that 'inspiration' which a firm belief in the reality of the spiritual alone can afford. He is not of those who manage to content themselves, or to think that they content themselves, with the narrow range and the arid pasture which the sphere of 'the seen and temporal' offers to man's yearning nature. He saw clearly, he felt intensely the need of some such enlargement and quickening as spiritual belief and aspiration bring to man. But his keen penetrating intellect could find, or thought that it could find, no certain ground on which to rest a conviction; and so it gave up the quest with what sounds to instructed ears like an ill-suppressed wail of despair.

Mr. Mill's last legacy is simply fatal to his reputation as a philosopher. Few men in our time have been the objects of more fulsome and exaggerated praise. He was the prophet of a school of keen, but shallow and arrogant thinkers, to whose ideas the recoil of the intellectual world from the theological tension of the past generation gave a prominence and influence which are by no means their lawful due. This school listened to the words of their great master with the kind of reverence with which men of another and deeper school accept the teaching of the oracles of God. His essay on Liberty, for instance, seemed to the world outside his porch a singularly inconsequent and futile argument; but the shout of acclamation with which it was received by the disciples of the 'advanced school' which followed him as a leader could hardly have been louder if a chapter of a new gospel had been promulgated to the world. Now these very disciples are scornfully tearing his philosophic reputation to tatters; they find his last utterances utterly incongruous with the first principles of the system which he spent his life in formulating and expounding; and they give him up in despair as a philosopher, for reasons which, while we entirely agree with them, will probably draw him as a man closer to us and to the great human heart.

Mr. Mill's character as a philosopher must inevitably suffer in the estimation of 'the ermine-robed great world,' which is the ultimate judge even of philosophies, from the revelation which his posthumous works afford of those higher interests, hopes, and aspirations of which he recognised the value, but of which his philosophy could give absolutely no account. He was not as the scorners to whom the spiritual world represents nothing more than the fancies of women, and the fictions of priests; who hold that it is always baneful in its influence on human character and conduct; and who systematically ignore it as a region with which they have nothing whatever to do. On the contrary, he feels keenly all that it has been worth to our race in the past ages of its development, and all that it might be worth, the still more precious fruits which it might bear in human experience and hope, if man could bring it within the range of his faculties, and satisfy himself that it was real. There is something deeply sad, coming from such a man, in the confession, which we give in his own words – 'To me it seems that human life, small and confined as it is, and as, considered merely in the present, it is likely to remain, even when the progress of material and moral improvement may have freed it from the greater part of its present calamities, stands greatly in need of any wider range and greater depth of aspiration for itself and its destination, which the exercise of imagination can yield to it, without running counter to the evidence of fact; and that it is a part of wisdom to make the most of any, even small, probabilities on this subject which furnish imagination with any footing to support itself upon.'

Here is a region of knowledge, or what man in all his ages has believed to be knowledge, which he recognises as of boundless worth to humanity, which would afford to our sad, poor life precisely the enlargement and inspiration which it needs, but he can tell us nothing about it, he has no room for it in his philosophy. The mere idea that it may be real is utterly inconsistent with the fundamental principles of the system which has become almost identified with his name; and yet his thoughts haunt it, his spirit clings to it, and he gravely advises his disciples to get all the comfort and strength which they can from such belief in it as they can persuade themselves to cherish, though his philosophic texts give no indication of its reality, and his intellectual system casts it out contemptuously from its sphere.

This 'uncertain sound' in his utterance about the themes on which men desire passionately clear and firm deliverance from their teachers is utterly fatal to his reputation as a great master in the realm of thought. But, as we have said, it may draw him closer in bonds of sympathy and fellowship to the great mass of his fellow-men. Multitudes who have thought of him as a cold, hard, incarnate thinking-machine will be profoundly thankful to find that he shared that aspiration for a wider and nobler field of thought and activity than this life can furnish, which has been in all ages the human characteristic – that which distinguishes men generically and absolutely from the brutes. He could get little comfort or hope from it for himself; but men will love him the better for having felt the yearning for it – it makes him a poorer philosopher in the judgment of his disciples, but a truer, larger, and nobler man. It may sound like a paradox, but I believe that Mr. Mill's many and palpable inconsistencies as a philosopher are the true key to the influence which he exerted on the world outside his school. Had he been merely the cold, bright, logical machine which his father did his very best to make him, the interest of the world at large in his life and labours would have been but limited. Men care most to hear those who can tell them most about the mysteries that are hidden behind the veil which Mr. Mill's hand was not strong enough to lift. Thinkers who ruthlessly shut them up in a world of sense and time, and bind them with the bands of an iron necessity, in all ages happily command but a limited audience, and bequeath their dreary legacy to but a little circle of legatees.

But Mr. Mill was always breaking out of the bounds of his dark and sad philosophy, and flashing out sentiments, resolutions, aspirations and hopes, which had their origin and justification in a quite higher sphere. Where can room be found for the brave resolution to face eternal torment rather than call a being good whom he believed to be malign, in any consistent utilitarian philosophy? What Necessarian ever before pleaded so passionately for liberty and for the free play of individuality, and all that can develop individuality in the ordering of the great world's affairs? What political economist ever left such range to purely sentimental considerations? What hard, keen logician ever idolized so fanatically a woman's intelligence, and submitted himself, or thought that he submitted himself, so humbly to a woman's judgment, in the domain of thought which was so peculiarly his own? or what Sceptic ever held the character of Christ in such supreme honour, or set Him on such a lofty eminence above all other teachers, exemplars, and martyrs of mankind? It is not too much to say that Mr. Mill did as much to break down the narrow bounds of his philosophy with the one hand as he did to establish them with the other. The day may come when he will chiefly be remembered for services to the cause of human progress, which his whole philosophical system would have led him and his followers to decry.

Well may he groan over 'the small and confined' creeds within which our life, if this be all, is allowed to range. He and his school did their utmost to contract it further, and to convince men that they are sent into a hard world, to live a hard life, under the hand of a hard Necessity, which is the nearest approach that they can make to the name of God. Those who read the account of Mr. Mill's childhood and youth which is given in his Autobiography, will find little to wonder at in the hard, stern, cruel aspect in which both Nature and the order of the human world presented themselves to his sight. He knew no childhood, no youth, none of the gay, glad hours which the music of merry laughter lightens; none of the careless play that supples the mental limbs and muscles for the tasks of life. His task was measured out to him by hours, his recreation by minutes. His father's dry, stern, ruthless discipline must have made his home dull and formal as a workshop, not to use a stronger image, and the saddest thing is that he never seems to have been fully conscious of the dreary conditions under which his childhood was hardened into manhood, and he was thus carefully prepared to find a hard, stern, and cruel system of things around him when he went forth at length into a wider world. Speaking of the God of Nature, he says, 'The worshipper must learn to think blind partiality, atrocious cruelty, and reckless injustice, not blemishes in an object of worship, since all these abound to excess in the commonest phenomena of Nature.' He sees no benignity in the sentence of toil and struggle which has been passed on man, and of whose execution Nature takes the oversight. The stimulus and education of human faculty and energy, the development of human sympathy and ministry, which are the direct and blessed fruits of the stern but benign ordinance under which man toils and suffers, occupy but a slight space in his field of vision, which is filled with the confusion, the caprice, the cruelty, the wrong that are malignly busy in the management of the world. No wonder life seemed poor and sad to him as it seemed to his stronger and sterner father; while the dearest treasure of his heart, the being whom he loved with a fond idolatry was certain to be torn from him, he thought for ever, by the hand of inexorable Death.

Sorely does such a life stand in need of comfort and inspiration. Mr. Mill has rendered an essential service to religion: he has demonstrated and brought home to the hearts of his readers the poverty, the worthlessness of life without it. He has taught us how a great famine must needs arise in the land, on which shines no sunlight from the spiritual and eternal world. And he has rendered another service, all unconsciously, hardly less precious; he has justified all the homage and Divine honour which Christendom has paid to Christ through all the Christian ages, and has helped to explain to others, though apparently not to himself, how near to the root of all the higher development of Christian society lies the Incarnation, and the passionate devotion which it has kindled in human hearts. True he has some vague sentimental ideas about the religion of humanity, and the way in which devotion to the race may be hoped to supply both stimulus and nourishment to the loftiest human virtues, in a measure which shall cast all the vaunted influences of religion into the shade. But his faith in it is not a power. Unlike the Kingdom of Heaven, his Kingdom of Humanity is in word, and not in power. He derived little joy and little hope from his prophecies; and his heart evidently strained towards the spiritual as the one home in which, if he could find it, he could rest. This sad book, which is as the voice

> 'Of children crying in the night;
> Of children crying for the light;
> And with no language but a cry,'

is fitly mated by the epitaph which, in an able estimate of the life and labours of John Stuart Mill, Mr. John Morley wrote over his grave, in which he uttered his sad conviction, that this keen intellect and earnest spirit – so sad as we have seen, so struggling, so full of yearnings for help and inspiration from a sphere which it felt itself unable to reach – had vanished out of the universe for ever.

# [REVIEW OF]
# THREE ESSAYS ON RELIGION
## Henry Shaen Solly

We now know all that we are likely to learn of our author's opinions on religion from his own pen. The book has been eagerly anticipated in many quarters, and will not disappoint those who have already learned from his autobiography and other writings what manner of man he was, and what he might legitimately be expected to contribute in this particular field of knowledge. It is another warning to the orthodox world to set its house in order, and to the sensational philosophy to look to its most fundamental principles, but to our own modern liberal theology it bears a message of the most inspiring encouragement. For if we ask what *made* Mill such a sceptic, these essays answer with unmistakable clearness – the obsolete and therefore false phases of religion which we have abandoned; and if we further ask what was the obstacle which *kept* him in such a state of doubt, the answer will come no less decisively – the false philosophy which we have relinquished. The reader will find proof enough that the impelling force which drove Mill into scepticism was his moral revolt against a superstitious dread of inquiring into the secrets of nature, against the consecration given to blind impulse to the prejudice of reason, against the ordinary unscientific mode of treating the Bible, especially the Old Testament, and finally against the vulgar identification of religion with other worldliness and with unfeeling and immoral Optimism (see pp. 23, 44, 88, 110, and 112–117). No doubt James Mill is primarily responsible for his son's bent of thought, but it was a very similar moral revolt with the father, and the causes we have mentioned seem to have been actively at work all through life on the far nobler nature of the son. But we do not doubt that J. S. Mill would have risen superior alike to the stifling influences of education and the repellant force of perverted theology, and have ultimately grasped the pure creed of a reasonable faith, had he not been fatally encompassed and blinded by his Necessarian, Emperistic, and Eudaimonistic tenets. The contradiction between an assured religion and such philosophy was felt in a similar way by the followers of Priestley. There were two positions which could not be held together. They surrendered the one, Mill gave up the other.

All that was best and most lovable in our author's character, his sympathy for suffering, his earnest zeal in striving to redress the wrongs which he saw so plainly, and his unswerving truthfulness, formed an absolute barrier to his believing both in the literal Omnipotence of the Deity and in his goodness. If God *could* have made a better world than this abode of sin and woe, He is not good; if He could not, if all you can do is to say with Leibnitz that it is the best of all *possible* worlds, then He is not all-powerful, and the belief that He possesses both attributes is a most demoralising error. The force of this argument is increased enormously by the position assigned by our author to happiness. And certainly if this be the *summum bonum*, the proper aim and project of goodness, then benevolent omnipotence would have left Adam and Eve in Paradise without any tree of knowledge or legged serpent to tempt them. Nor is it easy to see how he can arrive at any higher good than happiness, as long as his trust is given exclusively to the revelations of sensuous experience.

We do not say that Free Will and Intuitive Morals entirely remove these religious difficulties. It is hard to see why God should have made the law of the survival of the fittest, the condition of development in the animal world, if he could have secured the same end, as far as we understand it, by a less harsh method. Rather than believe that so much suffering was inflicted without an adequate reason, we would accept limitations to the divine power to any extent, and restore to matter all the obstructiveness with which Plato endowed it. But where our ignorance is so profound, when it is so manifest that 'we know and see but in part,' as is the case with regard to animal suffering, then our wisdom as obviously consists in waiting for more light, and we are amply justified in refusing the whole subject admission into our inquiry. When, however, we pass to the consideration of human misery, it does not seem extravagant to claim for our beliefs, that while they immeasurably exalt the divine nature, they also dispose of most of the difficulties which had so fatal an influence on Mill's convictions. It may, indeed, be necessary to believe that God *could not* make man morally good without making him a free agent, capable of sinning and causing misery, and without, may be, training him up through many generations, developing the divine Son-ship from its germ in the savage to its perfection in the Christ. But this inability is of the same sort as an incapacity to make two and two equal to five, or to make selfishness nobler than benevolence. There is a certain eternal order of things which *cannot* be reversed, or in any way interfered with, and in so far as this is incompatible with omnipotence, the latter term is misleading when used as a divine attribute. But so far from this being opposed to the requirements of a pure faith, it is indispensable to them. Right and wrong cannot be arbitrarily settled by a *righteous* God; the only question can be where do the conditions cease under which he must work? This may be freely admitted. But those who have had any experience of the slowness with which, it seems, spiritual progress must be made, and to whose minds immortality is a sublime and awful reality, will not find it difficult to believe that God is not less good because He is so patient, any more than those who realise the meaning of the verse, 'Be ye, therefore, perfect, even as your Father which is in heaven is perfect,' will think the suffering of the world too heavy a price to pay for the opportunity of attaining unto such a destiny. Mr. Mill brings a heavy a price to pay for the opportunity of attaining unto such a destiny. Mr. Mill brings a heavy indictment against Nature, saying, 'in sober truth, nearly all the things which men are hanged or imprisoned for doing to one another, are Nature's every-day performances,' and he proceeds to develop this charge with remarkable vigour. But in most of the instances he cites it is easy enough to see in Nature's harshness only a reparation or else a discipline. Take the case of the Irish potato famine. A million of people starved is, no doubt, a horrible thing; but given Ireland in the degraded, yet contented state in which she was prior to that event, and faith will not find it hard to believe that, under the circumstances, so impressive an occurrence was the best thing possible. Our author, of course, sees that this reply could be made, and thinks that it yields the whole point at issue. No doubt it does with regard to absolute omnipotence; his argument may be conclusive against one type of theology. If Jehovah hardened Pharaoh's heart, *as well as* sent the plagues, he was no holy being. But we cannot find anything in it to disprove any power which a pure and rational religion requires in the object of her adoration. For perfect trust in Divine Providence it is, indeed, necessary to believe that all things will work together for the good of those who serve the Lord with fidelity; that if we obey our consciences we need take no anxious thought for the morrow. For the perfect love of God it is, indeed, needful that we should be able to see His hand in all the changes of our outward lot, and He must therefore have sufficient power to discharge these functions. But that human suffering can do nothing to disprove the existence of this kind and extent of power has surely been shown in the tale of every martyrdom. Faith has never burned more brightly than in the days of persecution; and even if the extremity of mortal anguish wrings forth the cry, 'My God, why hast thou forsaken me?' that reveals the conviction, not the doubt, of the divine ability.

This view of religion, however, was *terra incognita* to our author, who rarely shows any acquaintance with the thoughts of the real prophets of his time. He tells us (p. 103) that 'religion as distinguished from poetry is the product of the craving to know whether these imaginative conceptions have realities answering to them in some other world than ours.' This reminds us of Professor Tyndall's assignment of religion to the *creative* faculties of the mind, but neither here nor there do we find a real inquiry as to whether the 'product of the craving' can afford us any insight into spiritual things. The point is superficially touched upon in relation to the belief in immortality. The desire that we actually have he thinks is a desire for life. Well, we have some amount of life given us; the fact that we desire more does not prove that we shall get it, any more than the desire for wealth or political power makes every man a Cræsus or a Prime Minister. The real arguments on the subject as they are drawn from the hunger and thirst of the soul by such teachers as Dr. Channing and Dr. Martineau, are wholly ignored, just as the manifest inequality with which rewards and punishments are distributed in this life, is only cited to show the injustice of nature (p. 37–8). Again, he not unfrequently himself identifies religion with other-worldliness, and speaks of a certain impulse being 'a divine enthusiasm – a self-forgetting devotion to an idea; a state of exalted feeling, by no means peculiar to religion, but which it is the privilege of every great cause to inspire' (p. 95). Thus as long as he is criticising the views of others, he misses the real characteristic of his theme, and will not allow religion to consist essentially in that which helps us to rise above the dictates of a self-regarding prudence. Yet when he comes to develop his own ideas as to the proper substitute for the old faiths, he claims the name of religion (p. 109) for the very thing he has hitherto refused to recognise distinctively as such. Christianity our author seems to identify with the belief that Christ was the Creator (pp. 112–113), and scientific Biblical criticism was only one degree less unfamiliar to him than to a Low Church curate. The reader will, however, find on p. 114 a doubt 'whether Christianity is really responsible for atonement and redemption, original sin and vicarious punishment: and the same may be said respecting the doctrine which makes belief in the divine mission of Christ a necessary condition of salvation. It is nowhere represented that Christ himself made this statement, except in the huddled-up account of the Resurrection contained in the concluding verses of St. Mark, which some critics (I believe the best) consider to be an interpolation.' What is this but verbal inspiration for everything which is not interpolated? The Christian revelation, if it was really made, is supposed to have been miraculous in its origin and attestation. Of course with regard to the Old Testament, any new views were still further from entering into our author's estimation of religion. Moses is the author of the Pentateuch. The history of the Jews is 'a mere succession of lapses into Paganism,' though 'if ever any people were taught they were under divine government,' they were so; and the utility of a religion which was such a failure is contrasted in no favourable light with the achievements in moral discipline made by the Spartans and the Romans without, as Mr. Mill supposes, religion playing any part in the latter case. Accordingly he thinks that the new Christian duties having been once manifested to humanity, will be a secure possession to the race, whatever may have been their source. No doubt they do need no miraculous credentials, and shine by their own light as long as they are practised, but it is difficult to believe that they would be long in existence if men ceased to draw strength to discharge them from religion. Mr. Mill should have compared the different effects produced by political misfortune on the Jews and on the Greeks. But to have done this truly, we confess he would have had to have studied some of the very latest criticisms of Jewish history.

We should have liked to show how easy it is for a rational faith to solve many of the other problems that perplexed him. It is not difficult to understand the significance of the word natural in its moral sense when we admit a moral scale of motives, and a free-will which can decide for a higher when without such interference the lower would win the day, and can see how such decisions produce a state in which the higher is at length followed *naturally*, without any supplementary effort of the will. An unnatural crime is one to which no temptation should have been felt, where the natural man should have been on the side of what is right, and only the greatest negligence or sinfulness can have given preponderating force to the evil desire. Again, we only need this moral scale to see that all real progress is due not to triumphs of reason over instinct (p. 46), but of higher impulses over lower. Miss Cobbe[1] has lately supplied us with an instructive instance of this. Twenty years ago Miss Nightingale was publicly complimented by a distinguished living statesman 'on having achieved her task in the Crimea "not for the sake of any reward which her country could offer, but for a much greater one which she would receive hereafter."' Such a calculation would indeed have been a triumph of reason over instinct, but it is hardly that for which England reveres her name. We fully agree with our author as to the evil of 'ascribing a supernatural origin to the received maxims of morality' (p. 99), unless the authority which consecrates them be internal, an alternative to Utilitarianism which is altogether ignored.

Of course it will be said that Mr. Mill is addressing himself not to Unitarians or any advanced thinkers, but to the great bulk of orthodox believers, and that it was their point of view alone which he was bound to study. But it was always his pride in controversy to seek out the strongest, *latest*, expositions of his opponents' views, and we cannot help thinking that had he adhered to this custom in the present instance, the result of his investigation into religion might have been different. But his philosophy may have repelled him here at the outset, pre-

---

[1] *Theological Review*, October, 1874, p. 465.

venting him from caring to inquire into a faith which rested on principles which he never doubted all his life were false.

We have confined ourselves hitherto to speaking of the first two Essays, the only ones which are properly elaborated. In the third, on Theism, there is far less from which we differ. We suppose it gives, on the whole, a fair account of how far the intellect can lead us towards religion; and we only wish that the argument might have the effect it merits. We should not then hear so much of logical proofs of theological propositions, and should learn our need of another faculty for the vision of spiritual things, and should, perhaps, give more consideration to the investigation of its claims. Mr. Mill calls it hope; the early Christians called it faith; both agree that it deals with the things that are unseen. But we can have little religion till we know what it is evidence for, and our author's last thoughts on the subject will not help us much in solving this question.

# [FROM] SCIENCE, THEISM AND REVELATION, CONSIDERED IN RELATION TO MR. MILL'S ESSAYS ON NATURE, RELIGION, AND THEISM
John T. Seccombe

### CONCLUSION

The general result at which we have arrived may be summarized in the following manner.

*Particulars in which the Essays are in accordance with the general belief of Christians:* –

1. The arguments from efficient and final causes tend to prove that God exists.

'Appearances point to the existence of a Being who has great power over us – all the power implied in the creation of the Kosmos, or of its organized beings at least' (p. 210).

2. Apart from revelation, the light of nature is not sufficient to assure us that God is at once an all-powerful and benevolent Being.

'If we are not obliged to believe the animal creation to be the work of a demon, it is because we need not suppose it to have been made by a Being of infinite power' (p. 58).

3. The highest known manifestation of power is in the Kosmos – of goodness in Jesus Christ.

As to power, see above from p. 210.

'The Author of the Sermon on the Mount is assuredly a far more benignant Being than the Author of Nature' (p. 112).

4. 'There is, in science, no evidence against the immortality of the soul but that negative evidence which consists in the absence of evidence in its favour. And even the negative evidence is not as strong as negative evidence often is' (p. 201).

5. No one can, upon principles of reason, be satisfied that Christianity is not true.

'The argument of Butler's Analogy is, from its own point of view, conclusive; the Christian religion is open to no objections, either moral or intellectual, which do not apply at least equally to the common theory of Deism' (p. 214).

6. That miracles are not impossible, and that they may be proved by trustworthy evidence.

'Divine interference with nature could be proved if we had the same sort of evidence for it which we have for human interferences.'

7. Christ was a unique Being in respect of His moral excellence, which has been well termed 'inexplicable.'[1]

'Whatever else may be taken away from us by rational criticism, Christ is still left, a unique figure' (p. 253).

8. 'To the conception of the rational sceptic, it remains a possibility that Christ actually was what He supposed Himself to be' (p. 255).

*Particulars in which the Essays are at variance with the general belief of Christians:* –

1. That the constitution and course of nature contain indications contradictory of the Divine attributes of power, wisdom, and goodness.

This conclusion is supported by the application of certain views respecting the origin and nature of evil. Our ignorance upon these subjects is such as to make it certain that any such application will lead us astray.

2. That the evidence in favour of miraculous interferences is insufficient.

We have the same evidence for miracles as we have for the life and teaching of Christ, and these are admitted to be unique. The miraculous element is so closely interwoven with the gospel narrative that no criticism can separate them on any other principle than that of taking it for granted beforehand that miracles are impossible or what cannot be proved, and this assumption is shown in the Essays to be groundless.

3. That Christ did not suppose Himself to be God.

It is admitted that Christ was a teacher, reformer, and martyr of surpassing excellence. His followers, from the first, believed Him to be God. There is the strongest reason, therefore, for concluding that He taught them so, especially as there is no antecedent improbability against it.

---

[1] Channing. Sermon 1. *On the Evidences of the Christian Religion*; in which he also says, in remarkable correspondence with the above, speaking of Christ, 'His history shows Him to us a solitary being.'

4. The existence of a hell is inconsistent with the benevolence of God.

This depends upon the application of a particular view respecting the origin of evil, which cannot be admitted.

These being the separate conclusions arrived at, we can hardly be unprepared for the verdict on the whole case, which stands as follows: 'The rational attitude of a thinking mind towards the supernatural, whether in natural or in revealed religion, is that of scepticism as distinguished from belief on the one hand, and from atheism on the other; including in the present case, under atheism, the negative as well as the positive form of disbelief in a God, viz., not only the dogmatic denial of His existence, but the denial that there is any evidence on either side, which for most practical purposes amounts to the same thing as if the existence of a God had been disproved. If we are right in the conclusions to which we have been led by the preceding inquiry, there is evidence, but insufficient for proof, and amounting only to one of the lower degrees of probability' (p. 242).

Here, then, at last we have the result of what is, I believe, on the whole, the most complete, and by far the most candid, inquiry into the evidences of religion which has proceeded from the so-called rationalistic school of our day. We have an edifice of argument raised up, from which great results might fairly be expected, but when we regard it as a whole it is seen to be so artificially raised that it resembles a pyramid supported on its apex. The equilibrium is so unstable, so utterly precarious, the balance is so nicely even, that a grain of solid evidence on one side or the other must suffice to overturn the whole. It is for others to judge whether what has been submitted in these pages will suffice to yield the disturbing element. But unless Mr. Mill has estimated the weight of the evidence on both sides with something like a miraculous correctness, it is evident that the balance will soon be overthrown. Meanwhile, there are some points of great value which we may secure in favour of Christianity. One is the confirmation here afforded to the statement of the Analogy. 'Some persons, upon pretence of the light of nature; avowedly reject all revelation, as in its very notion incredible and what must be fictitious.' Mr. Mill has, in these three Essays, disposed of this objection as completely as if he had written them for no other purpose. And he has illustrated with equal clearness the force of one-half of the saying of Pascal: 'Reason confounds the dogmatists.' Some persons may be inclined to think that he has also corroborated its other half: 'Nature refutes the sceptics.' In the summary of particulars I have just given I believe there will be found the framework of a line of argument in favour of Christianity founded entirely on positions taken from the Essays, while there is nothing on the other side which properly amounts to an objection, though there are undoubtedly many difficulties. But there is an important distinction to be drawn between a difficulty and an objection. The difficulties alleged in the Essays do not apply particularly to Christianity, but are equally obnoxious to any system which attempts to account for the existing state of the world. Christianity alone affords some kind of solution of these difficulties, and it is surprising that Mr. Mill should not have seen this. He has shown an acute perception of the difficulties themselves, and of many of the strong points in favour of the Christian revelation, but has just stopped short of that one central doctrine which goes so far to remove all obscurities and reconcile all apparent inconsistencies. For while the Gospel assures us that all nature groaned in travail for the coming of Christ, His advent, His life, and death, were for the very purpose of effecting an atonement, of removing the curse, of eventually overcoming evil with good, and of giving us the assurance of the goodness of God. But this could only be effected by supreme goodness in person; no other assurance would suffice, and accordingly He has transmitted to us, by the hands of His beloved disciple, and last surviving apostle, the sublime utterance, so consolatory to the perplexed, so assuring to believers, so inexplicable to the sceptic – Εγω ειμι το Α και το Ω, ἀρχη και τελος, ὁ ὤυ και ὁ ἦν και ὁ ἐρχόμενος, ὁ παντοκράτωρ.

# [REVIEW OF] THREE ESSAYS ON RELIGION
Anonymous

A book by Mr. Mill on the highest subjects must always be an important book. But a book like this, published after his death, and after his autobiography has been given to the world, has a twofold value: one arising from its relation to his philosophy and system of truth, another from its relation to that striking personal history whose significance is still far from being exhausted.

Take the contents first. 1. The earliest of these three essays, that on Nature, the author was just about to publish when he died in 1873. It had been written fifteen years before, and had thus undergone 'many revisions, which it was the author's habit to make peculiarly searching and thorough;' and as Miss Helen Taylor, his editor, goes on to tell us, on religious subjects 'he was peculiarly deliberate and slow in forming opinions, and had a special dislike to the utterance of half-formed opinions.' The result justifies this account of the process, for this first essay we take to be by far the best in a literary point of view, and the only one thoroughly thought out as a piece of philosophy. Had it been published separately, it would unquestionably have made a sharper sensation in the world of thought than has been effected by the whole volume. It is the best statement in modern times of Manichæanism, untinged with Christianity; and in conjunction with Mr. Greg's more eloquent but less powerful *Enigmas of Life*, it makes an important turning-point in this modern revival of an ancient tendency in speculation. Its professed purpose is to deal with the maxim, 'Naturam sequi;' 'to inquire into the truth of the doctrines which make nature a test of right and wrong, good and evil, or which in any mode or degree attach merit or approval to following, imitating, or obeying nature.' The maxim and the doctrine he denies out and out, arguing against both with great power. Take external nature first. Its great characteristic is its 'absolute and perfect recklessness.' In sober truth, 'nearly all the things which men are hanged or imprisoned for doing to one another are nature's every-day performances. Killing, the most criminal act recognised by human laws, nature does once to every being that lives,' and torture is its ordinary work and pastime. Now, of course the maxim to follow nature, has always meant to follow it in its whole tendency, presumed to be beneficent. Mill argues, with great energy, that its tendency is not beneficent as a whole, but at best neutral. But he pushes his position farther when he asserts, that if we are to follow nature at all, we must be at liberty to follow her in *all* she does, even in details. Here, of course, he stumbles up against the causation of evil; and to solve it, denies with passion the omnipotence of God, defined as a being supreme and beneficent. Then, in the latter part of the paper he denies that we are to follow *human* nature. Our instincts, he says roundly, are not good, and the 'vein of sentiment so common in the modern world (though unknown to the philosophic ancients),' which exalts them – a vein originally opened by Rousseau – has no truth in it. This part of the essay is much weaker than the other, lying open to all the well-known objections to our author's ethical theory. He does not even attempt to meet Butler's old view, that conscience is not one instinct or tendency among others, but a feeling which asserts a certain supremacy over, and so co-ordinates, the selfish and savage instincts. 2. The second essay, that on the Utility of Religion, is not a very valuable one in a theoretical point of view. It, like the last, was written many years ago; but it is not said that the author intended to publish it before his death; and there is a certain conflict between its views and those of the concluding treatise. It deals with the question, whether, not this or that religion, but religion in the abstract, is a good thing (a thesis discussed hitherto from the sceptical side only by Bentham). It lapses frequently into the mere *quantum potuit suadere malorum*; but it finally comes to the conclusion that a religion of humanity is enough, excluding both immortality and all consciousness of the divine. 3. The last essay, on Theism, was sketched shortly before his death, and is in its first rude draft. It is longer and more complicated in design than the others; but we have left too little space to analyse what perhaps is most appropriate for our pages. He commences with the First Cause argument, the value of which by itself he denies, 'because matter and force have had, so far as our experience can teach us, no beginning,' and need no cause – mere *changes* in things may proceed from many causes. The reasoning plainly omits the tendency the many causes have to run themselves back into a unity, both in fact and in our mind. The argument from the general consent of mankind, and that from consciousness, are both also denied; and that from design is treated (consistently enough on Mr. Mill's philosophical principles) as the only one having value. His conclusion is, that the *strength* of even this argument has been very much cut down by Darwin's doctrine; but that 'in the present state of our knowledge, the adaptations in nature afford a large balance of probability in favour of creation by intelligence.' Under the head of attributes, the old difficulties about the presence of evil of course come into view; and the 'net results' of his natural theology he sums up as 'a Being of great but limited power, who desires and pays some regard to the happiness of His creatures, but who seems to have other motives of action which He cares more for, and who can hardly be supposed to have created the universe for that purpose alone.' For immortality, however, 'apart from express revelation,' he finds no presumption; and under the head of revelation he re-states, with power, his own and Hume's argument against miracles. The general result of the essay is, that 'the whole domain of the super natural is thus removed from the region of belief into that of simple *hope*.'

'There is a man, saith the preacher, whose labour is in wisdom, and in knowledge, and in equity.' But 'how *dieth* the wise man? Even as the fool.' Seldom, we think, has the old lament of *Ars longa, vita brevis* rung out with more significance than over the grave of this brave and noble thinker. These essays on religion are essays *towards* religion – one or two steps, taken slowly at intervals of a quarter of a lifetime, all in the right direction, and needing only five hundred or a thousand years of the same steadfast thinking to have brought the thinker to the altar of the universe. But John Stuart Mill commenced his religious speculations at the chill and arctic distance where a cruel father placed his nobler child. He was nursed in the Utilitarianism of Bentham, under which the right and good means the happiness of the individual. In middle life he struck out, illogically (but the light that led him so astray was light from heaven), a Utilitarianism, meaning the devotion of the individual to the good of the whole. Now, his religious theory, especially his Manichæanism or doctrine of nature, *springs from the earlier, not the later*, idea of his ethics. It is the selfish system, pure and simple, whose voice is heard through these essays. 'It is wrong to hurt any one,' is his whole definition; and he charges upon nature as a crime every infliction of pain upon any sentient being. Now, it is of importance to remark how far this theory falls short, in the higher or religious sphere, of what Mill had already attained in the lower sphere of morals. In that lower sphere he had come to hold that a man was entitled, and bound, to look to the utility of his actions, with a view to the *good of the whole*, and that the mere avoidance of pain, or the incurring of pain by the individual acting, or the individual acted upon, was in no respect an ethical test. Now, whether this new step was warranted by his original theory or not, it was a great step in advance. Henceforth, before you could judge morally of the action of any human being, you required to know how it bore upon the good of the whole, and even how it seemed to him, the actor, to bear upon the good of the whole. Now, all that Mill needed to have carried him over the greater difficulties which entangle him in this book, was the application of his own simple and broad principle of mere morals to the higher sphere of the morals of religion. But he failed to attain this. The principle of mere fairness, which he asserted in judging men, he refused to his God. A *man's* act you shall not judge, unless you know the whole of things, at least as it appears to the actor; but the actings of God and nature you may judge fiercely, rashly, prematurely, never pausing even to consider whether you see the whole as it is seen by 'greater, other, eyes than ours'! The famous parable of the critic fly, outside the dome of St. Paul's, has never had a more just or a more important application, than to the present book. Of course, there are other ways in which the shortcomings of Mill's moral theory tell heavily upon his religious views. The problem of evil and sorrow – the riddle of the painful earth – is not to be solved by any facts known to us. But no one has ever been other than infinitely far from it, who has ignored that fact in human nature – *the sense of sin*. To this, also, Mill had not attained, – scarcely even to the recognition of its existence in others. To a consciousness of the obligation of righteousness he had come, and he twisted his theory in order to suit it;

and ennobles all his work. But the farther consciousness of shortcoming and evil he had not yet worked out; and we must ascribe it very much to this, that he attacked the problem of the universe by postulates borrowed from the swine-trough of his forgotten Epicureanism. The instructive connection between this lack of the conscience of evil and the new Manichæan theory, we need not point out. A very weak and unhistorical school has recently got into the habit of speaking of that old system as if it had some resemblance to doctrines which, like those of Calvinism, lay stress on the deadly and absolute contrast between moral good and evil. Books like this of Mill will, we believe, bring out that these systems, instead of being like each other, are deeply contrasted. The recognition of the implacable hostility between moral good and evil does *not* tend to acquiescence in them as equal and counter-balancing powers. For if the sense of the contrast, as a moral contrast, is deep enough, it necessarily includes in the idea of moral evil a crushing sense of demerit, and in that of moral good a sense of present and absolute supremacy, which make the present inequalities and injustices of earth a subordinate part of the tremendous problem, and teach man long patience with Almighty God.

We have only space further to suggest to our readers that the same defect in our author's philosophy, traceable to a defect in his still more interesting experience, is the key to the weakness of his theology proper. The *moral* argument for the existence of God, that which to some of us has always been the strongest, has scarcely any place in his speculations here. And that which deprives him of faith in God and in immortality, and reduces him to a faint hope, is fatal also, alike to his discussion of the antecedent probability of revelation, and to his estimate of the revelation which claims to have come. On the former matter the striking contrast between the negative conclusions of his old essay on the Utility of Religion, and the more hopeful suggestions of his last and unfinished paper on Theism, has been noticed by all readers. Heavy and sad as this volume is, those of us who never can read anything of John Stuart Mill without a glow of personal admiration and affection, find a certain mournful alleviation in the ever onward course of that unfinished career to which all too soon

'Came the blind Fury with the abhorred shears,
And slit the thin-spun life.'

So on the last subject, that of the Christian Revelation, the farthest double landmark is his description, on the one hand, of the Gospel of John as 'poor stuff,' which might have been stolen from any Gnostic, and his confession, on the other, that Christ is an historical person, and such an unique figure in history, that 'even now it would not be easy, even for an unbeliever, to find a better translation of the rule of virtue from the abstract into the concrete, than to endeavour so to live that Christ would approve our life' – nay, more, that 'it remains a possibility, to the conception of the rational sceptic, that Christ actually was what He supposed himself to be' – not God, which He never claimed, but 'a man charged with a special, express, and unique commission from God to lead mankind to truth and virtue.'

# [REVIEW OF] THREE ESSAYS ON RELIGION
Anonymous

These essays have received from so many hands exposition and criticism, that the former seems now almost unnecessary, while the latter has already become a very complicated task. The comments by distinguished admirers or honourable opponents of Mill's philosophical career already form a body of disquisition far exceeding in bulk the original essays. One of the most noticeable features of the reception they have met with has been the pious alarm which some religious disbelievers in the possibility of the existence of the Living God have manifested, at the supposed recreance of the hardy positivist, at the few but perilous concessions which the supernaturalist will discover in these melancholy broodings, at the faint glimmer of hope which hovers like a phosphorescent glow over this posthumous production. They seem to murmur, 'If John Stuart Mill can be quoted as having seen dimly the gateway into the realm of transcendental illusion; if *he* can be appealed to, as having perceived a purpose in the Cosmos, or a ray of kind or gracious intention behind the veil of phenomena; if the phantasm of immortality or of future life appeared to him – though but the shadow of a dream, and the faintest of hopes – to be of any "utility" now in the progressive civilization of man; then the ignorant and prejudiced ranks of Christian believers will make such capital out of it, that the blessed calm of a holy nihilism will be unnecessarily disturbed!' This phantom-ship, with the weird form of that 'Ancient Mariner' upon its quarter-deck, floating in without a breeze from the dark waters of death, and with a story to tell, which the smartest positivist is bound to hear, has made a commotion that will not soon be forgotten. It is not very edifying, however, when the angry believers in the great NOTHING throw stones at that Ancient Mariner.

The first of these essays, which was written between the

years 1850–58, is the most startling of the three. It appears to reflect the heartless training to which this remarkable personage was submitted in his youth. There are no signs of the spiritual progress which he describes in his autobiography as the result of his study of Wordsworth's poetry. He certainly never learned to look at Nature with the eyes of Wordsworth; and in this essay he proclaims war to the knife against her. The bare supposition that an ethical standard or a moral order, or a beneficent purpose, or a spirit of justice, could be discovered in her spontaneous operations, almost fills him with indignation. He accuses the sum of things – the ordinary course of Nature apart from human intervention – of every conceivable offence against goodness and equity, and with characteristic audacity exalts the skill and forethought of man above the most favourable interpretation of Providence.

Man's work, according to him, is to thwart, to counteract, to improve upon the proceedings of Nature. The 'following of Nature' is most irrational and immoral, and Mill closed his eyes on the great plan of God manifested in Nature. In each of the essays before us, he returns upon the thesis, that the facts of the universe are incompatible with either the goodness or the omnipotence of the supposed Creator. 'If good He could not be all-powerful.' In passages which must have become familiar to most of our readers by frequent quotation, he tries to show that Nature is ever doing that with human beings which, if men were to imitate in their treatment of each other, would be punished with ignominy or death. He would impale the believer on the horns of the dilemma, if Nature *could* not accomplish benevolent or equitable ends on a grand scale without such tremendous sacrifice, she *must* be limited in power.

He frequently speaks of Omnipotence, as though believers in it were bound to show that Omnipotence involved the blending of contradictories and the doing of impossibilities. It is not enough, says Mr. Mill, to maintain a 'thesis, which could only avail to explain and justify the works of limited beings, compelled to labour under conditions independent of their own will, but can have no application to a Creator assumed to be omnipotent, who, if He bends to a supposed necessity Himself, makes the necessity He bends to.' But, surely even *Omnipotence* CANNOT determine the existence of two mountains without originating a valley between them. Every property of things, all the modes of force, and all the forms of life, involve millions on millions of incessant consequences, which the Omnipotence that determined their character and quantity *cannot* modify or invert in individual cases without infinite chaos. 'Nature,' or the sum of these properties, forces, forms and activities, has, apart from any of the spontaneous efforts of man to improve upon her, during numberless ages and æons, been preparing a complicated equilibrium, in which, through the agency of perpetual death and boundless complexity of relationship, a place has been found for One, who, in the course of those few thousand years which are but as the twinkling of an eye, would see through the mystery, and learn to appreciate the order, and commune with the Eternal Source of every change, and use the boundless reserve of force which is never expended – that is, the right hand of God – for His own comfort, progress, and the prolongation of His being. How should the Omnipotent Goodness teach this great Companion of His eternity the nature of the universe, but by letting Him discover all its properties and forces. Mr. Mill might as well take us into a vast manufactory, all dizzy with its revolving machinery, the sole object of the maker and managers of which, moreover, we learn to be the production of some useful article of food or clothing, and which we know to be instinct with boundless benefits to mankind; and then because we see under our very eyes some poor blind child caught by the flying wheels and destroyed, or because we know that some of the workpeople suffer from its atmosphere, he might inform us, to our amazement, that there is neither wisdom nor justice, nor adequate power, nor any goodness, in the heart of the engineer or manager of that machine.

To some extent we agree with the argument. The whole creation groans; and it is because we know that the order and the teachings of Nature are inadequate as a guide to moral life; it is because Nature is too much of a machine, and is not a person, that without more help than itself we cannot learn all the character of its Maker, or feel all the pulsations of the Father's heart. Therefore it is that we look to other and deeper revelations of the Supreme will. Moreover, it is because the Sublime Ideal of humanity presents so many crushing contrasts with our actual life, that we find ourselves burdened by a sense of ruptured relation with God, which it is the aim of revelation to remedy.

Mr. Mill, in his 'Essay on the Utility of Religion,' pursues this theme; but, as it seems to us, without a hint or glimmer of true religious experience. His malignant antagonism to the Author of Nature, which recalls the old Gnostic and Manichæan dualism, prevents his seeing the significance of Christ's teaching about the Author of Nature, and condemns those who accept it, as being either most stupid observers, or most confused or deluded in their moral perceptions. If the ignorance of some spectators of the sacrifice of the blind child were to accuse the benevolent architect or engineer of deliberate murder, and of being utterly destitute of all moral qualities besides, it would be surely time for those who saw the misconception and could correct it, to speak out. We believe that the whole aspect of modern science, which Mr. Mill strangely ignores, contradicts his one-sided estimate, his narrow and bigoted rendering of the meaning of Nature.

He seems, moreover, to magnify the bitterness of death and suffering, and not to have got a ray of light on the significance of *death* either to God or man.

The essay on 'Theism' was produced at a later period in Mr. Mill's career, and it lacks his final revision. It is an ambitious and comprehensive attempt to review the entire field of natural theology and apologetics, and touches many questions, every one of which requires and deserves much more attention than he seems willing to have bestowed upon it. He admits that 'there is nothing to disprove the creation and 'government of nature by a sovereign will,' and then proceeds to criticise, as it seems to us, in the crudest fashion, the evidences *for* the truth of such an hypothesis. The strongest point against the intelligent character of the 'force' which produced 'mind,' is a reference to the law of the evolution of the higher form of life from the lower. It is remarkable, and to be regretted, that he did not grapple more heartily with that law, and criticise the doctrine of the 'persistence of force' and the 'correlation of the forces,' in which we believe he would have found the reply to his own position. The arguments from 'consent of mankind,' 'consciousness,' 'design,' are hastily touched; the last he admits to possess 'considerable strength.' The repetition of his previously expressed views on 'the attributes' of God makes the same approach to dualism, and to the discovery of the feebleness, fickleness, and blundering of the Almighty.

Then he endeavours oracularly to deny the faintest *evidence* for 'immortality' from natural religion, although admitting that if a man finds 'the hope of future life conducive to satisfaction or usefulness,' it will do him no harm to cherish it. He recapitulates his well-known argument concerning miracles, which appeared in his 'System of Logic,' and then, though showing that the presumptions against miraculous facts are great, he allows, that if the hypothesis of a God be admitted, then one *prima facie* objection to their occurrence would be removed, and that a philosophical mind, if this, that, and the other evidence be forthcoming, need not be precluded from hoping that the revelation in Christ may be true.

The concluding passages have been so often quoted that we will not repeat them. There is a flash of light over the sad and hopeless meditations. The character of Christ and the morality of Christ are provisionally allowed to be a noble ideal of excellence. No loftier rule of life, or more stimulating imagination, can present itself, even to the mind of Mr. Mill, than that a man should so conduct his life as that Christ would approve it. We put down this volume with intense sorrowfulness, and a passionate and now vain wish, that John Stuart Mill, with his love of man, his candour, nobility of soul, and his desire for truth, had ever come into real contact with Christian ideas. A blind man discoursing of art would have made a better exposition of the mysteries of colour, the charms of beauty and of form, than this great thinker has effected in his estimate of 'the utility of religion,' or the hope of eternal life.

# JOHN STUART MILL AS A RELIGIOUS PHILOSOPHER
## Noah Porter

Three distinguished English writers, all notorious for their negative attitude toward Theism and Christianity, have left their maturest and ablest writings upon these topics, to be published after their death. Lord Bolingbroke committed his 'Letters on History,' which had already been privately printed, to David Mallett, who published them in 1753. This procedure elicited from Dr. Johnson the well-known emphatic comment: 'Sir, he was a scoundrel and a coward: a scoundrel for charging a blunderbuss against religion and morality; a coward because he had not resolution to fire it off himself, but left half-a-crown to a beggarly Scotchman, to draw the trigger after his death.'

The ablest work of David Hume, the 'Dialogues on Natural Religion' – perhaps the most subtle anti-theistic treatise ever published in the English language – was written in 1751, but was not published till 1779, some three years after his death. Hume, by his will, appointed Adam Smith his executor, and left him two hundred pounds for the services he might render in editing this work. But fearing that Smith would be unwilling to execute the task, on account of the odium it might excite, he gave the matter in charge to his publisher, and in the event of Smith's failure to issue the treatise within two and a half years, to a nephew, by whom it was published in fact.

Mr. John Stuart Mill was more reserved in his life-time, in the expression of his religious opinions, than either Bolingbroke or Hume. Had not his autobiography in part prepared the public for what they had reason to expect, these theological essays would have been looked for with a more eager curiosity than they received. There seems to have been no good reason for the delay of the publication of the first two essays contained in this volume, both of which were written between 1850 and 1858. The editor confidently avers that their author did not withhold them from publication 'on account of reluctance to encounter whatever odium might result from the free expression of his opinions on religion.' She ascribes his delay to his well-known deliberation in forming his opinions, and his special dislike to express opinions when half-formed. The careful student of Mr. Mill's other writings could not fail to notice, however, that he uniformly avoided any reference to religious questions, or, in the few cases where they have been forced upon his attention, so carefully avoided committing himself, as to seem wanting in both frankness and courage. His actual opinions were so generally understood, and the conclusions to which his philosophy must lead him were so inevitable, that his cautious and studied statements were interpreted as indicating a certain sardonic contempt of the faith or feelings of the most of his countrymen. These feelings were distinctly expressed by the remark in his autobiography, that from his childhood 'I looked upon the modern as I did upon the ancient religion, as something which in no way concerned me.' His studied and long-delayed reticence cannot easily be reconciled with the emphatic assertion in the same connection, that the time had already come in which it was not only safe for, but obligatory upon, all those who held opinions opposed to those commonly received, to assert them freely and boldly. For many reasons, the revelations of this autobiography did not open the way for the most favourable reception of his mature and yet long-withheld opinions upon Theism and Christianity. The avowals made in that notable work, of the conclusions which he had reached, and the contemptuous or unsympathetic air assumed toward all forms of earnest religious belief, were not fitted to conciliate a very favourable judgment from very many readers, who are not wanting in candour. Nor should it be overlooked, that not a few rejectors of supernaturalism in England and this country, hold a philosophy and a faith which are very far removed from those of Mr. Mill; nor again that Mr. Mill's prestige as an authority in metaphysical philosophy ... has been somewhat diminished by the more imposing proportions and claims of the philosophy of Mr. Herbert Spencer. This writer, although his system rests upon the same psychological basis of inseparable associations, claims that it meets all the requirements of the intuitional metaphysics, and even provides for faith in an inscrutable force or being or person, who or which is at once the necessary assumption of science, the verified result of all experiments, and the satisfying though ever-changing object of faith and worship.

It might seem scarcely necessary to solicit attention to the religious philosophy of so modest a thinker as Mr. Mill, at a time when his ineffectual fires are paling before the radiant splendours of so imposing a teacher as Mr. Spencer. But Mill's system of religious philosophy is, to say the least, a metaphysical curiosity. The analysis of it may also be presumed to give some important indirect results, even though it may not be required for the refutation of his arguments.

The first of the three essays contained in this volume is entitled 'Nature,' and in matter and form is the least interesting. We cannot be mistaken when we pronounce it one of the feeblest of Mr. Mill's productions, for the ambitiousness of its pretensions, the narrowness of its definitions, the defectiveness of its logic, and the repulsiveness of its conclusions. Though written in the maturity of the powers of the author, after he had felt and acknowledged the liberalizing and elevating influences of both poetry and love, and had learned to be catholic in judging, and kindly in appreciating, the opinions and feelings of men from whom he differed very widely, this essay seems to reflect the narrowest and the most acrid spirit of his unripe youth, as well as the bitterest prejudices against all who believe in God's goodness, which characterized his early manhood. It would seem that his temper must have been for the most part greatly disturbed, while he thought and wrote out this essay....

It might seem to be a useless and thankless undertaking, to dwell so long upon an argument which is so perverse and unsatisfactory as this. It is, indeed, in every respect, unsatisfactory; it is unsatisfactory as a statement of the theory which the author takes such useless pains to refute; it is unsatisfactory as an argument for the views which the author asserts; while as an argument against the benevolence of an unlimited Creator, it is pre-eminently superficial and dogmatic. In two respects, however, the essay is very significant: that the author attaches great importance to its reasonings and doctrines, which is evident from the confidence with which he refers to this essay in the two which follow it, as further developments of his Religious Philosophy; that it also expresses the creed of a school which is becoming not inconsiderable, even among

English and American writers, and is likely to prove a somewhat formidable antagonist even to a wholesome and hopeful theism.

The essay is also instructive, as we have already intimated, as showing how completely inadequate is Mr. Mill's metaphysical system for the construction of a satisfactory or even a fixed philosophy of religion. Mr. Mill makes no show of his philosophical views in his reasonings. He rather conceals it from view, as he is apt to do. He now and then even abandons it, and reasons from the ordinary principles of conscience and common sense. But he is none the less completely swayed by its influence. To us it is no matter of wonder that a system made up of associational psychology, empirical metaphysics, prudential ethics, and necessitarian fatalism should be incompetent to lay the foundations or rear the superstructure of a religious theory of the universe. Mr. Mill has no need to obtrude upon our attention the peculiarities of his instrument and method. The results make them but too conspicuous. A telescope which stands upon an unstable pedestal, and is furnished with imperfect lenses, and moved by imperfect machinery, must of necessity give images of vague outlines and blurred surfaces. Mr. Mill's philosophy appears to a bad advantage when it is applied in the service of a science of nature considered as the aggregate of finite, physical, and spiritual existence. It is not surprising that it should fail altogether to justify the belief in a self-existent Originator and Moral Ruler of this finite universe, who is unlimited in power and perfect in goodness.

The weakness of Mr. Mill's philosophy is singularly conspicuous in the reasonings of both father and son in respect to the goodness of God. We learn from the autobiography of the son, that there was no opinion to which the father adhered more positively than that the universe was to a certain extent under the control of some principle or source of evil which limited and checked the benevolence of the Creator. He was led to this conclusion by the argument in Butler's Analogy. This argument was, in his view, decisive to the conclusion that the same difficulties which inhere in the scriptural representations of God are found in the moral administration of the universe. For a while the argument satisfied him that the Revelations of the Scriptures were from God, and ought to command his confidence and his complacency. But on farther reflection he found himself drawn back to the more radical conclusion that the administration of nature itself could not be vindicated to his reason and conscience, except on the theory that the benevolence of God is in some way thwarted and controlled by the limitations of his power. This doctrine was held with fanatical dogmatism by the father, and was literally *inculcated* by his hard and positive temper into the receptive and plastic nature of the son. It is the strong and ever reappearing warp of the argument in these essays, into and athwart which are wrought all the minor arguments which make up the tissue. Even at the very close of the last essay, after the ample and almost pathetic concessions to Christian theism which he makes, out of the gentle and truth-loving impulses of his better nature, he gives as his last thought to the world, that in addition to the other moving influences to love and duty which proceed from God, and Christ, and Immortality, the motive should not be overlooked that by our personal love and duty, we give aid and sympathy to God himself in the unequal conflict which he is maintaining with the inevitable and persistent evil.

In all this argument, as conducted by both father and son, there seems not to have been the faintest approach to a suspicion that the difficulty in the way of receiving the doctrine of a benevolent God was created by the bald and outspoken necessitarianism of their psychological philosophy. The associational psychology involves by a logical necessity the conclusion that every man's character and actions are the product of circumstances. It necessarily excludes the possibility of individual responsibility in any proper sense of the phrase. Any science of sociology, and any philosophy of history, would be impossible, in the judgment of Mr. James Mill, Mr. John Stuart Mill, and Mr. John Morley, unless every individual man and all the societies of men were formed by the environment of each according to laws the operation of which is as fixed and inevitable as is the operation of gravitation and chemical affinity. The distinction between fatalism and necessity made by Mr. Stuart Mill is designed to meet a difficulty which is simply practical, and does not alter in the least his views of responsibility, and of moral liabilities.

Now it ought to have been no secret to any of these gentlemen that the majority of theists who have attempted to explain and vindicate the divine goodness, have derived most of their arguments from the essential nature of freedom as the necessary condition of moral responsibility. It was entirely a proper question for them to discuss, whether or not these arguments were pertinent or satisfactory, but it was not left to their option as courteous or even as well informed critics to leave this class of arguments unnoticed, or to ignore their existence and importance, at least as matters of philosophical history. An impartial critic will readily see that it must make the greatest possible difference in the judgments which we form of God's benevolence, whether we do or do not include as an essential element to be considered, the reality and the importance of individual responsibility, and that a reasoner who denies the freedom which is its essential condition and accepts in its place the doctrine of necessity, is driven by a logical necessity to the conclusion that either God is not supreme in goodness or not unlimited in power. But Mr. Mill had never the capacity to look at any argument from any other point of view than that which his own philosophy permitted. The weak, and false, and vacillating conclusions which he so often reached, very often illustrate nothing so strikingly as the uncertainty or the falseness of his underlying philosophy.

The second essay on 'The Utility of Religion' is less speculative in its character than the essay on 'Nature.' And yet it is scarcely less important as an exposition of certain practical features of his religious philosophy. The drift of its argument is against the almost universal impression that some form of positive religion is useful and even necessary for the moral well-being of man. The author in opposition to this view, contends that many of the elevating and restraining influences usually ascribed to religion alone, are in fact due to the influence of authority by which the principles and impulses of men are so largely moulded. Authority, he urges, can be exercised as efficiently without as with religious motives; overlooking very strangely as it seems to us, the fact that the force and energy of authority must be intensified when the authority of God is superadded to that of any and all human beings. Even if it were conceded that the force from these two sources was similar in kind, it might still remain true that the authority of religion is not only useful but indispensable. Mr. Mill urges next, that education has done vastly more than religion in elevating the human race, and that the Grecian states especially are examples of what education can do with the least possible assistance from any religious force. He also contends that public opinion exerts a potent formative influence upon the character, overlooking the often unnoticed yet always energetic part which religion has uniformly played in moulding and animating both education and public opinion. Next, he borrows from Mr. Bentham an argument, the object of which is to show, that the influence of religion is conspicuously weak in deterring men from perjury, duelling, and illicit sexual intercourse, an argument of which it is difficult to see the force, so long as decisive evidence is not adduced, that men who are manifestly swayed by religious influences are as little restrained as other men when tempted to these three forms of sin. That religious motives are very often impotent to deter many from these offences, proves nothing except that temptations to commit them are specially powerful with the majority of the race. The special power of religion to sustain men under severe persecution and even extreme torture, is disposed of by referring it to 'a divine enthusiasm – a self-forgetting devotion to an idea; a state of exalted feeling by no means peculiar to religion, but which it is the privilege of every great cause to inspire' – which is met by the query whether religion is not in its motives and inspiration the greatest of all causes. From these general considerations the author advances to the special position that if it be granted, as it should be in all fairness, that in the past, religion has been efficient and necessary in teaching and enforcing morality, its aid is required no longer, for the reason that when ethical truth is accepted and approved, it shines by its own light and attracts by its own radiance. Religion is no longer useful because the occasion for its influence has been outgrown. Its addresses to the fears of men may be laid aside, and it is desirable they should be dispensed with as ignoble, and consequently in the present state of society as anything but useful. Its power to elevate and kindle the imagination may be conceded, and its actual influence in this direction may be gratefully acknowledged. But if the imagination can be stimulated and purified by ideal pictures, the same results will follow:

> 'It has still to be considered whether in order to obtain this good, it is necessary to travel beyond the boundaries of the world which we inhabit; or whether the idealization of our earthly life, the cultivation of a high conception of what IT

may be made, is not capable of supplying a poetry, and, in the best sense of the word religion, equally fitted to exalt the feelings, and (with the same aid from education) still better calculated to enable the conduct than any belief respecting the unseen powers.'

That present and finite objects and motives are capable of producing these effects, is argued as follows:

'When we consider how ardent a sentiment, in favourable circumstances of education, the love of country has become, we cannot judge it impossible that the love of that larger country the world, may be nursed into similar strength, both as a source of elevated emotion and as a principle of duty.' 'This exalted morality would not depend for its ascendancy on any hope of reward; but the reward which might be looked for, and the thought of which would be a consolation in suffering and a support in moments of weakness, would not a problematical future existence, but the approbation, in this, of those whom we respect, and, ideally, of all those, dead or living, whom we admire or venerate.'

The author therefore infers that for all the exigencies of men, the *Religion of Humanity* is better than any *Supernatural Religion:*

'For, in the first place, it is disinterested. It carries the thoughts and feelings out of self, and fixes them on an unselfish object, loved and pursued for its own sake. The religions which deal in promises and threats regarding a future life, do exactly the contrary; they fasten down the thoughts to the person's own posthumous interests,' etc.

'Secondly, it is an immense abatement from the worth of the old religions as a means of elevating and improving human character, that it is nearly, if not quite impossible for them to produce their best moral effects, unless we suppose a certain torpidity, if not positive twist in the intellectual faculties. For it is impossible that any one who habitually thinks, and who is unable to blunt inquiring intellect by sophistry, should be able without misgiving to go on ascribing absolute perfection to the author and ruler of so clumsily made and capriciously governed a creation as this planet, and the life of its inhabitants.'

If a man, to adjust the strip between his moral convictions and his faith, accepts the conclusion that morality in himself and in God are different attributes –

'The worship of the Deity ceases to be the adoration of abstract moral perfection. It becomes the bowing down to a gigantic image of something not fit for us to imitate. It is the worship of power only.'

The Religion of Humanity has the still further advantage, that it relieves men of intellectual and moral independence, from believing that God, as represented in the Scriptures, can possibly be good.

'He who can believe these [and the characteristics of God as set forth in and through the Scriptures] to be the intentional shortcomings of a perfectly good Being, must impose silence on every prompting of the sense of goodness and justice, as received among men.'

'Only one form of belief in the supernatural – one only theory respecting the origin and government of the universe – stands wholly clear both of intellectual contradiction and of moral obliquity. It is that which, resigning irrevocably the idea of an omnipotent Creator, regards nature and life not as the expression throughout of the moral character and purpose of the Deity, but as the product of a struggle between contriving goodness and an intractable material, as was believed by Plato, or a Principle of Evil as was the doctrine of the Manicheans.' 'Against the moral tendency of this creed no possible objection can lie; it can produce on whoever can succeed in believing it, no other than an ennobling effect.'

The author concedes that the supernatural religions possess one advantage over the Religion of Humanity, in the prospect they hold out to the individual to a life after death. But he urges that man has no rational desire for continued existence in itself, and that as man rises in intellectual culture and in unselfish desire he will be trained by degrees, rather to prefer annihilation to immortality. As he expresses himself:

'It seems to me not only possible but probable, that in a higher and above all in a happier condition of human life, not annihilation but immortality may be the burdensome idea; and that human nature, though pleased with the present and by no means impatient to quit it, would find comfort and not sadness in the thought that it is not chained through eternity to a conscious existence, which it cannot be assured that it will always wish to preserve.'

To a conclusion so lame and impotent as this, is the author reduced in order to sustain his position that supernatural religion is no longer useful for the moral elevation or the happiness of man. As man does not need religion for his moral culture because though he may have risen by means of its aid, he has outgrown the capacity of any longer receiving help from its authority or its inspiration, so he does not require religion for his comfort, because he does not care for the immortality which it reveals and promises. It is a significant fact that similar sentiments in disdain of immortality are rapidly becoming current among certain literary circles. It is worth notice how those who cherish and defend them, assume that they are more unselfish than the vulgar longings for continued personal existence – how pantheists and empiricists both unite in rejecting with supercilious pride or affected indifference the gift of eternal life, if it is to be received as a gift of God. Mr. John Morley uses all the pomp of words and the splendour of pictorial imagery to set forth the blessedness of prospective annihilation and the peace of anticipated non-existence, in a memorable and most eloquent passage which concludes in these words:

> 'And a man will be already in no mean paradise if at the hour of sunset a good hope can fall upon him like harmonies of music, that the earth shall still be fair, and the happiness of every feeling creature still receive a constant augmentation, and each good cause yet find worthy defenders, when the memory of his own poor name and personality have long been blotted out of the brief recollection of men for ever.'

George Eliot expresses the same in a poetic prayer, the splendid imagery and elevated moral aspirations of which are impotent to weaken the impression upon the reader that the language of inspiring hope is made to do service to depressing despair.

> 'O may I join the choir invisible
> Of those immortal dead who live again
> In minds made better by their presence: live

In pulses stirred to generosity,
In deeds of daring rectitude, in scorn
For miserable aims that end with self,
In thoughts sublime that pierce the night like stars,
And with their mild persistence urge man's search
To vaster issues....
               This is life to come,
Which martyred men have made more glorious
For us who strive to follow.'

The last and the longest of these essays is for many reasons the most interesting and significant of the three. Its title is 'Theism,' but it treats also of Immortality, of Revelation, of Miracles, of Christianity and Christ, and of the beneficent and powerful influences of supernatural religion as compared with the Religion of Humanity. It was written only a few years before the death of Mr. Mill. It indicates a fairer intellectual spirit, and a more kindly feeling toward Christ and Christian believers than the first two essays. In respect to many points, the author retains and re-asserts the same opinions contained in these earlier essays. In respect to others he modifies his opinions very considerably. The argument for the Being and attributes of God is scrutinized with great earnestness and logical acumen from the point of view given in Mr. Mill's philosophy and psychology as re-enforced by the doctrines of the conservation of force and the struggle for existence. There are philosophers, however, who do not accept his philosophy. There are those who do not believe that the belief in causation, and in the unity of the universe, is derived from experience or verified by experiment. Such might be willing to concede that on the basis of any philosophy whatever, whether it be intuitional or experiential, the Being of God cannot be proved by induction or demonstrated by syllogism. To such, Mr. Mill's failure to reach intellectual satisfaction by an argument only adds to the demonstration furnished by many similar failures, that truths like these are incapable of demonstration. But Mr. Mill's objection to accepting the truth as *a priori*, that it is deduced from *an idea* or *an instinct*, would only excite the wonder, if it did not the ridicule of any intelligent advocate of this theory as held in modern times. But for a practiced controversialist, Mr. Mill is singularly incapable of justly appreciating and faithfully representing the views of any school but his own, and almost uniformly fails to conceive how any man can possibly reason or think in any other way than he does. That the belief in an intelligent originator is the necessary assumption to the belief in an orderly universe, and therefore the condition of all special induction, is a proposition which Mr. Mill would seem to be incapable of understanding, so far as to conceive how any sane man should hold it. That a man, with these limitations, should fail to find what he calls an argument decisively proving that God exists, is to us altogether intelligible.

Of the natural attributes of God, he asserts that omnipotence is incompatible with design – an old assertion which gains no new force as repeated by Mr. Mill. He adds that if matter and force are eternal, as would seem to be probable, we can see an additional reason for believing that the power of God is limited. When he adds that there is no decisive proof that God is absolutely omniscient, and that God's fore-knowledge need not extend to all future events, he simply expands and enforces what he had already announced in the Essay upon Nature. In respect to the Benevolence of God, he re-affirms what he asserted so positively in that essay, but with far less bitterness of spirit.

He gives the following as

'The net results of natural theology on the question of the divine attributes. A Being of great but limited power, how or by what limited we cannot even conjecture; of great, and perhaps unlimited intelligence, but perhaps, also, more narrowly limited than his power; who desires, and pays some regard to, the happiness of his creatures, but who seems to have other motives of action which he cares more for, and who can hardly be supposed to have created the universe for that purpose alone.'

Leaving the doctrine of God as so far established, the author proceeds to the discussion of immortality. The conclusions which he reaches are that, apart from the designs of the Creator, there is no evidence for the future existence of the soul from its own essence or from its aspirations or desires. If we reason from the power or goodness of God, both of which have been proved to be limited, we can infer only, that there is room to hope that both the one and the other may extend to granting us this gift, provided it would really be beneficial to us.

Strangely enough Mr. Mill next proposes the problem of Revelation in a general sense, including the possibility and credibility and actuality of miracles. The chapter on this topic is singularly fair and even-handed, and in the discussion of this subject, the author shows himself an able expounder of the principles of evidence. Possibly his philosophical theory of the grounds of our faith in the laws of nature and in the power of God may have had some influence in determining his positions. Still the conclusion which he draws is 'that miracles have no claim whatever to the character of historical facts, and are wholly invalid as evidences of any revelation.'

Thus far, Mr. Mill seems to proceed in a line of thought in which he is, with here and there an exception, consistent with himself. But in the 'general result' in which he proposes to gather together the several lines of argument and to bring them to a consistent and well-supported conclusion, he opens a new line of thought, and as it were turns back upon and reverses his previous course of argumentation. This general result covers less than fifteen pages, but in these few pages Mr. Mill presents himself in a new attitude, and seems to reason from a new point of view in a direction which is opposed to that of the entire volume. The sentiments expressed in this general result are doubly interesting from the fact that this is the last utterance of the author upon a subject which had occupied many earnest thoughts during his life-time.

The new point of view is what he himself, in the second essay, has somewhat naively described as 'the theism of the imagination and feelings,' as not incompatible with the 'scepticism of the understanding.' How he could possibly satisfy himself with any conclusions reached from this point of view, especially after the abundant and almost passionate protests which he urged in all these essays, against reasoning from what he calls 'instincts' and 'ideas,' it is not our duty to explain. That he did do this is evident in almost every line of this concluding chapter. That he did it deliberately and upon a theory is manifest from his autobiography, in which he speaks of his 'conversion' to the position that it is absolutely essential to cultivate and exercise the sentiments and the imagination for the sake of their effect upon character and happiness. The theory as he held it not only entirely overlooks any necessary or even any conceivable connection between the sentiments and the imagination and intellectual conviction, but it proceeds on the supposition that the truth for which the understanding fails to provide, or which it is forced entirely to reject, may be accepted by the imagination and embraced by the feelings. In a similar spirit Tyndall asserts in the address delivered at Belfast:

> 'For science, however, no exclusive claim is here made; you are not urged to erect it into an idol. The inexorable advance of man's understanding in the path of knowledge, and those unquenchable claims of his moral and emotional nature which the understanding can never satisfy, are here equally set forth.' ... ' "Fill thy heart with it," said Goethe, "and then name it as thou wilt." '

It is worth noticing as a sign of the tendencies of the times, that this gross form of sentimentalism seems to be epidemic among a very large class of anti-supernaturalists and negative thinkers. Even Mr. John Morley, who, in the 'Fortnightly Review' for November 1874 and January 1875, argues very earnestly and ably against the sentimental argumentations of Mr. Mill, in this draws very largely upon the imagination for the gorgeous drapery which he requires to hide and to adorn the repulsive hideousness of his own ghastly creed, and places great reliance upon the noblest and the tenderest emotions which in their nature are stronger than death, to persuade the soul that shrinks from the extinction of its being, that it can only attain to the apotheosis of self-forgetfulness by being willing to forego the hope of immortality. Even George Eliot depends upon the richness of her own affluent and soaring imagination, and the pathos of her singularly tender and sympathizing heart, for the splendid imagery and moving appeals, that almost reconcile herself and her reader to the abnegation of the most exalted hopes and the noblest faith of our nature.

The conclusions which Mr. Mill sets forth in this remarkable conclusion are that

> 'the whole domain of the supernatural is removed from the region of belief into that of simple hope; and in that, for anything we can see, it is likely always to remain.'

He then asks

'whether the indulgence of hope, in a region of imagination only,' 'is irrational, and ought to be discouraged as a departure from the rational principle of regulating our feelings as well as opinions, strictly by evidence?'

To this question of his own asking, he replies that human life stands greatly in need of 'a wider range and greater height of aspiration for itself and its destination,'

'and that it is the part of wisdom to make the most of any, even small probabilities on the subject, which furnish imagination with any footing to support itself upon.' 'On these principles it appears to me that the indulgence of a hope, with regard to the universe and the destiny of man after death, while we recognize as a clear truth, that we have no ground for more than a hope, is legitimate and philosophically defensible.'

What Mill called only a hope, resting on the slightest and scarcely preponderating probabilities, others regard as so nearly self-evident as to be the most trustworthy truth. The sentiments which he would cherish for the sake of their elevating tendency and their kindling power, others would say were justified by the most obvious and decisive analogies. What he would inculcate as worthy and uplifting sentiments, others would enforce as the natural result of the most elevating truths. The processes which are often dignified by the appellation of faith, as an activity justified by reason, while it quickens the imagination and kindles the sensibility, Mill would lower to the regions of the imagination and sensibility, with the faintest and feeblest suggestions of reason. But while Mill remands the truths and faiths of religion to the limbo of mere possibility, he fully concedes their beneficent influence even where they are regarded as only imaginary ideals. In the second essay, he had elaborately argued the point that the need of religion is so completely outgrown as to have become utterly useless. In the conclusion of the third essay he concedes that although as a matter of faith, and as requiring and resting on objective truth, religion may be outgrown, yet even as presenting definite and elevating ideals to the imagination, it is infinitely precious to mankind. He dwells upon the familiarity of

'the imagination with the conception of a morally perfect Being, and the habit of taking the approbation of such a

Being as the *norma*, or standard, to which to refer and by which to regulate our own characters and lives.'

He even concedes

'that the *undoubting belief* of the real existence of a Being who realizes even our best ideas of perfection, and our being in the hands of that Being as the ruler of the universe, gives an increase of force to these feelings beyond what they can receive from reference to a merely ideal conception.'

This undoubting belief is not indeed warranted by evidence. Those who carefully weigh the considerations for and against, must lose somewhat of this 'increase of force to these feelings.' But what they lose in respect to force, they gain in the purity of their ideal. They find no moral contradictions in the object of their faith. If they cannot believe in a God of infinite power, they can believe in a God who is as good as his limited power will allow.

Even the absolute unbeliever can avail himself of the ideal Christ which Christianity presents, and which can never be lost to the world whatever may be thought of the origin of the ideal, or of the history which records it.

'Whatever else may be taken away from us by rational criticism, Christ is still left; a unique figure not more unlike all his precursors than all his followers.' 'But Christ stands alone, for who among his disciples or among their proselytes, was capable of inventing the saying ascribed to Jesus, or of imagining the life and character revealed in the Gospels.'

Christ must have been

'in the very first rank of the men of sublime genius of whom our species can boast.' 'When this prominent genius is combined with the qualities of probably the greatest moral reformer and martyr to that mission who ever existed upon earth, religion cannot be said to have made a bad choice in pitching on this man as the ideal representative and guide of humanity: nor, even now, would it be easy, even for an unbeliever, to find a better translation of the rule of virtue from the abstract into the concrete, than to endeavour so to live that Christ should approve his life.'

When we add the possibility that Christ was more than this, i.e.

> 'a man charged with a special, express, and unique commission from God, to lead mankind to truth and virtue,'

we may conclude that the influences of religion on the character are well worth preserving, and that

> 'what they lack in direct strength, as compared with those of a firmer belief, is more than compensated by the greater truth and rectitude of the morality which they sustain.'

With these concessions, Mill leaves his readers. That he should make them, is a far higher and more decisive testimony to the sensibility of Mill, as a man, to the necessities of his moral nature, than to his sagacity as a philosopher and his self-consistency as a logician. His admiring or apologetic disciples may explain or excuse these concessions as they will, but his impartial though not unkindly critics cannot fail to find in his last utterances upon religion a decisive, because an unconscious and even a reluctant testimony to the truth and importance of Christian theism.

The autobiography of Mr. Mill, and those three Essays upon Religion, are his last legacies of thought and feeling. The autobiography leaves him 'in a cottage as close as possible to the place where she was buried,' declaring that her memory was to him a religion, and her approbation the standard by which he endeavoured to regulate his life. His Essays on Religion conclude with his honest testimony to the value of faith in a personal God, and a glowing tribute to Christ the perfect ideal of human excellence, and a possible extraordinary furnished and commissioned messenger from God to man. Both these volumes are remarkable for many things, but for none which are more worthy to be pondered than these passages.

# [REVIEW OF]
# THREE ESSAYS ON RELIGION
Anonymous

We hardly know so remarkable a fact in the history of philosophy, as the collapse of Mr. Mill's fame which has so speedily followed on his death. To us the reaction seems as exaggerated on one side, as his philosophical name was indubitably exaggerated on the other. But when his opinion became publicly known, that it would not be easy even for an unbeliever to find a better rule of conduct than 'to endeavour so to live that Christ would approve our life' – nay, that not impossibly Jesus Christ was 'a man charged with a special, express, and unique commission from God to lead mankind to truth and virtue' – we may well understand with what contempt his memory is regarded by some of his former admirers. His very particular friend, Mr. Morley, has published in the *Fortnightly* what we must pronounce to be a crushing criticism of his work.

In fact, we are bound to admit that it is by far the weakest thing he has ever published. His philosophical principles lead to antitheism by legitimate consequence; and his passionate attempts to construct some kind of religious edifice do more credit (if we may use the common antithesis) to his heart than to his head. Such attempts, we think, are due to that passionate emotionism, which was so very prominent and so very singular a part of his character.

It is certain that his writings had more powerful effect in promoting speculative irreligion than any other of his time, and that his great influence was predominantly directed against the cause of God. Without, however, attempting to deny this, we may say that the present volume has much confirmed an opinion which we have frequently expressed, that in several points he was distinguished for the better from the body of his brother irreligionists.

As to the contents of this volume, our time for discussing

them will be at the appropriate period of the controversy which we are still carrying on against his philosophy. When we began that controversy, his was confessedly the greatest English name on his own philosophical side; whereas there is now hardly one which carries with it so little authority.

# [REVIEW OF] THREE ESSAYS ON RELIGION
[Henry Reeve]

... The posthumous Essays of Mr. John Stuart Mill ... are, as we are informed by the Editor of this volume, 'the carefully balanced result of the deliberations of a lifetime.' There is something solemn in a voice which comes from the grave, though in the opinion of the author it be the grave of annihilation: and it was no light motive which induced Mr. Mill, having committed his thoughts on these subjects to paper, to withhold them during his lifetime, and to order them to be published as soon as possible after his death. ...

As Mr. Mill has mainly to deal with what is termed Natural Religion, he wisely commences his work by an attempt to define the terms *natural* and *nature*. The task is not an easy one, for few terms in language have acquired a greater variety of significations. M. Littre, in a consummate analysis of the word 'nature' as used by French authors, in his admirable dictionary, assigns to it no less than twenty-eight shades of meaning, some of them extremely dissimilar. Dr. Johnson confined himself in English to thirteen. ...

Mr. Mill's own definition is as follows: –

'The Nature of a thing means its entire capacity of exhibiting phenomena. And since the phenomena which a thing exhibits, however much they vary in different circumstances, are always the same in the same circumstances, they admit of being described in general forms of words, which are called the *laws* of the thing's nature. Thus it is a law of the nature of water that under the mean pressure of the atmosphere at the level of the sea, it boils at 212° Fahrenheit.

As the nature of any given thing is the aggregate of its powers and properties, so Nature in the abstract is the aggregate of the powers and properties of all things. Nature means the sum of all phenomena, together with the causes which produce them; including not only all that happens, but all that is capable of happening; the unused capabilities of causes being as much a part of the idea of Nature, as those which take effect. Since all phenomena which have been sufficiently examined are found to take place with regularity, each having certain fixed conditions, positive and negative, on the occurrence of which it invariably happens; mankind have been able to ascertain, either by direct observation or by reasoning processes grounded on it, the conditions of the occurrence of many phenomena; and the progress of science mainly consists in ascertaining those conditions.'

We very much question whether this definition can be supported. To assert that Nature means the sum of all phenomena, *together with the causes which produce them*, is to assume the main question in dispute, and amounts in fact to saying that Nature includes the causes of Nature. A law of Nature is not the efficient cause – the *vera causa* – of any event. It is only the rule according to which the efficient cause acts.

The sum of all phenomena includes, we presume, the manifestation in every form of power and will with its results; yet these can hardly be termed natural, nor are they regular. Mr. Mill, however, is of the opposite opinion, for he says in the next page, 'Art is as much Nature as anything else, and anything which is artificial is natural. Art has no independent powers of its own: Art is but the employment of the powers of Nature for an end.' Yes; but the *employment* is the Art. That use or employment of natural elements is precisely the function of the intelligence and the will, which differs from Nature in its proper sense as the active differs from the passive. These philosophers do not always agree. If Mr. Mill had turned to a well-known dialogue of Voltaire, he would have found precisely the opposite statement: –

> '*Euhémere.* – Et si je vous disais qu'il n'y a point de nature, que tout est art dans l'univers, et que l'art annonce un ouvrier?
>
> *Callicrate.* – Comment donc, point de nature, et tout est art! Quelle idée creuse!
>
> *Euhémere.* – Vous m'avouerez que vous ne pouvez entendre par ce mot vague *nature* qu'un assemblage de choses qui existent et dont la plupart n'existeront pas demain – certes, des arbres, des pierres, des legumes, des chenilles,

des chevres, des filles et des singes ne composent point un etre absolu quel qu'il soit: des effets qui n'existaient point hier ne peuvent etre la cause eternelle, necessaire et productive. Votre nature, encore une fois, n'est qu'un mot invente pour signifier l'universalite des choses. Pour vous faire voir a present que l'art a tout fait, observez seulement un insecte, un limaçon, une mouche; vous y verrez un art infini qu'aucune industrie humaine ne peut imiter: il faut donc qu'il y ait un artiste infiniment habile, et c'est ce que les sages appellent Dieu.' (*Voltaire*, Dialogue xxix. 2.)

Or to borrow a line from our own Cowper which expresses the same sentiment –

'Nature is but a name for an effect,
Whose cause is God.'

We cannot conceive on what grounds Mr. Mill asserts that the office of man in the artificial operations of constructing an engine or composing a picture *'is a very limited one.'* The office of man in the invention of such works is strictly creative, for he makes something that did not exist before; it is the adjustment of the powers of Nature which produces the result; but the intelligence which contrives and the volition that constructs cannot be called powers of Nature without a distortion of language, since they are precisely the powers that control Nature. Take a tube of metal, place in it some vitreous plates fused of soda and sand, and ground to a particular curve by a rough powder – no great natural elements, but a good deal of skill in combining them. For this tube, by means of the laws of optics and the properties of light, will conquer distance, as a cord of wire stretched along a row of poles has, by the properties of electricity, conquered time. With this instrument man will range the solar system, and sound immeasurable depths of space beyond it, till he arrives at the mathematical truths which are the basis of the universe. Is the office of man in the construction and use of the telescope and the electric battery a 'very limited one,' because they are composed of natural substances and worked by natural agents; or is it Mr. Mill's purpose to lower the artificer, be he human or divine, to the level of the substances on which he works? The merit of these inventions is not merely an ingenious use of natural substances, but the discovery of the laws which natural substances obey. This confusion of terms is the more remarkable on the part of Mr. Mill, because the chief object of this Essay is to prove that it is the duty and glory of man to combat and subdue Nature – to conquer and resist our natural tendencies – and to amend the world by endeavouring to improve a world 'so clumsily made and so capriciously governed' (p. 112). No Calvinist ever took a darker view than Mr. Mill of this eternal conflict of Nature and Grace, only he calls it by another name: and we are not sure that something of the hereditary theology of Scotland does not lurk under all his philosophy....

It is a morbid and saturnine view of creation: the sense of terror exciting the abject superstition of a savage incapable of a sense of excellence – feeling awe without admiration, fearing vastness without a moral perception of universal wisdom and power. For if, as Mr. Mill says, he is affected not by these considerations but by mere enormity allied to terror, these sentiments are equally excited in the mind by the belief in a maleficent power; and as with the lowest order of Polynesian or African savages, Mr. Mill's best reason for the worship of gods is the fear of their capacity to inflict evil. We doubt whether so monstrous a theory was ever propounded by a cultivated man, and we shall presently see to what it leads.

His picture of man is charged with the same gloomy colours. Having sneered at p. 10 at most denominations of Christians for affirming that man is by nature wicked, he himself asserts at p. 46 that it is only in a highly artificialised condition of human nature that the notion grows up, or ever could grow up, that goodness was natural. On the contrary, man was a sort of wild animal, distinguished chiefly 'by being craftier than the other beasts of the field' – (he was then himself one of them) – all worth of character was the result of taming; and, in short, Mr. Mill holds that 'there is hardly a single point of excellence in the human character which is not decidedly repugnant to the untutored feelings of human nature.' That seems to us very like saying that man is by nature wicked, and much more akin to the teaching of the Genevese theologian Calvin than to that of the Genevese philosopher Rousseau. Man, according to Mr. Mill, is naturally a coward. Fear is his most constant attribute. It may fairly be questioned if any human being is naturally courageous. As Mr. Mill appears to have no conception of moral power or force in his view of our miserable nature, man is in his eyes the most degraded of material beings only to be stimulated by artificial discipline. He is not even a cleanly animal; selfishness is his most intense and natural characteristic, and he is a born liar.

Another great English writer has drawn a picture of his fellow-creatures which differs not materially from that of Mr. John Stuart Mill, but he called them Yahoos; but there is this distinction between them, that whilst Swift abhorred and despised mankind, Mill affects to believe in what he terms the Religion of Humanity as the last hope of an unbelieving world. Neither of these philosophers appears to have perceived that however degraded man may be by circumstances or by nature, there is in him the potentiality of the highest known order of finite beings – gifts which he does not share with perishable brutes, and faculties which require but to be awakened to reflect truths and ideas infinitely beyond his own present condition. It is this strange absence of the sense of beauty, order, and rational powers which seems to us to be the characteristic of Mr. Mill's system. Like his father, when he exclaimed 'How poor a thing is life!' he has destroyed life by rejecting all that ennobles it. It is a mere truism to assert that 'if Nature and Man are both the works of a Being of perfect goodness, that Being intended Nature as a scheme to be amended, not imitated, by Man' (p. 41). All philosophy agrees in the belief that it is the prerogative of Man to seek to penetrate the secrets of Nature, to control her elements, to apply her powers: and all civilisation and knowledge are the result of these efforts. But the faculties we bring to this great task are natural faculties; that is, they are the gift of the same Being who brought Man and Nature into existence, and who

'Binding Nature fast as Fate,
Left free the human will.'

We now arrive at the central point of Mr. Mill's theory. Struck by the existence of evil in the world, recoiling with horror from the spectacle of pain and death, and the relentless tortures of the course of Nature, he arrives at the conclusion that 'if the Maker of the world *can* all that he will, he wills misery. . . .'

Mr. Mill does not appear to have perceived that the limited knowledge of a finite being renders it impossible for him to conceive and apprehend all the elements of the question. 'To have sufficient grounds for believing in God,' says Dean

Mansel, 'is a very different thing from having sufficient grounds for reasoning about him.' Mr. Mill has not got the data necessary for his argument; and with a presumption which savours of infatuation he proceeds to arraign and convict infinite wisdom on finite evidence. 'To resolve to believe,' says Whateley, 'that God *must* have dealt with mankind just in the way *we* could wish as the most desirable, and in the way that seems to *us* the most probable – this is, in fact, *to set up ourselves as his judges*.' The conclusion of such reasoning is simply that an omnipotent and beneficent Being was bound by the conditions of his existence to banish evil from the universe, and if he did not do so that he was either not omnipotent or not beneficent. But it is surely more consistent with reason and probability to suppose that there are limits to the faculties and philosophy of Mr. Mill, than to the power and benevolence of God.

We shall not follow Mr. Mill into the most difficult of all questions, and the most impenetrable to the human understanding – the origin of evil. Be it enough to say that the conscience of mankind, and the voice alike of philosophy and of religion, reject with equal horror his alternative solution that the Creator of the world is either the Author of evil or the slave of it.[1]

We are so sensible of the utter inadequacy of our own faculties, and indeed of the powers of thought and language, to deal with these speculations, into which Mr. Mill plunges with all the confidence of one who believes in the power of logic to explain a universe, that it is with the utmost diffidence and reluctance that we follow him to the brink of these abysses. The very terms 'Omnipotence' and 'Omniscience,' if they are taken to convey more than an assertion of unlimited power and universal knowledge, are unfathomable, for we can ourselves discern a limit to omnipotence inasmuch as a thing cannot exist at variance with its own conditions of existence, or be and not be at the same time; and the attribute of universal

---

[1] Every one of the arguments or objections advanced by Mr. Mill will be found in the second chapter of Cudworth's 'Intellectual System,' in which that author recapitulates the doctrines of Leucippus, Democritus, and Protagoras, for the purpose of refuting them. There is a noble passage in the tenth book of 'The Laws' of Plato in which he disdainfully describes them; for these opinions were professed in Greece long before Epicurus was born.

knowledge or prescience cannot be reconciled with what we know of the liberty of man. These propositions, and many others equally incomprehensible to us, are just as difficult of solution by our systems of logic as the existence of evil in a world created by a just and all-powerful Being.

There is, nevertheless, one unassailable method of dealing with such arguments as those Mr. Mill presents to us. It is a profound remark of Pascal that although man is always prone to deny the incomprehensible, yet nothing is demonstrably certain but those things *whose converse is manifestly false.* Hence whenever a proposition is unintelligible, instead of passing judgement on it and rejecting it on that account, the wiser course is to *examine its opposite*, and if that be manifestly false it may boldly be affirmed that the former proposition is true, though it may be incomprehensible.[2] Pascal applies this method of reasoning to some of the most abstruse and inconceivable propositions in geometry, such as the infinite divisibility of matter; and indeed something analogous to it is in common use in ordinary mathematical demonstrations. You prove the truth of a proposition by showing that the converse of it is absurd. This is a test which, if we are not mistaken, many of Mr. Mill's propositions will not support. They all converge towards the absurd. And however difficult it may be to meet affirmatively objections which are deeply seated in the nature of things beyond human knowledge, it is much easier to show that to these objections he supplies no rational solution, but, on the contrary, offers and adopts an absurd one....

Whatever be the limited powers of the Creator, according to Mr. Mill, he will scarcely deny that the Power which called into being the universe, filled the globe we inhabit with animated beings, and gave birth to that intellect of man, which, with all its imperfections, is able in some faint degree to conceive and love the attributes of its Author, is a Power of a very high order, and there is something incredibly absurd in the conception that it is the duty of man to supply the deficiencies of the Being who gave him life and every faculty he can exercise or enjoy. But, says Mr. Mill, it is incomprehensible to me that the Creator should be at once all-powerful and just. This

---

[2] Pascal, 'De l'Esprit Géométrique.' Ed. Faugère. Vol. i. p. 149.

is the old argument of Callicrates: either God could not expel evil, and in that case, is He omnipotent? or He could, but has not done so, is He then just? The answer appears to us to be that which we gave a few lines back in the words of Montesquieu – if God exists, He must be just, for to conceive him otherwise is to conceive him as the worst and most imperfect of beings, which is impossible.

But Mr. Mill resorts throughout these Essays to the strange hypothesis that as it is impossible to believe that an all-powerful Being created a world, as he terms it, 'so clumsily made and capriciously governed,' the Demiurgus, or maker of the universe, must be held to be a Being of limited powers.[3] This hypothesis appears to us to leave Mr. Mill little choice but in Polytheism, Manicheism, or devil-worship. For if the powers of the Maker of the world are limited, they must be controlled by the superior power of some being greater than himself. There is therefore a plurality, or at least a duality, of these supernatural existences, of which man and nature are at once the creatures and the victims. The Jupiter of Homer laments that there is a Fate, which even he cannot overrule. But as, according to Mr. Mill, the scheme of Nature cannot be supposed to have for its object the good of sentient beings, it follows that the Evil principle is more powerful than the Good principle, or, if these supernatural beings are beings of limited powers, there is no reason to assign any limit to their numbers, and we relapse into something not unlike the system of the Hindoo mythology. Mr. Mill has told us that the feeling chiefly excited in his mind by the contemplation of the grandeur and vastness of the physical universe, was that of terror – not admiration, not gratitude, not humility, not religion. But if terror at the vastness of the physical universe is the sentiment excited in the mind of man instead of the religious sentiment, the ultimate conclusion would be precisely that of the savage

---

[3] Mr. Mill is not entitled to the merit of originality in this view of the Creator. He was to a great extent anticipated about one hundred and twenty years ago by Soame Jenyns in his 'Free Enquiry into the Nature and Origin of Evil' (1757). Jenyns laid it down that Omnipotence cannot work contradictions: which is true enough; that all evils owe their existence to the necessity of their own nature; and that the Almighty is limited and circumscribed by the nature of things (pp. 14, 16). This however is very vague language. Who created the 'nature of things' by which the Almighty is limited and circumscribed?

who seeks to avert the wrath of an infernal deity, and sees the Supreme Being in an incarnation of destructive ferocity. He must needs worship and propitiate whatever is Most High and most powerful, but by this theory the Most High is not a God but a devil; therefore religion assumes in his mind the form of devil-worship. We will carry this extraordinary chain of reasoning but one step further. Mr. Mill holds that the design of Nature is no evidence of any moral attributes, and its end is not a moral end at all (p. 189). Indeed throughout this work it is hard to trace any sense at all of those finer perceptions of moral evidence which, as Mr. Gibbon says, really govern our thoughts and motives. Mr. Mill's sole conception of a moral end of our being appears to be the hope that some thousands of years hence the world may become, by dint of the enlightened exertions of the human race, a little less intolerable than it is at present.

We might apply severe language to such propositions as these, for they are more offensive to the most cherished sentiments of mankind than those which Voltaire denounced as horrible and impious, and we do not remember that in the whole range of sceptical literature any writer ever adopted conclusions so atrocious. But our object in quoting such passages is simply the demolition of Mr. Mill's argument by the weight of its own absurdity. 'I cannot understand,' we hear him saying in substance (the words are our own), 'that the power and goodness of a Supreme Being are compatible with what I see around me. Therefore I resort to the converse, and have arrived at the conclusion that if there be a Deity at all, he must be a Being of limited power or malevolent disposition,' or (as he says elsewhere, p. 184) 'a single Creator with divided purposes.' But, we rejoin, your converse proposition is manifestly absurd and totally incompatible with the very existence of God or any rational scheme of Nature. Bishop Berkeley remarks that the expression 'a blind agent' is a contradiction in terms, for an agent, to merit the name, must have intelligence and will. Much more is the idea of an impotent and maleficent God a preposterous contradiction, if God be the 'Ens summe perfectum et absolute infinitum.' Therefore, we say, applying the test of Pascal, it is much easier to believe that in some way unknown to our finite intelligence the power and goodness of God are compatible with the existence of evil, than that the world is the work of an inferior demiurgus or of a demon.

We confess that it is a relief to us, after dealing with these monstrous paradoxes, to fall back on the more sober argument of the teleogists, who, no doubt, cannot prove from the works of creation infinite wisdom, goodness, and power, but who do prove an amount of wisdom, goodness, and power which satisfies the mind. Take, for instance, the charming and instructive volume of Sir Charles Bell on 'the Hand,' and say whether it is possible to follow him through the niceties and beauty of adaptation which he demonstrates, without acknowledging an inconceivable amount of ingenious contrivance and benevolent design. Mr. Mill admits that the argument from marks of design in Nature is one of the most important proofs of superior intelligence in creation. But here he strangely misconceives or misstates the well-known illustration of Paley's watch. Mill says, 'If I found a watch on an apparently desolate island I should indeed infer *that it had been left there* by a human being; but the inference would not be from marks of design, but because I already knew from direct experience that watches are made by men:' and he adds that he should draw the same inference no less confidently from a foot-print, as geologists infer the past existence of animals from a coprolite. But Paley did not introduce this illustration of the watch merely to prove the former presence of a human being. He infers from the inspection of the watch that its parts are framed and put together for a purpose; viz. to measure time with great mechanical accuracy, and that consequently it had a maker who comprehended its construction and designed its use. Mr. Mill's illustration of the foot-print or the coprolite suggests no such inference: they prove no more than the mere passage of a man or an animal. We are surprised at so gross a misstatement of a well-known proposition. In the same chapter he deals with an equal want of candour or intelligence with the argument derived from the faculty of sight. The structure of the eye and the combination of the organic elements which enable an animal to see are no doubt the result of some common cause, though Mr. Mill is not disinclined to favour the Darwinian theory that sight and the organs of sight are only the result of 'the survival of the fittest,' which has led by gradual evolution to the extraordinary perfection of structures and functions which exist in the eye of man and of the more important animals. Mr. Mill is pleased to say for Mr. Darwin that this theory is not so absurd as it looks. But when they have by this process endowed the animal with an eye, they are as far as ever from the faculty of sight. That consists not only in the particular structure of the optic nerves and all the marvellous parts of that living instrument, but in the adaptation of this organ to the influence of light emanating from sources hundreds of millions of miles from this planet. The adaptation of the retina to the momentum of light, says Dugald Stewart, is one of the most astonishing facts that falls within the sphere of our observation: –

'How beautifully is the same organ adapted to that property of light in consequence of which it alters its course when it passes obliquely from one medium to another of different density, insomuch that the course of the visual rays through the humours of the eye, till they paint the image on the retina, may be traced on the same dioptrical principles on which we explain the theory of the telescope and the microscope.'[4]

The argument of design is not adequately stated until it is shown that the parts of creation, the most remote, are indissolubly adapted to each other. Rays of light which have been travelling to this earth with inconceivable velocity for thousands of years, from the more distant stars, are received by the eye of every animated creature, and even exercise a mysterious influence over the vegetable and mineral kingdoms. Is it possible to conceive a more direct proof that He who said 'Let there be light,' also provided the organs and functions to which this ocean of light was to bear the countless impressions of sight and life? The argument is far beyond a mere argument of analogy: it is the argument of causation by intelligence and will, which includes things the most remote in a common purpose.

For, in fact, it includes all things in a common purpose. Mr. Mill speaks of the nice and intricate combinations of vegetable and animal life as an argument of considerable strength. But this is a very narrow and contracted view of the theory of design. It is not enough to trace in the combinations of vegetable and animal life the combinations which subserve the existence of the individual or the species. These, it may be

---

[4] Stewart's Philosophy of the Moral Powers, chap. ii. § 2.

conceived, might be the results of evolution caused by the wants or hereditary faculties of each particular race of beings. But every individual and every species, in every act and incident of its existence, bears some necessary relation to everything else existing in the universe. 'According to the doctrine of infinite divisibility,' says Berkeley, 'there must be some smell of a rose at an infinite distance from it.' And these combinations are infinite in number and extent. The harmony and adjustment of these countless elements is the greatest marvel of creation: every created thing has its function and its place in relation to every other thing, however remote from it. 'All natural consequences,' says the Duke of Argyll in his 'Reign of Law,' 'meet and fit into each other in endless circles of harmony and purpose. And this can only be explained by the fact that what we call natural consequence is always the conjoint effect of an infinite number of elementary forces, whose action and reaction are under the direction of the Will which we see obeyed and of the Purposes which we see actually attained.' The reduction of this infinite variety of causes and results, all interdependent on each other, to unity of purpose in one great Whole, is the most direct evidence of omniscience and omnipotence which we can arrive at, because it is inconceivable that any Power short of an infinite intelligence and will should embrace and direct an infinite multiplicity of effects, every one of which is more or less dependent on all the rest. The government of the material and moral universe by fixed laws, or in other words the substitution of a Kosmos for a Chaos, is precisely the most evident proof of the prodigious power and wisdom which controls all phenomena, and has been well pointed out by Mr. Page Roberts in some simple village discourses that contain a great deal of sound philosophy. When laws exist they cannot be broken with impunity. The effect of an interruption of these is destruction. Hence the very laws which are designed for the good of sentient beings and are necessary for their existence, become when they are violated the cause of suffering and death: the evidence of a sovereign will is as strong in the one case as in the other....

Mr. Mill coldly admits that there is a large balance of probability in favour of creation by intelligence. We contend that creation, and more especially the harmony of the infinite variety of the universe, is absolutely inconceivable without it.

For, to borrow an expressive sentence from Dr. James Martineau's address: –

> 'It is precisely here and now that a Divine Agent is needed, to be the fountain of orderly power and to render the tissue of laws intelligible by his presence; his witness is found not only in the gaps but in the continuity of being – not in the suspense but in the everlasting flow of change; for the universe as known, being throughout a system of *Thought-relations*, can subsist only in an eternal Mind that thinks it.' (P. 11.)

If this be true of the material conditions of the universe, it is still more true of the moral ends for which the universe subsists, as far as we can discern them. Mr. Mill denies that Nature affords evidence of any moral end in creation: we think, on the contrary, that it is solely for moral ends that creation subsists at all, that all material life and being is but the mechanism subservient to that moral purpose, and that the moral purposes of God will survive the dissolution of the universe. The difference between us therefore becomes more palpable. Mr. Mill, confining his view to the functions of life and nature in the globe, or extending it at furthest to the terrestrial condition of mankind in future ages, sees no moral end at all but the improvement of society, and on that the bearing of each individual life and effort must be so small that we derive no consolation from the 'Religion of Humanity,' and must confess that we are wholly without faith in it: –

> 'For all our yesterdays have lighted fools
> The way to dusty death. Out, out, brief candle!'

It is the correlation of the moral purposes of being with the functions of life and matter which gives a meaning and purpose to existence: but this adjustment of the visible and the invisible, of the finite and the infinite, though here and there discernible even to ourselves, demands for its preservation an amount of wisdom and power immeasurably beyond the most sublime results of the material universe.

This consideration alone may suffice to refute, in passing, Mr. Mill's strange propensity to favour the Manichean doctrine, or to represent the Author of the world as a God of divided purposes and limited powers. The difficulty is sufficiently great for man to conceive a Supreme Being of such infinite wisdom and power, that all the issues of creation resolve themselves into one universal Whole, governed by law and directed by unity of purpose. But this difficulty is increased beyond the verge of possibility by the theory that there is not one Supreme Being, but two principles in active hostility, the one perpetually frustrating the designs of the other – that the relations of every part to the whole are not guided by one intelligence, but torn asunder by conflicting wills – and that the conception of Deity as the source of Law, Order, and Power is degraded to the strifes of a mythological Olympus. Intolerable discords and total anarchy would then take the place of harmony, and the universe itself would sink into chaos.

It follows from the mutual dependence of all things and of all the conditions of existence, that those conditions of life which appear to Mr. Mill to be noxious, cruel, and unjust are just as necessary and useful as those which he conceives to be pleasurable; for, except in the utilitarian philosophy, to seek pleasure and to fly from pain are not the sole ends of existence. We do not assert that Omnipotence could not have made a different sort of world, but we do contend that the world, being designed for the moral purposes we discern in it, could not be very different from its actual condition. Take for example the great facts of mutual destruction, disease, decay, and death, which appear so revolting to Mr. Mill. These are obviously the inseparable conditions of a state of being of brief duration, by means of which an inexhaustible *flow* of successive generations passes onwards through a limited sphere of space and time, and the world is perpetually renewed.[5] Life supports life, but by losing it, for whilst vegetables draw their nutriment directly from the chemical ingredients of the soil, animals only subsist upon organic productions. Water and salt are perhaps the only inorganic exceptions in the diet of man,

---

[5] Mr. Mill himself observes that 'the destroying agencies are *a necessary part* of the preserving agencies; the chemical compositions by which life is carried on could not take place without a parallel series of decompositions.' Nothing can be more profound and true. If Mr. Mill had followed that line of thought, it might have guided him a long way. A stranger who seeks the tomb of Lord Bacon in St. Michael's Church, near Gorhambury, may still read upon his monument the words placed there by the faithful Meautys, '*Composita solvuntur.*' That is perhaps the secret of the world. For, as Tertullian has it, '*Omnia pereundo servantur; omnia interitu reformantur.*'

but these alone will not support life, though they are essential to it. If the globe were inhabited by a fixed number of creatures, incapable of destruction or of increase, the whole movement of animated nature would cease: we should live in what Professor Tyndall calls the stagnation of the marsh instead of the leap of the torrent. So in the moral world, if it had pleased the Creator to place us in a perfect state of being, all those faculties which Mr. Mill admires in common with ourselves – energy, resource, effort, thought, self-sacrifice – would have lacked all scope of action. A perfect state of existence, being alike incapable of change or improvement, differs not materially from the Nirvana of the Buddhists; it is the extinction of the active powers and an absorption in the perfection of God. These are happily not the conditions of human life, and we prefer it a thousand times, with all its pains and perils, its brevity and its obscurity, to a state of being in which man would lose all the incentives and the freedom of action.

We now proceed to consider Mr. Mill's chapter on the Immortality of the Soul – not the least singular and painful portion of this volume. A writer who would speak of the immortality of the soul labours under some difficulty when he entertains doubts of the existence of any spiritual faculties and nature in man. 'Those,' says Mill, 'who would deduce the immortality of the soul from its own nature have first to prove that the attributes in question are not attributes of the body but of a separate substance.' The body is certainly perishable: hence if we hold that '*all thought and feeling* has some action of the bodily organism for its immediate antecedent and accompaniment,' and that 'our senses are all that we have to trust to' (both these propositions are laid down by Mr. Mill), it is not easy to imagine that out of this purely material frame should spring an immortal and spiritual being. But here we come across one of those singular contradictions which we had occasion to notice some time ago in reviewing Mr. Mill's answer to Sir William Hamilton. For though he seems in places to deny the existence of mind, it is in reality matter and material certainty that he holds to be undemonstrable. . . .

Mr. Mill says fairly enough that weighed by the light of Nature there is rather more to be said in favour of our immortal nature than against it. We ourselves should go further. The inference to be drawn from the brevity and incompleteness of human life seems to us to warrant the strongest belief that this is no more than a phase of existence; and that the greatest realities lie beyond it; whilst it is obvious that nothing but a future state of being can fulfil our conceptions of justice and moral responsibility. These Mr. Mill peremptorily rejects, and we do not think his whole work contains a passage more entirely destructive of faith and morals than the following: –

> 'Nothing can be more opposed to every estimate we can form of probability, than the common idea of the future life as a state of rewards and punishments in any other sense than the consequences of our actions upon our own character and susceptibilities will follow us in the future as they have done in the past and present.' (P. 211.)

That is, in other words, to say, if we understand the author's meaning, that there is no objective law of rectitude, administered by a Being to whom all hearts are open and all desires known – that no consequences follow the performance of any human actions except those which they may produce on our own characters – and consequently that the ideas of retributive justice and moral responsibility are delusions or impostures. This opinion, if it were entertained, is obviously subversive of all law whatsoever. It is the negation of the moral government of the universe, and that is the logical conclusion to which a reasoner like Mr. Mill is led, when he disputes the most essential of the Divine attributes and the immortality of the soul. For, as has been demonstrated by Mr. John Austin, himself a Utilitarian writer, the first principle of ethics and jurisprudence is that there can be no such thing as a law without a sovereign and without a sanction. Mill annihilates the sovereignty of the Deity by reducing the conception of him to that of a being of limited powers, and he annihilates the sanction of law by denying the system of retributive justice. His conception of the evil results of crime would seem to be purely subjective, that is, he holds that the consequences of our bad actions may unpleasantly affect our character. Such a theory would let loose all the bad passions of the human race, and turn earth into hell, just as we have seen the mere temporary suspension of human law in a great city open all the sluices of destruction. Mr. Mill, as a moralist, would certainly contend that he does not underrate the moral obligation of man to do what conduces to the welfare of mankind, but of the extent of that obligation each man is himself the judge. The objective laws of right and wrong disappear with the lawgiver: and, to borrow another sentence from Dean Mansel, 'If man is absolutely a law unto himself, his duty and his pleasure are undistinguishable from each other; for he is subject to no one and accountable to no one.' (*Bampton Lectures*, p. 112.)

If this be all the evidence in favour of religion and a supreme morality which Mr. Mill and the advanced thinkers of our age are able to draw from the study and comparison of Nature, it must be acknowledged that their failure supplies an argument of considerable strength in favour of Revelation. If without Revelation man cannot be assured of the existence of God or of the immortality of the soul, that is an additional reason for believing that those great facts have been communicated to man by some messenger of divine truth. Mr. Mill acknowledges that, admitting the existence of God, 'there are grounds which, though insufficient for proof, are sufficient to take away all antecedent improbability that a message may really have been received from him.' Indeed Mr. Mill's chapter on Revelation is by far the least irreligious portion of his book; and he seems at moments to have been brought, by the stress and vacuity of scepticism, almost to the verge of Christianity. Indeed he is at one with the most exclusive and dogmatical of Christian sects in affirming that by nature the secrets of life and religion are totally impenetrable, whence they draw the corollary that if solved at all, they must be solved by what theologians call the gifts of grace. If this be so, and if it be impossible to ascertain or demonstrate the first elements of religious truth by any evidence derived from Nature or by any effort of the human reason, the probability is greatly increased that God should by supernatural means have imparted some knowledge of his existence, his attributes, and his moral law to his creatures. Mr. Mill seems to admit as much, and he adds that 'the Christian religion is open to no objections, either moral or intellectual, which do not apply at least equally to the common theory of Deism.' That is a large concession, for it extends very nearly to the length contended for by the Doctors of the Roman Catholic Church, that there is no halting ground in strict logic between their own dogmatic theology and atheism. Mr. Mill then acknowledges that the only question to be entertained is one of evidence. Can any evidence prove a Divine

Revelation? Does such evidence exist in support of the Revelation believed by Christians to be divine? Mr. Mill rejects, as might be expected, all miraculous evidence of Revelation, but the historical evidence in favour of Christianity obtains even from him some acknowledgment. It is impossible to deny that the Christian religion exists – that it has existed for more than eighteen hundred years – that it has changed the face of society – that, as he himself expresses it, 'religion, since the birth of Christianity, has inculcated the belief that our highest conceptions of combined wisdom and goodness exist in the concrete in a living Being, who has his eyes on us and cares for our good. Through the darkest and most corrupt periods Christianity has raised this torch on high – has kept this object of veneration and imitation before the eyes of man.'

> 'Above all, the most valuable part of the effect on the character which Christianity has produced by holding up in a Divine Person a standard of excellence and a model for imitation, is available even to the absolute unbeliever and can never more be lost to humanity. For it is Christ, rather than God, whom Christianity has held up to believers as the pattern of perfection for humanity. . . .'

If all the phenomena of life succeed each other with undeviating regularity, whence came this astounding apparition? In a semi-barbarous province of the Roman Empire, in a brutal age, amongst the lowest class of a fanatical people, appears one figure absolutely unparalleled in history and in fiction – one man who displays in perfect humility the qualities of transcendent humanity, completely free from all human infirmities of passion, of false judgment, and frailty. A few simple sentences delivered from his lips, and preserved in the scanty pages of a broken record, suffice to regenerate the world, as he himself announced. Nothing *aut simile aut secundum* has been known to exist, or has even pretended to exist, in the history of our race. But that he did exist, and did hold this language, and did produce these effects, is as indisputable as any occurrence in the annals of mankind. The evidence of the fact is certain. Can the fact be explained by natural causes? Are any natural causes known to us which could lead to such a result? If not, is not the supernatural origin of Christianity by far the least improbable solution of the question?[6]

According to Mr. Mill, 'the whole domain of the supernatural is removed from the region of Belief into that of simple Hope;' but he admits that the imagination of man stands greatly in need of wider range and greater height of aspiration for itself and its destination, than human life affords. Other writers of the same school have acknowledged that however inconsistent religious belief may be with what they call scientific reasoning, yet that it is essential to purify and elevate the emotions of man. This faint homage to the Power they have sought to dethrone cannot alter our judgment of the fatal perversity of their systems. The primary condition of religious belief is the Truth of the objects to which it is directed – that Truth being the basis of all other truths, and without it there being no truth or certainty at all. To substitute a dream of imagination, or a thrill of emotion, for that which is, if it exist at all, the foundation of all Being and all Knowledge, appears to us to be but a feeble attempt to dispel the gloom of this philosophy of despair. When the light that should lighten the world is darkened, how great is that darkness!

---

[6] This argument is pursued with great ability by Mr. Henry Rogers in an excellent work, entitled 'The Superhuman Origin of the Bible,' being the Congregational Lecture for 1873. Mr. Rogers is a philosophical writer of very high merit, as is well known to the readers of this Review, and without any appeals to dogmatic theology, he has in this volume set forth the overwhelming difficulties to be surmounted by those who assign to the Bible a merely human origin. [For Henry Rogers see Alan P. F. Sell, *Dissenting Thought and the Life of the Churches. Studies in an English Tradition*, Lewiston, NY: Edwin Mellen Press, 1990, ch. 6.]

# [REVIEW OF] THREE ESSAYS ON RELIGION
Anonymous

Whether respect for the memory of the late John Stuart Mill called for the posthumous publication of his unfinished Essays, it is not for us to say. Respect for the opinion of the living would have suggested a very different course. They were not called for from any quarter. They are more displeasing even to his followers of the sceptical school than to those whose faith in Revelation is fixed and firm. The book has been received with a chorus of disappointment on the part of those who call themselves philosophers, principally because they shut their eyes to the sunlight from above, and are content with the glimmering of their own imaginations. We do not remember a case in literature of such unanimous disapproval on the part of a man's own following. What useful purpose, then, could they serve?

We can only accept these essays of Mr. Mill as the testimony, all the more decisive because it is that of an unwilling witness, that by wisdom the world cannot find out God. Without intending to do so, these essays throw light on a question upon which divines have long disputed – viz., the respective claims of natural and revealed religion. Into that controversy which was kept up with much warmth during the whole of last century we do not mean here to enter, but content ourselves with remarking that natural religion, which is logically prior to revealed, is chronologically posterior. In the order of idea we should know God first in his works and afterwards in his word; but in the order of fact it is the reverse. God reveals himself in his word and then we see him in his works. Natural religion, as we call the latter for convenience' sake, thus follows on revealed. It is an old-fashioned but a true way of putting the same thing to say that, except as a covenant-keeping God, the El, or the Almighty, is not to be known by his creatures. But as soon as he has made a covenant with us and we with him – in other words, as soon as he has revealed himself to us in his word – then we can turn to his works and there trace the lines on which he has written the proofs of his eternal power and majesty. He has written them in lines of light in the heavens, and furrowed them deep in the earth's valleys and mountains. It is possible to see design in everything, from an eagle's wing to an insect's eye, if we set out with some conception, drawn from our own awakened spiritual consciousness, of the Designer himself. If 'we are his offspring,' as the Apostle is able to show from one of the deeper and devouter utterances of the Greek poets, and if, moreover, as his offspring he has not left us orphans and outcast, but has revealed himself in a series of progressive lessons, educating and enfolding the spiritual consciousness through patriarchs and prophets, by type and by ritual, on to the full manifestation in Him who is the brightness of his Father's glory, and the express image of his person; if, to sum up all, we thus know God as the covenant-keeping Jehovah, then what is called natural religion becomes as simple and obvious as it is otherwise complicated and confused. As we love Him because He first loved us, so we may equally say that we know Him because He first knew us, and made Himself known to us. Knowing Him, then, in one direction we desire to know Him in every other; confiding in Him, as well in providence as in grace, we desire to see some trace of Him in nature; and turning thus with these prepossessions, as some would call them – prejudices they certainly are not – we open the page of nature, and see it written within and without with proofs of benevolent design. 'The works of the Lord are great, sought out of all them that have pleasure therein.'

The mistake of the divines of last century was not in making much of natural religion, or of its connection with revealed. Too much cannot be made of that connection. Their error was in putting them in the wrong order, and mistaking the ideal or logical order for the actual or chronological. In theory, at least, natural religion should lead up to revealed. But experience and history both attest that the true order is the reverse, and consequently that whoever, whether wilfully by putting himself out of the pale of the covenant, or ignorantly by being born outside it, tries to construct for himself a scheme of natural religion – a pure Deism, as we may describe it – desiccated of every positive element of historical or revealed religion, must end in failure. Naturalism, as soon as it comes out from the cold, dark cave of Atheism, as if blinded with excessive light, either sees two suns or can see nothing but the sun. Some form of Manichæism or some form of Pantheism is the invariable conclusion of every thinker, from Zerdusht the Persian to Schopenhauer the German. We challenge philosophy to point to a single instance of a pure Theist. Theism, pure and undiluted, is as perfect a fiction as one fixed centre of gravity in a moving body. It never existed and never can exist. It either takes shape in some form of historical religion, or it falls back into one of those theories which we commonly describe as Pantheism or Manichæism.

We have made this preliminary explanation in order that we may by anticipation account for some of those conclusions to which Mr. Mill came which have surprised so many of his followers. That he should have rested all his life in the Comtist conclusion, either that there is no God at all, or that it is no matter whether he exists or not, this would not have surprised or scandalised the Benthamite school, with which he was connected during the early years of his life. But that, in his declining years, and under softer influence, he fell under what they would describe as superstition, this is the scandal which they cannot get over, and we are not surprised, therefore, that the 'Pall Mall Gazette' should condemn these essays of a philosopher as unphilosophical. We do not presume to define what unphilosophical means, since the clique who arrogate to themselves the high name of philosophers have a very conventional sense of what it is. We have nothing to say to caste ideas on the subject, but the impression which these posthumous 'Essays' of Mr. Mill produces on our mind confirms that of the 'Autobiography.' Mr. Mill there traced the development of his own mind. From the ice-house of materialism, where he was trained on a diet of hard facts by a schoolmaster-father, he passed, by some strange gradations in his latter years, into the hot-house of mysticism. The 'Autobiography' shows us the revolt of a nature in which the imagination had been systematically starved, breaking out in the direction of a life beyond. The following passage from the 'Essays' illustrates this: –

'Human life,' he observes, 'stands greatly in need of any wider range and greater height of aspiration for itself and its destination which the exercise of the imagination can yield to it without running counter to the evidence of fact; and that it is a part of wisdom to make the most of any even small possibilities on the subject which furnish the imagination with any footing to support itself upon. And I am satisfied that the cultivation of such a tendency in the imagination, provided it goes on *pari passu* with the cultivation of severe reason, has no necessary tendency to pervert the judgment, but that it is possible to form a perfectly sober estimate of the evidence on both sides of a question, and yet to let the imagination dwell by preference on those possibilities which are the most comforting and the most improving, without in the least degree overrating the solidity of the grounds for expecting that these, rather than any others, will be the possibilities actually realised.'

It is clear from this and other expressions which recur in these 'Essays,' that Mr. Mill had become deeply dissatisfied with the Benthamite ideal of existence in which he had grown up, and at the same time was unable to reject it for some other. Hence that state of unhappy division between his intellect and his emotions. He was drawn forward by a strange attraction towards the unseen and the unknown, and then forcibly held back by the prejudices of his early bringing-up. It is not singular, therefore, that in this divided state of mind he fell into one of those strange theories of existence which for awhile held captive the acute intellect of Augustine. The stages by which he was led to this appear to have been as follows.

'The notion,' he observes, 'of a providential government by an omnipotent Being for the good of his creatures must be entirely dismissed;' and yet with great inconsistency Mr. Mill goes on to remark – 'To one who feels it conducive either to his satisfaction or to his usefulness to hope for a future state as a possibility there is no hindrance to his indulging this hope. Appearances point to the existence of a Being who has great power over us – all the power implied in the creation of the cosmos or its organised beings at least; and of whose goodness we have evidence – though not of its being his predominant attribute; and we do not know the limits either of his power or of his goodness. There is room to hope that both the one and the other may extend to granting us this gift, provided that it is beneficial to us.'

He had brought himself, then, to this state of mind. Anxious for some evidence for a life beyond the present, and longing for some proofs of it in the existence of a Being who is himself eternal, he looked around to see what evidence there is from nature for the being of God. The facts of the case seemed to warrant that there was a Being 'whose predominant attribute was benevolence; but, since we do not know the limits either of his power or goodness,' all that we can conjecture is that 'there is room to hope that both the one and the other may extend to granting us this gift, provided that it is beneficial to us.' Surely a more lame and impotent conclusion was never penned by a philosopher. A theology of Manichæism ending in a 'perhaps' with regard to the life beyond the grave! A being a little less than the All-wise and the All-good sits on a precarious throne and borrows the right to be! Above him and behind him there is the iron reign of law, like that Μοιρα or Destiny which, according to the Greeks, was stronger than Jove himself. Is it to be wondered at that with conceptions of God so dim and depressing, the possibility of a future and an endless life had dwindled down to a 'perhaps'?

Mr. Mill was far too acute a logician to reason from his wishes and to exalt the ontological argument of Anselm into an actual proof that man is immortal because he can entertain the idea of immortality and has a natural dread of extinction. He points out, as Kant has done before, the fallacy of this argument, which is no more a sure proof of immortality than a man's desire to be rich and great is that he is sure to be rich or great. Our wishes deceive us with regard to present good, and therefore equally with regard to future. The ontological proof, therefore, as worth little apart from the theological, and this Mill felt as clearly as Kant himself. But he was unable to go back and see where the source of his inconsistency lay. He was in that miserable state of fluctuation of mind which Augustine has made us only too familiar with in his 'Confessions.' Undecided as to any unity of purpose in the Divine mind, and unable to see that evil only exists as the tares among the wheat and because an enemy has done this, he came in a hesitating kind of way to a compromise between philosophy and religion which both philosophers and religionists repudiate with equal emphasis, and which has never laid any serious hold on minds in the least. In Augustine's case the Manichæan heresy was only a halting-stage between a sensual philosophy and faith. We wish we could say the same of Mr. Mill. But the 'Autobiography' and the 'Essays' break off at the point where he has begun to see that there are capacities in a man which the things of time and sense cannot satisfy. Would that Augustine's experience had been realised in this case. There was no voice which seemed to whisper to him the words, '*Tolle lege*' (Take and Lead), when, as Augustine tells us in his 'Confessions,' opening his Bible his eye fell on the words, 'But put ye on the Lord Jesus Christ, and make not provision for the flesh to fulfil the lusts thereof.'

One of the most perplexing problems of our existence here is that which is suggested by the supplementary chapter, as we may describe it, to Mr. Mill's 'Confessions.' He seemed to be making his way to the light – as far as reason could guide him, his face at least was set in the direction of religious truth – when his life came to an end, and the curtain dropped on a truth-loving but unhappily incomplete nature. If a 'culture,' as it is called, is the final end of man, meaning by that the harmonious development of two only of the three inalienable faculties of man, then Mr. Mill was, after Goethe perhaps, one of the most cultured men of modern times. Differing from Goethe only in this, that he was a scientist first, and a man of imagination and sentiment afterwards, it was his life study, as it had been Goethe's before him, to make incursions into other regions of thought than those in which his life studies lay. Goethe, for instance, was a poet and an artist, but he felt that, to round off his intellectual life and complete his ideal of culture, he must include also exact science, and therefore in his old days he studied botany and comparative physiology, though his researches in morphology, or the doctrine of typical form, were, after all, little more than a poet's dream. Mill, on the other hand, whose education was on a different plan, began as a student of exact science and branched off in his latter days into sentimental theories, and what were called by political economists of the old school his heresies, as to the rights of women, the unearned increment of land, and other such sentimental views of the laws of wealth. It was the desire of culture in both cases which drew these men off in directions the very opposite to that which they had set out with – the poet dabbling in science and throwing out theories in optics and botany which were little else than poet's dreams, the man of exact science falling into sentimentalisms quite as far-fetched or alien to his true genius. But in neither case did culture carry them on to the true conclusion to which Solomon was led, that to fear God and keep his commandments, this is the whole duty, or rather is the true end, of human existence. The spiritual side of human nature was to them a blank, and culture, therefore, in the highest and truest sense of the word, unknown.

There is a mournful sadness in the closing pages of the book. Had he studied the evidences of Christianity at an earlier age and under happier conditions, he could hardly have rested satisfied with a mere admiration of the ethics of Christianity. Of the Founder of Christianity, as well as of the morality he taught, he makes what will be to many unexpected admissions, as when he says 'Whatever else may be taken away from us by rational criticism, Christ is still left, – a unique figure, not more unlike all his precursors than all his followers, even those who had the direct benefit of his personal teaching.' And again, he speaks of Jesus of Nazareth as 'the ideal representative and guide of humanity; nor even now would it be easy, even for an unbeliever, to find a better translation of the rule of virtue from the abstract into the concrete than to endeavour so to live that Christ would approve our life.'

These 'Essays,' then, of Mr. Mill, the last gleanings of an intellectual harvest of remarkable completeness, are a melancholy confirmation of the old adage –

'Unless above himself he can
Exalt himself, how mean a thing is man.'

The book is disappointing to philosophers and to religionists, but more especially to the former. To the Christian, indeed, it is a confirmation of the truth of God's word that man is made for God and eternity, and that no less good than the highest will really satisfy him long. If there are any timid Christians who think that the tendency of such a book as this of Mr. Mill's is to promote scepticism we can only say that our impression is the very reverse. It is, in fact, a testimony to the truth of Revelation, and though Mill does not break off with the same conclusion as Augustine in his 'Confessions,' every line in it leads that way. 'Fecisti nos ad te et inquietum est cor nostrum donec requiescat in te.' (Thou hast made us for thyself, and our heart is restless till it rest in thee.) – *Aug. Conf.* i. 1.

# [FROM] RELIGIOUS OPINIONS OF J. STUART MILL
## James Allen Brown

An apology, if one be needed, for referring so frequently in the REVIEW to the opinions of such a man as J. Stuart Mill, is the prominence which he occupied, and the position awarded him by so many, as a leader in modern thought and speculation. He was regarded by his followers as little less than an oracle. His writings have done much to shape the thinking of this generation. On the general subject of religion Mr. Mill preserved a remarkable reticence. His views were interpreted from his general position in science and philosophy, but he was at no pains to let the world know what he thought on the most momentous of all subjects. This silence of Mr. Mill has been broken by the publication of three Essays of his since his death. In an Introductory note, we are assured that these Essays exhibit *'the carefully balanced result of the deliberations of a life time.'* We do not propose any elaborate review of these Essays. They have surprised alike the friends and opponents of Mr. Mill, and are satisfactory to neither. That he should have deliberated for a life time on such subjects, and left the world in ignorance of his opinion until after his death, is no very strong evidence of candor or zeal in the cause of truth. It is, however, in harmony with the conduct of others of this school of thought and religion. The world would have been better satisfied with Mr. Mill, if he had published his views while living, and evinced a willingness to assume the responsibility of defending them before the bar of public opinion. It is not pleasant to carry on controversy over the grave. Death usually quiets animosities and silences discussion. But Mr. Mill has chosen to leave his religious opinions to be learned when he was beyond the reach of attacks or reply.

We propose simply to exhibit, in his own language, and without discussion, the views of Mr. Mill on a few leading topics of religion, believing that their presentation will be sufficient.

# [FROM REVIEW OF] THREE ESSAYS ON RELIGION
## James Elliott Cabot

... What strikes us first of all, as we follow these interesting conjectures, is that there is a drawback attending the investigation of morals and religion by methods which exclude from consideration all hypotheses involving real existences which the senses give us no means of imagining, this, namely, that we have to place ourselves out of sight of the facts we are investigating. In the Essay on Nature, Mr. Mill's definition of Nature ought to have shown him that in stating his question he had emptied it of all meaning. If Nature is only a general name for our sensations, it is easy to see that it cannot serve as a guide, an ideal, or a rule of conduct. But the difficulty remains to imagine what can be in the minds of those who (p. 110) still continue to talk of the intrinsic capacities of human nature, as distinct from the forms in which those capacities happen to have been historically developed, and who would make out of these non-apparent capacities the proper object of religious worship. Avoiding all *a priori* reasoning, human nature must be the sum of those impressions which we have received from the people we have met; and these impressions can have no capacity except to exist or be felt; to distinguish what is intrinsic in them from what is actually experienced, is to substitute imaginations for facts. Evidently, however, Mr. Mill, when he is not hindered by the theory that the senses are the inlet of knowledge, feels, as every one does, that the reality of a thing is not the sensuous impression, but what the impression presupposes; the Notion or *nature* which manifests itself to us through the senses, but only on the condition that we *understand* our sensations, – that is, draw from them the proper inferences. Those who bid us follow Nature do not mean that we are to do what we do, or what others do, or what the elements or the beasts do; but that we are to bring our lives into accordance with that notion of Man with which

Conscience supplies us; as the plant or the animal, though here involuntarily, embodies the notion of the genus. Something of this sort seems to lie at the bottom of the 'Religion of Humanity,' only that, instead of hearing in the intimations of conscience the voice of that divine spirit which animates every man that comes into the world and makes him man, Mr. Mill is forced to attach them to an abstraction, an endless succession of human beings, whose possible happiness and indefinite capability of improvement we are to make the object of our aspirations. But, as Mr. Mill found in his own experience, as related in his Autobiography, such a sentiment, however real, is much too vague to constitute a religion. It contents itself with averages and tendencies; it does not come home to each one of us as the sufficient object of life.

In all Mr. Mill's discussions of Religion, we hear the theories of an ingenious and candid man about facts which he cannot overlook, but which do not fit into his framework of thought. They are like the speculations of a blind man about pictures, – or rather of a man having the power of sight, but conceiving it to be his duty not to use his eyes, and so in perfect good faith exploring the surface of the canvas with his fingers, candidly admitting a sort of attraction, which ought to be accounted for, and endeavouring to hit upon the particular confusion of thought to which it is due. That there is no such matter to be *seen* as is pretended, he is quite clear; but then, if people do in fact find satisfaction and elevation of mind in pacing the galleries and gazing at these parti-colored parallelograms, it would be a pity to disturb them, only we cannot pretend to be taken in by the cant which artists are sagacious enough to encourage about the momentous differences between this and that. There is, beyond doubt, a distinct satisfaction in the act of looking, and this being so, there must be something to look at; but when mankind are once sufficiently educated, the bare canvases will serve the turn as well, and make no false pretences.

In spite of the earnest and even religious temper of these Essays, there is something fairly comic in the conception of a probable God, of limited capacities, whom we may perhaps help out in his desperate task of governing the world. Believers and sceptics, we think, will unite in protesting that nothing can be more improbable. We may find the hypothesis of a divine ruler of the universe incredible or superfluous, but it must at any rate be adequate. God is the necessary implication of every fact of our experience, more conspicuously of the phenomena of conscience, yet of all phenomena. We may decide that the implication is unnecessary; that the facts can very well take care of themselves; but it cannot be *partly* necessary.

But if there is no room in Mr. Mill's philosophy for the idea of God, this need the less surprise us when we remember that there is no room either for the idea of Self. The Self, as the unity of the separate facts of consciousness, cannot, Mr. Mill says,[1] be conceived as a reality, because in reality they are separate; a series of impressions and emotions, each occupying its own place and its own moment. The Self cannot be a unit, because experience shows that it is a stream of feelings, each of them capable of a faint repetition, but each itself and not any other. So the conception of God as the explanation of the universe; the comprehensive unity in which all things live and move and have their being, contradicts experience, for there is in fact no such Cosmos as it would suppose, but rather a Chaos: at least the only conceivable end and aim of sentient being, happiness, is attained in a very incomplete and intermittent fashion in the world as we know it. In the brute creation we find no distinct provision for the prevention of cruelty and suffering; still less in the life of man any settled successful purpose to make him comfortable: but rather the purpose to lure him away from the enjoyment of ease and security, in the pursuit of a happiness that is never reached. Some dream of wealth, power, liberty, knowledge, love, is forever plucking him up from his snug repose, and sending him forth to toil and suffer his life long, – and for what? Not for any gain of personal satisfaction that we can discover. Still, in the case of the Self, by far the wisest thing we can do, Mr. Mill decides, is to accept the inexplicable fact of personal identity, without any theory of how it takes place. By parity of reasoning it might seem wisest to accept the fact of a divine order of the universe, if we find ourselves compelled to do so, even though Creation, if looked at as the work of a utilitarian philosopher, seems palpably a failure. Especially for Mr. Mill, since he confesses in the Essay on Liberty that increased freedom to

---

[1] An Examination of Sir William Hamilton's Philosophy (Am. ed), I. p. 262.

seek each his own satisfaction in his own way has not tended to better the condition of mankind, to bring men nearer to the best thing they can be, but rather to produce a stunted type of humanity, incapable of suffering or of enjoying much, and, as he says, to make mediocrity the ascendant power among mankind. Here and in the Autobiography, and indeed throughout Mr. Mill's later writings, are glimpses of a far different end for human life than happiness; namely, the purpose to bring human beings themselves nearer to 'the ideal conception embodied in them.' Such a thought, whatever it leaves unaccounted for in our fortunes, seems fitted to take away the sense of hostility in the forces that govern our lives, and so to dispose of the indictment which Mr. Mill brings against Providence. Such ideas, however, are excluded by the postulates of Mr. Mill's philosophy, and remain only as hopes, aspirations to be indulged in the region of the imagination; or as probabilities, not in the sense of facts imperfectly proved, but in the sense of haunting conjectures which reason can neither sanction nor shake off, phantoms to which passing emotion may lend the momentary semblance of life, not realities having any proper place in the actual world. Hence the uncertainty of treatment remarked upon by disciples and opponents in these and other recent Essays of Mr. Mill. It seems often like mere inconsistency, but it is only the legitimate effect of an exorbitant cultivation of the faculties of analysis and discussion at the expense of the faculty of perception. Each concrete fact of experience is reduced to a *caput mortuum*, and no longer corresponds to its real self. The act of knowing destroys its object, which comes to life again, but outside the pale of philosophy, so that we can never be sure whether we are dealing with the ghost which alone can be proved and known, or with the real fact which can be only hoped for and aspired after.

To the American edition has been added an Essay on Berkeley from the Fortnightly Review; the last publication, we believe, of its author. It shows the same method applied to Metaphysics. Berkeley, as a consistent empiricist, saw that Sensation shuts itself up within its own home, and does not include its object. The object must be supplied from without, and he supplied it provisionally by the name of God. Mr. Mill's improvement was to substitute as the object 'the permanent possibility of sensations,' not seeing apparently that this is another way of saying that knowledge is an illusion, that we never really get beyond our own sensations, but only come, through their repetition, to fancy that they are something more.

# [FROM] THEISTIC REACTIONS IN MODERN SPECULATION
## John William Mears

... In the recently published posthumous essays of John Stuart Mill, there are two which stand in marked contrast to each other: 'The Utility of Religion' and 'Theism.' The former seems designed to vindicate the melancholy impression made upon his youthful mind by the atheistic teachings of his father, and might, with equal or greater propriety, have been entitled, 'The Uselessness and Injuriousness of Religion in General, and of the Evangelical Type of Christian Belief in Particular.' Not only are the views of Mr. Mill narrow and bigoted, as might be expected from his education, but they reveal often a complete ignorance of the common defenses of the orthodox faith. His treatment of the problem of evil under the government of God is crude, puerile, and shallow. He knows nothing, apparently, of the approximate solution of the problem which the tyro in moral philosophy draws from the bare fact of the existence of finite moral beings. Such, as far as we can see, there cannot be, without the possibility at least of sin and fall and all its evil consequences.[1] He never caught a glimpse of the profound ethical meaning of the Book of Job, in which the uses of suffering, in the discipline and development of the imperfect

---

[1] The late Gerrit Smith, although maintaining his profession of Christianity to the last, held views of the immoral tendencies of certain orthodox doctrines very similar to these extravagant opinions of John Stuart Mill. They appeared in his 'Letter to Albert Barnes,' in 1868, from which arose a correspondence of profound interest between those distinguished men, on 'Sin and Suffering in the Universe.' Yet Mr. Smith's clear head and early familiarity with the grounds and defenses of leading orthodox doctrines saved him from the astonishing crudities of Mr. Mill. In the letter above-mentioned, he says (p. 5): 'It is true that man is so made that he can sin, but how low a being would man be if he were of necessity sinless? How far inferior to what he now is? He would be a mere machine, and his going right would no more argue wisdom and goodness in him than does the right-going of a clock argue wisdom and goodness it it.'

righteousness of the best of human characters, are set forth with all the richness of language and fertility of invention and singleness of aim of the highest type of poetry.

However, it was appointed to Mr. Mill himself to undergo no small share of these chastisements, and, all unconsciously to himself, he may have profited by their teachings. His wife, for whom he felt an affection more nearly approaching worship than perhaps anything in his whole experience, was removed from him by death in the fall of 1858. It was before her death (between the years 1850 and 1858, says Miss Taylor, in the Introductory Note) that this essay on 'The Utility of Religion' was written. Ten years after that event (1868–70) he composed the essay on 'Theism,' the last of the Posthumous Essays. So different is its spirit and, in several instances, its specific declarations, from those of the essay which preceded it, that his step-daughter, Miss Taylor, is constrained to spend a large part of her introductory notice, two pages out of three, in the effort to account for the discrepancy. It is certainly interesting to know that it was 'the last considerable work' of the author, and, consequently, that 'it shows the latest state of the author's mind – the carefully-balanced result of the deliberations of a lifetime.' This is Miss Taylor's opinion of the essay, notwithstanding the fact of which she admonishes us, that it had not undergone 'the revision to which, from time to time, he subjected most of his writings before making them public.'

In fact, the whole draft of the two essays may be described as mutually contradictory. The first is atheistic; the second is theistic. The first aims to reconcile the reader to dispensing with the idea of religion; the second, by a halting, timorous, and yet careful, analysis, develops the scientific grounds of a possible faith in natural and revealed religion. The first breathes unmistakable hostility to Christianity – at times it reminds us of the truculence of the bar-room and of the itinerant infidel lecturer; the other sounds a truce, offers the olive branch, and makes reserved but actual advances to the position the writer had been so bitterly assailing before.

In the first essay, following the hint given him by his father, Mr. Mill applauds the doctrine of the Manicheans (a good and an evil principle, dividing the government of the world between them). He says (Three Essays, Am. Ed. p. 116): 'One only form of belief in the supernatural – one only theory respecting the origin and government of the universe – stands wholly clear, both of intellectual contradiction and of moral obliquity, . . . the doctrine of the Manicheans.'

In the second essay, on the contrary, he asserts that Monotheism is the only Theism which can claim for itself any footing on scientific ground. (Three Essays, p. 133; comp. also, p. 186.)

It is freely conceded in this Essay on Theism, that 'Science contains nothing repugnant to the supposition that every event which takes place results from a specific volition of the presiding power, provided that this power adheres in its particular volitions to general laws laid down by itself' (p. 136). Widely different is this from Mr. Tyndall's labored attempt to prove that science excludes the idea of a Creator and Preserver of the universe. Even the reservation, with which Mr. Mill closes the above statement, seems to be withdrawn at a later stage of the argument, where the credibility of miracles is discussed (p. 232).

This admission introduces the main argument of the essay, viz., whether there is sufficient evidence to prove 'the creation and government of nature by a sovereign will?' It is in entire accordance with the philosophical prejudices instilled into his mind, that he can appreciate none of the deductive arguments for the being of a God; that he seems utterly unconscious of any metaphysical necessity for a first cause; that he denies the general consent of mankind to the doctrine, and argues against any and every form of intuitive knowledge of the divine existence in the human mind. To be sure, in this last position he is able to quote as high authority, on the theistic side, as Sir William Hamilton. 'Whatever relates to God,' he says, in another place,[2] 'I hold, with Sir William Hamilton, to be matter of inference; I would add of inference *a posteriori.*' Then passing beyond Sir William's position, he proceeds to argue that a knowledge of the infinite (in the concrete) can be and is reached by that method. He thus appears rather as a defender of the common idea, that the infinite God, in some true sense, is known by the mind. Whether this idea, gained *a posteriori*, is to be regarded as having a corresponding reality outside the mind any more than the *a priori* notion, we are not informed.

But the most surprising feature of Mr. Mill's attempt to

---

[2] Examination of Sir William Hamilton's Philosophy, New York, 1874, Vol. I, p. 48.

discredit the *a priori* argument is his explanation of its continued existence in the world, in spite of the absence of all adequate grounds for its support. He regards it as an instance of the absurdity of assuming that, in the order of the universe, whatever is desirable is true. It is 'a *naif* expression of the tendency of the human mind to believe what is agreeable to it.' Instead of the belief in God being a fact which man cannot shake off, in spite of his natural distaste for the idea, according to Mr. Mill, he likes it so much that he has actually formed it without adequate ground! Nothing is clearer throughout this whole volume, than that the author himself is utterly without that fine moral sensibility, that awakened conscience, which, under the teachings of the gospel and the Holy Spirit, reveals to us the deep dislike of the natural man to God.

It is when Mr. Mill reaches the argument from Marks of Design for the Being of a God, that he speaks like a man who is at home. 'We now, at last,' he says, 'reach an argument of a really scientific character, which does not shrink from scientific tests, but claims to be judged by the established canons of induction' (p. 167). Mr. Mill applies these canons most rigorously to the argument, as stated by Paley; holds the argument closely to experience, declares it amounts only to the inferior kind of inductive evidence, called analogy, and that it can never be equal in validity to a real induction (pp. 168, 169.) Yet, a moment after (pp. 169 and 170), he gives a different shape to the arrangement; says the previous view 'does not do full justice to the evidence,' and points out the fact of nature's arrangements *conspiring to an end*, as constituting an inductive argument. 'This,' he now says, 'I think is undeniable.' Selecting the eye as an illustration, he argues that, by induction of particulars, under the 'Method of Agreement,' we are brought to the conclusion that it is the work of an intelligent, designing will.

With an expression of regret (is it mere Attic courtesy, or does it reveal a slight improvement in his own state of mind?) he sees this argument for creative forethought in the formation of the eye diminished in conclusiveness by the principle of the 'Survival of the Fittest.' The reality of such a principle, we are told, cannot be doubted, though its adequacy to account for such truly admirable combinations as some of those in nature is still, and will probably long remain, problematical. The theory, if admitted, would be in no way inconsistent with creation. 'But it must be acknowledged that it would greatly attenuate the evidence for it. Leaving this remarkable speculation to whatever fate the progress of discovery may have in store for it, I think it must be allowed that, in the present state of our knowledge, the adaptations in nature afford a large balance of probability in favor of creation by intelligence.'

With all his deductions and extenuations, Mr. Mill has thus conceded to the argument, as it now stands – for the existence not only of a God, but for a creator – *a large balance of probability*. An accumulation of probabilities reaching to moral certainty, not to demonstration, is all that natural theology can give us. The argument for design, doubtless from design, is not compulsory, but such as is adopted to influence beings endowed with moral sense and with common sense. For them 'a large balance of probability' should be and is enough, at least in the sphere of natural theology. What may be needed more is furnished in the Evidences of Revelation.

In turning to this part of the subject (Part IV., p. 212), Mr. Mill makes the remark, that 'the indications of the creator and of his attributes, which we are able to find in nature, ... are sufficient to give to the supposition of a revelation a standing point, which it would not otherwise have had; it has not to prove the very existence of the being from whom it professes to come.' His characteristic narrowness and insensibility to any form of *a priori*, or deductive, mode of thought, appears in his rejection of the internal evidence of a revelation, except as having negative weight. It may be of a character to discredit – it can never establish – the superhuman origin of the document. He confines himself entirely to the external evidence, *i.e.*, to miracles.

Here, as in his logic, he puts himself upon ground entirely different from that of the unbelieving naturalists of our day. Hume's argument against miracles, he admits, may be conclusive with them. 'But it is far from being equally so when the existence of a being who created the present order of nature – and, therefore, may well be thought to have power to modify it – is accepted as a fact, or even as a probability, resting on independent evidence. Once admit a God, and the production, by his direct volition, of an effect, which, in any case, owed its origin to his creative will, is no longer a purely arbitrary hypothesis to account for the fact, but must be reckoned with as a serious possibility.' It is a point which may be settled by evidence in the affirmative. Whether the evidence in case of the Christian miracles was sufficient is the true question. Mr. Mill is not willing to admit its sufficiency; he will only go so far as to say that 'there is nothing so inherently or absolutely incredible in this supposition (of a revelation attested by miracles) as to preclude any one from hoping that it may, perhaps, be true.'

But we hasten to lay before our readers the 'general result' of the discussion, as presented by the writer. It is here especially, that the tone of the essay is in contrast with that which precedes it, and here we cannot fail to detect a hopeful progress in the author's mode of conceiving his subject. Before, religion was a foe of good – worse than useless in the world. Now, it appears to him 'that the indulgence of hope with regard to the government of the universe and the destiny of man after death – while we recognize as a clear truth, that we have no ground for more than a hope – is legitimate and philosophically defensible. The beneficial effect of such a hope is far from trifling. It makes life and human nature a far greater thing to the feelings, and gives greater strength as well as greater solemnity to all the sentiments which are awakened in us by our fellow creatures, and by mankind at large. The benefit consists less in the presence of any specific hope than in the enlargement of the general scale of the feelings, the loftier aspirations being no longer in the same degree checked and kept down by a sense of the insignificance of human life' (pp. 249, 250).

We wonder if Mr. Mill, in penning these sentences, thought of that period in his own life, so candidly and graphically described in his Autobiography (chap. 5: 'A crisis in my mental history'), when he seemed suddenly, and without any afflicting experience, 'to have nothing left to live for.' Mr. Thomas Hughes, M. P., explains this crisis, in his own way, as the result of a life without any 'back-ground of God' in it. Mr. Mill seems to have acquired at least the premises for a similar conclusion.

He continues by ascribing to religion the principal share in maintaining among men 'a most important,' an 'infinitely precious exercise of the imagination;' indeed, 'human excellence greatly depends upon the sufficiency of the provision made for its exercise.' 'This consists of the familiarity of the imagination with the conception of a morally perfect being, and the habit of taking the approbation of such a being as the standard by which to regulate our characters and lives.' Even when the being is conceived of as merely imaginary, this beneficial effect is quite possible. 'But religion, since the birth of Christianity, has rendered the special service of inculcating the belief, that our highest conceptions of combined wisdom and goodness exist in the concrete, in a living being, who has his eyes on us and cares for our good. Through the darkest and most corrupt periods, Christianity has raised this torch on high – has kept this object of veneration and imitation before the eyes of man' (pp. 250, 251).

As the essay draws to a close, its tone continues gradually to rise, until one cannot help believing that the long-fettered mind of this most exceptionally trained Englishman was working its way to truer freedom and to better light. There is almost a positively Christian tone in many of the sentences of the following paragraphs:

'Above all, the most valuable part of the effect on the character which Christianity has produced, by holding up in a divine person a standard of excellence and a model of imitation, is available even to the absolute unbeliever, and can never be lost to humanity. For it is Christ – it is the God incarnate; more than the God of the Jews, or of Nature, who, being idealized, has taken so great and salutary a hold on the modern mind. And whatever else may be taken away from us by rational criticism, Christ is still left; an unique figure, not more unlike all his precursors than all his followers, even those who had the direct benefit of his personal teaching. Who among his disciples, or among the proselytes, was capable of inventing the sayings ascribed to Jesus, or of imagining the life and character revealed in the gospel? Certainly not the fisherman of Galilee; as certainly not St. Paul, whose character and idiosyncracies were of a totally different sort; still less the early Christian writers, in whom nothing is more evident than that the good which was in them was all derived, as they all professed that it was derived, from the higher source.'

[We omit the sentences which show that Mr. Mill had not yet attained an insight into the significance of John's Gospel.]

About the life and sayings of Jesus he continues, 'There is a stamp of personal originality combined with profundity of insight, which, if we abandon the idle expectation of finding scientific precision where something very different was aimed at, must place the prophet of Nazareth, even in the estimation of those who have no belief in his inspiration, in the very first rank of the men of sublime genius of whom our species can boast. Nor would it be easy, now even, for an unbeliever to find a better translation of the rule of virtue, from the abstract to the concrete, than to endeavor so to live that Christ would approve our life. When to this we add, that to the rational skeptic it remains a possibility that Christ actually was what he supposed himself to be – not God, but a man charged with a special, express, and unique commission from God, to lead mankind to truth and virtue; we may well conclude that the influences of religion on the character, which will remain after rational criticism has done its utmost against the evidences of religion, are well worth preserving, and what they lack in direct strength, as compared with those of a firmer belief, is more than compensated by the greater truth and rectitude of the morality they sanction.'

With all the grave defects of the Essay on Theism, some of which we have passed over lightly, or without mention, we are inclined to regard it as one of the most remarkable and significant of all of the author's productions. We are heartily glad that Mr. Mill lived long enough to conceive and write it. It is a contribution, real, though slight, towards undoing the great mischiefs of his earlier writings, and of the general drift of his example during a long, able, and influential career. . . .

# [FROM REVIEW OF] THREE ESSAYS ON RELIGION
## Charles Barnes Upton

The eagerness with which thoughtful persons in all classes of society looked forward to the appearance of this book, was no doubt due in part to the world-wide reputation and to the pure and noble career of its author; but perhaps, to quite as great an extent, to the state of uneasy suspense in regard to religious belief which marks our present culture, and to the consequent hope that in the last words of this earnest and acute thinker would be found some valuable clue to the unravelling of that perplexing entanglement in which, for many minds, recently published facts and theories have involved all questionings concerning the cause and meaning of the universe. That it has furnished no such clue is now, we suppose, generally admitted. From neither the friends nor the foes of the Experiential Philosophy has it received a warm and unequivocal welcome. It does not make that clean sweep of theological sentiments and beliefs which thorough-going Positivists desiderate; nor, on the other hand, do its faint probabilities seem of any worth to those who believe that only in the immediate apprehension of a righteous and sympathizing God is to be found the basis of that Theistic faith which is worthy to overthrow and replace the decaying orthodoxy of our time. . . .

We know not how to characterize the book before us more exactly than by calling it the final utterance and confession of that eighteenth-century Deism, based on the Experience philosophy, which once paraded its so-called Natural Religion as a rival of Christianity, but which now confesses its own incompetency, acknowledges that it has no well-founded claim to *convictions* concerning the truths most dear to the human heart, that *hopes*, and those too somewhat of the faintest, are all it can pretend to supply in answer to the restless quest of the intellect for an adequate Cause, and to the pathetic cry of the affections for an eternal Father and a spiritual home. Throughout the book it is consistently maintained that the only reliable conclusions upon religious truth which the facts at our command enable us to infer are as follows: first, that there is some probability of the existence of an intelligent Governor of the universe; and that, secondly, there is a more slender probability that He is benevolent, and cares for the welfare and happiness of His sentient creation. These probabilities, however, vanish entirely, unless we are prepared to allow that He is of limited power, and that the happiness of His creatures forms neither the whole, nor perhaps the chief, object of His care and activity. When we pass on to the kindred question of Immortality, even these small probabilities fail us, and we must content ourselves with the bare possibility that death may be a transition to another life.

If the value of the book were confined to the attempt to justify this poor modicum of probability and hope, as all that the religious sentiment can rely on for satisfaction and for nourishment, there would be little fitness in our dwelling at any length on a performance which, in our view, is as devoid of novelty as it is of philosophical worth. But we believe, and shall endeavour to shew, that though these essays are of little account as a direct contribution to the solution of the intellectual and spiritual problems of the age, nevertheless, when we consider, not what they actually aim to prove, but rather the more substantial truths which they indirectly suggest and confirm, we shall find that they are utterances of the highest significance; and, if carefully studied in connection with the Autobiography and the other writings of their author, are seen to bear testimony, indirect and unintended indeed, but on that account only the more precious and conclusive, to the reality and influence of that Spiritual Environment of the human soul which it was the great object of Mr. Mill's philosophical career to declare illusory and fanciful, and from which, therefore, he earnestly strove to draw off all earnest attention and serious regard. It is not, however, till we reach the concluding essay, that on Theism, which forms about the latter half of the volume, and in which alone we have the reflex of his inner life during its closing years, that the great lesson of the book becomes apparent, and we discern, with as much interest and delight as Mr. Morley does with dissatisfaction and regret, indications which tell of the dawn of spiritual emotion and insight in the author's soul, – a dawn which simultaneously reveals to us the moral purity and genuine wealth of his nature, and the utter inadequacy of the philosophy, in which he had been trained, to embrace and explain the more precious experiences which never fail to enrich and sanctify the life of a truly noble man.

Before, however, proceeding to the more congenial business of pointing out these noble inconsistencies, which bear witness at once to the worth of the man and to the worthlessness of his philosophy, we must attempt the unpleasant task of criticising those direct teachings of the earlier essays in which we see rather the aberrations of a distorted intellect than the wise insight of a living and a loving soul. As we study the essay on Nature and that on the Utility of Religion, we are conscious throughout of a fundamental misunderstanding between the author and ourselves. The arguments in the former essay are based upon a conception of Omnipotence which we have never entertained; and in the latter, the Religion whose utility is questioned is one whose right to the name we strenuously deny, and of whose inutility for the furtherance of life's highest interests we have as strong a persuasion as Mr. Mill himself. For us, then, as might be expected, his reasonings and his rhetoric alike exhaust their energy upon the empty air; and though the spectacle of their vagaries is painful to the sentiment, the fabric of our convictions does not lie within their sweep. To consider, in the first place, the essay on Nature: we believe that in thoughtful minds it is rare to meet with such a conception of the unlimited power of the Almighty as would at all justify Mr. Mill's exaggerated and repulsive description of what he terms the immorality and reckless cruelty of Nature. We will revert presently to this topic, and consider how the Christian Theist may best deal with that most ancient and yet most recent of all perplexities, the existence of material and moral Evil. On the threshold, however, of this inquiry, we must call attention to the great and obvious inconsistency which pervades Mr. Mill's treatment of this question. . . .

As we read Mr. Mill's highly wrought description of Nature's criminalities, the question constantly arises, What right has Mr. Mill, on the principles of his own philosophy, thus to set man's moral judgments and sympathies over against Nature, that he may contrast the two, and shew how reckless, cruel and immoral, is the one; how judicious, benevolent and just, the other? An Intuitional philosopher and a believer in Freewill may possibly contrast his ideal of beauty and goodness with the moral character which he conceives to be displayed in Nature, and may pass a judgment to the disparagement of the latter; but that an Experientialist and Determinist (the writer of the chapter on 'Liberty and Necessity'), who must needs regard himself, and all his moral ideals and activities, as items in the phenomena which this same Nature has, on the principle of uniformity of sequence, steadily evolved, should thus turn round and revile the system of things which produced him, and of which he is the necessary consequent, seems grotesquely inconsistent and absurd. Nature, at all events, is not so bad but that in her own good time, it seems, she can and does climb the loftiest heights of Utilitarian ethics, and that too, as Mr. Mill has so often assured us, without any fresh aid and inspiration from a Creator, if such a Being exists. Surely, then, it should be no slight extenuation of her offences, in the eyes of a sensational philosopher, that now at length, in the person of one of her most elaborate and successful productions, she looks down upon her humbler handiwork and candidly acknowledges it is not good, and heaps upon her own devoted head the most bitter reproaches and scathing self-condemnation for her many shortcomings. And if it be said that the object of the argument is to shew that the Creator of the whole system of things is not perfectly wise and powerful, and at the same time benevolent, Mr. Mill should have been consistent in his philosophy, and have credited the Creative Intelligence with the origination of the highest types of human genius and virtue, with the ideals in the light of which the external world is criticised and condemned, and with the energy whereby it is to be amended, as well as with the sphere of physical and animated existence which requires amendment. It is not fair thus to play fast and loose with Intuitive Truth and Moral Freedom; first, to use the doctrine to obtain that severance from the stream of Nature's phenomena, and that independent standard of beauty and righteousness, which enables you to criticise and condemn her seeming blemishes, and then reject these self-same intuitions when they are brought forward by their advocates as furnishing some solution of the appearances of Evil in creation.[1]

But though we maintain that Mr. Mill's estimate of Nature is, from the point of view of his own philosophy, a flagrantly unjust one, and, even from the standpoint of those who do not identify man with Nature, a gross misrepresentation of a world in which the marks of beauty, harmony and benevolent intention vastly predominate; yet the most enthusiastic optimist cannot deny that the apparent exceptions are very formidable, and quite sufficient to remove all self-evidence from the assertion that the universe is produced and maintained by a Being of infinite resources and of unfathomable love. Did inference from the phenomena of the external world furnish the only ground for the Theistic doctrine, we do not see how, in

---

[1] Mr. Mill, we are well aware, would not acknowledge that his Determinism necessarily involves that view of the relation of man to nature which, so far as we can see, is the only possible deduction from his premisses. He speaks, for instance, elsewhere of man 'struggling upwards, against immense natural difficulties, into civilization, and making to himself a second nature far better and more unselfish than he was created with.' He might just as well, we think, have represented Nature as struggling upward along the subjective line in the endeavour to outdo her own achievements in the objective department. We remember once having an interesting conversation with a teacher of the Associational creed. Feeling curious to know how in his theory infants are regarded before the time when they give signs that they have awakened to the seriousness of the distinction between themselves and the external world, we inquired whether the sensations at that early date were supposed to inhere in any entity. Smiling at the ignorance of the true philosophy implied in the term 'entity,' he explained that he had watched the period of babyhood pretty carefully, and he had found that the Ego came into existence at from four to six weeks (if we remember rightly) after birth. Previous to that date there were sensations, it is true, but they had not yet differentiated themselves, and grouped themselves round the two distinct centres called the Self and the External World. We have not yet succeeded, though we have tried hard, in fathoming the depth of meaning involved in the words, 'sensations which have as yet no subject.' That the subject had not before that date become conscious of its own being, as contrasted with the beings around it, we readily admitted; but that the birth of knowledge is the birth of being also, we could neither understand nor accept. And when, having thus learned all that we could of the genesis of the Ego, we tried to investigate the human Will, in what Mr. Mill calls Dr. Bain's 'great work on mind,' we found that this Will likewise, neither in its origin nor in its growth, displays (according to this thinker) the smallest sign of any severance from the rest of nature, and for such a Will to attempt to exalt its own dignity at the expense of the rest of creation seems to us on a par with the absurdity of the man, mentioned by Dr. Tyndall, who should attempt to lift himself by his own waistband.

face of so much unhappiness, and so much physical and moral deformity, our faith could ever rise above the level of a moderate degree of probability. So far we are quite at one with Mr. Mill, and should have admitted the force of his arguments quite as readily and far more gratefully, if, instead of his too dismal and revolting portraiture, he had given due emphasis to the fact that the cases of pain and ugliness are in a small minority, and that the prevailing expression of Nature's countenance is cheerful, benign, and even joyous; for, as Miss Cobbe well puts it in reference to the balance of happiness or pain in the lives of animals, 'The scene which the woods and pastures present to a thoughtful eye on a summer morning is not one to "blacken" the character of the Creator, but to lift up the soul in rapture, and prompt us to add a human voice of thanksgiving to the chirp of the happy birds, the bleating of the playful lambs, and the hum of the bees in the cowslips and the clover.'

We hope, however, to be able to make clear in the concluding part of this article, that the belief in God does not take its rise or find its chief aliment in the study of nature. We shall endeavour to shew that the life and writings of Mr. Mill himself incidentally afford a strong confirmation of our own conviction that this fundamental truth has its ineradicable root in the very constitution of our volitional and moral being, and that it blooms and fructifies in the light and warmth of other influences than those which stream into the soul from the visible world. If it be true, as we believe it is, that, as the higher life of man unfolds its marvellous wealth, as the fountains of pure affection are opened, and intellectual culture assumes its normal relation to spiritual insight, the soul passes into distinctly-felt relations with a Spirit of infinite wisdom and goodness; if it be true, as mankind's greatest 'religious genius'[2] both proclaimed and gloriously exemplified, 'that the pure in heart shall see God,' and that those who do the will of the Eternal shall know of the doctrine whether it be of Him, then have we attained an independent ground of conviction, which will enable us to calmly envisage this problem of Evil, without being dismayed by its magnitude, or by the vastness of the personal interests which, else, would wholly depend on its

---

[2] P. 254.

solution. If the signs of intelligence and benevolence in nature do not originate, but only confirm, our faith, so, on the other hand, the partial absence of such marks, though it is competent to perplex that faith, can never wholly destroy it. Careful introspection of our own consciousness appears to us strongly to support this view. At times we are brought into such close and continued contact with sin and suffering, that our faith, too weak to bear the strain, bows for the moment to the earth; when lo! amid that scene of wretchedness, some lovely trait of self-sacrificing love arrests our glance; and at the inspiring touch of divine love in another, a gush of new spiritual energy flows into our inner life, our faith instantly regains its elasticity, throws off the incubus of doubt, and once more points thankfully and hopefully heavenward. No reasoning process has effected this recovery: the invigorating impulse that has restored our trust springs from the same supernatural sphere whence that trust derived its primal energy. But though neither the lighting of the lamp of faith nor its extinction depends essentially on inductions from the external world, yet the soul does not attain to perfect harmony with itself until it has intellectually framed such a conception of the general character of the universe as may render the appearance of the external world not incompatible with the heart's independent affirmations concerning Divine justice and love.

The only theory of the universe which ever approves itself to our reflection as fitted to afford 'reasonable satisfaction to that religious sentiment which has its immovable basis in the nature of man,'[3] is the doctrine of Leibnitz and Archbishop King, that out of all the possibilities that lie open before the volition of God, He gives actuality to that form of creation which involves the *minimum* of imperfections. That God is omnipotent in Mr. Mill's sense of the term, that He can not only do any one thing, but any combination of things, is a dogman which Faith does not demand, and one which we think has seldom commended itself to the belief of thoughtful men.

If God be that highest form of being that we know of and which we name Spirit, we have no *a-priori* reason to expect in regard to His activity the absence of those limiting conditions

---

[3] Professor Tyndall's Address, p. 60.

which appear intrinsic to the very essence of Mind. We do not see, for instance, how it is possible even for Him to create or suspend those mathematical relations which condition all physical phenomena. Nor, again, can we conceive how, when He has voluntarily imposed upon His activity those uniform modes which we call Laws of Nature, He can introduce fresh manifestations of His will into creation, which shall not lie under the necessity of duly recognizing the claims of the energies which already occupy the field. In a universe, for instance, where the modes of mechanical and chemical force are already determined, it would seem inconceivable that any Being, however powerful, should be able to preserve that perfect consistency in His activity which He may think desirable, and yet to introduce into creation a new energy, such as Life, which should not have to recognize, even in the very act of avoiding or overmastering them, the prior physical conditions already imposed. It is clear that this alone may vastly complicate the process of creation, and introduce insuperable difficulties, of which we can have but the faintest conception. Nor, again, if Matter be not identical with Force; if the Divine Will really moulds some substance external to His own being, such as that to which the Platonists gave the negative name of τo μη ov, and which Aristotle more positively terms ὕλη, how can we at all estimate the possible difficulties which may environ the Divine Idea, as it gradually by the might of its persuasive wisdom converts this matter into our present Kosmos? As Mr. Mill truly says, 'It may be possible to believe with Plato that perfect goodness, limited and thwarted in every direction by the intractableness of the material, has done this because it could do no better.' We prefer to conceive of the difficulty in the way we first mentioned, as being more consonant with the recent disclosures of science; but, in either case, it seems not impossible, nor perhaps improbable, that even God's Ideal may be but imperfectly manifested in the outward creation. We know how, throughout human experience, this disparity between the Ideal and the Actual universally prevails; is it, then, either irreverent or irrational to suppose it possible that in this respect, as in more essential ones, there is some parallelism between the finite spirit and its infinite Father in heaven? To our mind there is something sublime and inspiring in this conception, and we quite agree with Mr. Mill in the idea which he repeats in so many forms, that the feeling that we are really capable of genuine co-operation with the Eternal, and that, on the other hand, He understands and really sympathizes with our difficulties, is a grand stimulus to heroic effort, and is worthy to hold, as we indeed believe it does hold, a permanent place among the highest and most efficacious of man's religious ideas.

There is one point more, however, which must not be overlooked in connection with this controversy. It may be asked, Can we conceive of a sufficient reason why the Divine Spirit should persist in such uniform modes of energizing, when by accommodating His volitions to changing emergencies so many calamities might be avoided? The common reply to this question is surely adequate. If among the chief perfections of creation is the nurture of souls that can in some degree respond to the thought, the righteousness and the love of the Creator, it would seem that for the attainment of this transcendent end there is no other possible method than the one which we find in actual operation, namely, the co-existence and interaction of uniformity in nature and moral freedom in humanity. Take away either of these, and, so far as man's finite vision can discern, the possibility of intellectual and moral culture vanishes likewise. Leave them both, and we see not how the contingency of some amount of natural and moral evil can be avoided. With respect to very much indeed that Mr. Mill calls Evil, we see at once that it leads so directly to the possession of advantages far outbalancing it, as to fall rather into the category of Good. We need not dwell on that fertile theme of the intimate connection between difficult external conditions and the development of intellectual and moral greatness. Biography and History teem with interesting illustrations of this obvious truth, and of the companion truth, that suffering and sorrow elicit from human nature a spiritual loveliness and sanctity precious beyond all comparison. Mr. Mill's Eudæmonism does not prevent his reverent appreciation of this divine self-forgetfulness; but how it could arise in such a universe as he seems to expect from Omnipotence, we are utterly at a loss to conceive. Nay, even this very perplexity in which the appearances in nature at times involve our religious belief, is it not mercifully correlated to our spiritual needs; is it not a trial of our faith through which it is good that human character should pass on its way to become qualified for more satisfying sympathy with the Eternal?

We are far from saying that we have any knowledge that the Primal Cause of phenomena is limited in any of the ways that we have attempted to describe, but we do say that there is nothing in the idea of God, as it presents itself to the religious mind, and as it appears in the language of mankind's divinest teachers, which precludes the possibility of such limitation. Concerning the perfect wisdom and love of God, the awakened heart of humanity speaks with an emphasis which will admit of no deduction; but concerning the limits of His power, the inner voice declines to dogmatize. Enough for us if, in surveying the aspect and history of creation, we see no imperfections save such as may proceed from those limiting conditions which we know *must* environ the activity of any mind of which we can form an idea, and from which, therefore, it is possible that the Perfect Mind may not be wholly exempt.

It is in connection with the animal world that the seeming restriction of God's possibilities most forcibly arrests our attention and occasions perplexity. In the case of man there are always the resources of an infinite future upon which we may draw; and whatever unmerited suffering and unequal allotment the scheme of providence may necessitate here, are open to readjustment in the life to come. And further, as regards the human race, though externally God deals with them according to the unvarying methods of nature, yet we believe that He reserves for Himself such power of immediate influence upon their spirits, that under the most trying circumstances there may arise that inward accession of strength and enlightenment which shall restore harmony between man and his surroundings. But if for animals this life is all, it does seem certain that, had it been possible, the Creator, whose general purpose of benevolence Mr. Mill fully admits, would have spared them the element of bitterness which mingles in their cup of life (a bitterness very slight, it would seem, in proportion to their happiness, yet apparently subserving no ulterior purpose of moral health), and would have rendered their mode of preservation and progression less painful and less combative than science declares it to be. But when we attempt to suggest improvements in the plan of creation, and propound our schemes for the elimination of suffering from the sentient world, we discover on reflection that our method would involve a far more than proportional deduction from the sum-total of happiness.

Here, then, we can only pause and leave the question in suspense, as to whether it be stern necessity which determines this small infusion of pain in the lower animal realm, or whether, in the mysterious return of disembodied life to the spiritual world whence it originates, there may not be some compensations and further uses that we know not of.

One general confirmation of our Theistic faith, the teachings of Zoology and History clearly furnish, namely, that while it is evident that happiness and beauty are the real ends in creation, and pain and deformity only incidental and occasional accompaniments, so is it likewise evident that all is arranged to secure the advance of animated nature to higher types of perfection. For aught that we know, or that faith declares, to the contrary, the rising gradations of the animal kingdom may be indispensable steps through which the Divine Idea passes on the way to a more perfect expression in humanity. And as we study the development of mankind, we cannot but note the steady conquest which those mental attributes that we feel to be the more noble, gradually achieve over their lower but more intrusive and demonstrative competitors. We remember once hearing this truth most impressively unfolded by Professor Martineau. We cannot recall the eloquent words which conveyed the idea, but its substance was, we believe, somewhat as follows: The history of humanity teaches that those elements in human nature which have the Right on their side, always succeed at length in obtaining the Might also; that nations, for instance, who have begun to exercise their Will in self-control, inevitably take precedence over those who are governed by undisciplined impulse and desire; while those, again, in whom the sense of Duty has become a living power, acquire greater dignity and influence than those with whom prudent self-love is the highest inspiration; and that, finally, the progress of Christianity sanctions the conviction that the still higher type of character, in which the negative restraints of morality are superseded by the soul's willing and joyful self-surrender to the guiding influence of Faith and Love, will gradually subdue unto itself all the lower forms of personal force, and hold at length *de facto* that supreme sway in society which already belongs to it *de jure* in the estimation of the best and purest of mankind. Thus in Nature and in History we see the steady approximation to a Divine Ideal, to the realization of God's perfect thought and love. If in the external world (admirable though it be) that thought and love find but an imperfect and progressive expression, still we must remember that to our inner life, to the reason, the conscience and the heart, there comes a more perfect revelation of that ideal which nature has not yet realized. This is the invitation of the Eternal to strive with Him for the manifestation of all that is beautiful and good. It is the Creator of nature who inspires the impulse to improve nature; it is He likewise who furnishes the ideal pattern to guide man's activity. Thus the seeming imperfections of nature afford no sufficient ground for calling in question the boundless wisdom and goodness of God; but they do teach us that it is not to nature chiefly, but to the inner revelation which He makes of Himself to the loving and the prayerful heart, that we must look for all satisfying knowledge of Him and of His character.

Turning now to the essay on the Utility of Religion, we at once become aware that Mr. Mill's definition of Religion entirely misses the features which are most characteristic of the faith in which we find light and strength. He cannot divest himself of the idea that Religion means what has been aptly called 'other-worldliness,' and that Revelation is a system of rewards and punishments guaranteed by miracles. In respect to this idea of future happiness and misery, he is of opinion that it does not act very powerfully upon the moral character. If he had become familiar with the best writings of our most cultured theologians, he would have found that their estimate of the moral worth of the religion which Paley described is essentially identical with his own. His view is not even a caricature of Christian Theism, for it involves no reference to true spiritual experience, to the consciousness of personal obligation, and to that immediate insight of the affections, apart from which the reality of that which he attempts to criticise is wholly absent. Into the inner heart of Christianity he, at this period of his mental history, never penetrates. His valuation of it is altogether external and Deistic, having no point of contact with that Theistic conception which now largely pervades religious teaching, and, in truth, cannot be entirely dispensed with in any form of vital Christianity. Where, indeed, he encounters a class of religious facts that bring prominently into view the influence of religion as a mighty internal energy exercising marvellous controlling power over the other springs of action, he is particularly careful to explain that in such cases we have to do with merely an occasional accident, and not with the genuine essence of religion. Referring to the cruel deaths and bodily tortures which confessors and martyrs have so often undergone for conscience' sake, he says that he will not depreciate them by attributing any part of this admirable courage and constancy to the influence of human opinion.

'But,' he continues, 'if it was not the thought of glory in the eyes of their fellow-religionists which upheld these heroic sufferers in their agony, as little do I believe that it was, generally speaking, that of the pleasures of heaven or the pains of hell. Their impulse was a divine enthusiasm – a self-forgetting devotion to an idea; a state of exalted feeling by no means peculiar to religion, but which it is the privilege of every great cause to inspire; a phenomenon belonging to the critical moments of existence, not to the ordinary play of human motives, and from which nothing can be inferred as to the efficacy of the ideas which it sprung from, whether religious or any other, in over-coming ordinary temptations and regulating the course of daily life.'[4]

It seems strange that a writer who thus protests that 'a self-forgetting devotion to an idea' should not be regarded as a necessary property of religion, should, a few pages afterwards, pen the words, 'The essence of religion is the strong and earnest direction of the emotions and desires towards an ideal object recognized as of the highest excellence, and as rightfully paramount over all selfish objects of desire.'[5] In truth, however, the whole essay is utterly vitiated by the fact, that in his estimate of Christianity he never leaves the obsolete standpoint of Deism, whereas his own conception of religion, so far indeed as he can be said to have one, is an incipient and imperfect Theism, in which Hopes take the place of Beliefs, and ideal imaginations of spiritual realities. Had Mr. Mill at all imbibed the spirit of the liberal Christianity of the present day, he would have learned that it is enthusiastic reverence for a revealed perfection far transcending ourselves, that constitutes the very breath of the religious life, and that to its presence in the soul are due the gentle graces of character, the purity, the meekness and

[4] P. 94.
[5] P. 109.

the self-sacrifice which ordinarily characterize a truly religious heart, as well as the more sublime religious phenomena which are conspicuous in the history of the past. Heat is needful for the growth of the common daisy and for the ripening of the autumn grain, as well as for the upheaving earthquake and the purifying storm; and what Warmth is in the physical world, that is Divine Reverence and Love in the world of morals and religion.

The main thesis which this essay aims to establish is, that the great service which Christianity and other positive religions have confessedly rendered to morality, is not due to any exclusive fitness in these religions to perform this beneficent function, but is mainly owing to the fact that they have managed to enlist in their service three great social forces, and have in consequence obtained undue credit for the triumphs which these obedient genii have achieved. It is the forces of authority, of early education and of public opinion, whose energies Christianity has hitherto appropriated, but which, we are led to understand, may just as fitly be yoked in future to the chariot in which Utilitarianism, and by its side the Religion of Humanity, proceed to the accomplishment of social reformations which will throw into the shade all earlier victories. Mr. Mill, however, overlooks here, as he habitually does in these earlier essays, that religion is essentially an impelling and restraining power, and not an intellectual creed; that it is a power, too, which is awakened by felt contact with present spiritual reality, and not chiefly by anticipations or fears concerning future contingencies; that it has its vital seat in the affections and the will, and not in the understanding. Hence it comes to pass that he is utterly unable to furnish any *rationale* of the process by which religion has thus managed to exert a guiding influence over so large a portion of our social energies, and has turned them to such beneficent account. Public opinion, for instance, which he mentions as chief among the social forces which religion has hitherto wielded, does not spontaneously come and offer its services to religion. On the contrary, it is first indifferent to her appeals, and when importuned shews itself refractory and antagonistic, and only after long-sustained pressure and persuasion does it ally itself with religion in the carrying out of social reforms. Christianity at first made its way directly against public opinion, and not till later, when the grand spiritual impulse had done its mighty work, did public opinion act as a conservative power to retain the advantages already won and recognized. Thus, too, has it been with every victory which Christianity and Philanthropy have gained. In each one we see a divine idea and aspiration, originating in some reformer's soul, which gradually by its own native elasticity overcomes the dull inertia of public opinion; and only after it has affected this can it derive help and furtherance from the force which it has by its own inherent might subjugated to its nobler sway. And it is enabled thus to subdue and utilize these lower energies, because religion is itself the highest and mightiest energy which the influence of the Eternal ever kindles in the human soul. It uses them because it is intrinsically worthier than they, because it has an authority as well as a strength which they do not possess. Just as in the natural world, chemical force overcomes mechanical, while vital force controls both mechanical and chemical alike; so in the world of mind, the social sympathies by degrees pervade and overcome the lower forces of passion and self-love; while in their turn, passion, prudence and social and national affinities yield at length to the all-subduing might of religious enthusiasm.

To discuss the utility of that which inspires and sustains man's higher life, and which alone saves humanity from gravitating downwards to sensuality and covetousness, is as superfluous as it would be to discuss the use of caloric, the possible substitutes for oxygen, or the desirability of our daily bread. He who attempts to investigate the worth of religion in the spirit of this essay, simply demonstrates that he has not himself yet come consciously under its inspiring and edifying influence. To illustrate what is divine by what is human: M. Comte, no doubt, discoursed rationally enough about the utility of love when he married his first wife, on the ground that she was well qualified to supply his emotional deficiencies; and Mr. Mill was probably able to estimate calmly the gains and losses of the matrimonial union when in his earlier years he listened to the instructions of that parent of 'iron unfaith' who moulded his youthful intellect. But when the French philosopher had felt the wondrous influence of 'the incomparable Clotilde,' and his English admirer had entered upon his worthier devotion to her 'who inspired his best thoughts,' and whose 'incomparable worth' made her friendship the greatest source to him of happiness and improvement, they were hardly then in the mood to consider the utility of these choice experiences. How much more justly and impressively does this apply to that self-surrendering devotion to the Eternal, which in so far as it is real, becomes the source and sustenance of all the higher life – a holy and perennial enthusiasm, vivifying the homely sphere of daily duties and daily charities, but having the latent power to rise, if occasion calls, to sublimest heights of moral heroism! Nay, is it not manifest that it was precisely the want of the due presence of this supreme controlling energy, which springs out of felt personal relations with a Being of perfect Holiness and Love, which allowed the human affections in the hearts of these philosophers to assume so exaggerated and undisciplined a form? It is one of the chief utilities (if the word in this connection were not almost a profanation) of true religion in the heart, that it alone can bless and consecrate all our pure earthly loves and aspirations, and yet so restrain, exalt and organize them, as to produce in the noblest and saintliest natures that spiritual microcosm which is fashioned after the model of heavenly perfection.

In bringing to a close the first part of this article, we have only to express our conviction that the treatise on Nature, and that on the Utility of Religion, are of very slight intrinsic value. They give interpretations and criticisms of both Nature and Religion as unjust as they are unlovely; and but for the light which they throw by force of contrast on the after-awakenment of the author's religious sentiment, we almost think it would have been better for Mr. Mill's permanent reputation as a sound philosopher if they had been left to his executor with the hint,

'Quem criminosis cunque voles modum
Pones iambis, sive flamma
Sive mari libet Hadriano.'

There remains for us now the more agreeable task of reviewing the essay on Theism, and of endeavouring to shew what strong testimony it indirectly bears to the reality and true source of Spiritual Insight, and to the utter incompetency of the Experiential Philosophy to explain or justify the inevitable attitude of mind which such insight occasions. . . .

We have now to notice, however, that in the interval of ten or more years, which separates the composition of the last essay from that of its predecessors, it would seem that some potent though unobtrusive influence had greatly modified our author's valuation of the Theist's faith. Notwithstanding Miss Taylor's confident assertion in the Preface that 'the author considered the opinions expressed in these different essays as fundamentally consistent,' internal evidence of the strongest kind compels us to believe that in this intervening period the spiritual atmosphere of Mr. Mill's inner life passed through a remarkable and most salutary change. Religious belief for its own sake, and not merely as the handmaid of morality, has now become with him an object of earnest interest and study. Nor is the investigation into the truth of Theism carried on, as from the tone of the preceding extract we should naturally expect, in any hostile spirit. On the contrary, Mr. Mill is now ready to give the arguments in favour of the existence of God and of a Future Life the most friendly consideration, will go with them to the uttermost limit that his intellectual conscience permits, – a great deal farther, indeed, than in the view of his Positivist associates he has any right to go, – and then, when at last the tightly-stretched tether of his philosophical creed absolutely forbids all further advance, he stops short with manifest reluctance, and casts a wistful look at those realms of positive conviction whither the Intuitionalist is enabled to travel onward. We now read, in direct contravention of what he said above, that 'it cannot be questioned that the undoubting belief of the real existence of a Being who realizes our own best ideas of perfection, and of our being in the hands of that Being as the ruler of the universe, gives an increase of force to these feelings [i.e. aspirations towards goodness] beyond which they can receive from reference to a merely ideal conception.'[6] Surely this is nothing short of a distinct confession that liberal Christianity,[7] which combines the enthusiastic devotion to the service of mankind, towards which the Positivist aspires, with an assurance of the existence of such a Being as Mr. Mill describes, must, in so far as it takes a real hold on men's

---

[6] P. 252.

[7] Mr. J. S. Mill had evidently escaped from his father's unhappy misapprehension of the essence of Christianity, for he says 'it may be doubted whether Christianity is really responsible for atonement and redemption, original sin and vicarious punishment; and the same may be said of the doctrine which makes belief in the divine mission of Christ a necessary condition of salvation' (p. 114).

convictions, prove a far mightier power for good than that Religion of Humanity to which before he gave such marked pre-eminence. And not only does he now admit the surpassing efficacy of this Christian Theism, but he is also most anxious, as we have said, to lend it all the support which Experientialism can allow. Only two possible lines of argument in the direction of Theism are left open to him by the tenets of his philosophy – the one is by way of well-attested Miracle, the other through the evidence for the action of a Designing Intelligence in nature. The section of the essay devoted to the question of Miracle eminently exhibits that clearness of thought and grace of diction for which Mr. Mill's writings are so justly distinguished. After a careful review of David Hume's reasoning, he arrives at the following decision:

'The existence of God cannot possibly be proved by miracle; for unless a God is already recognized, the apparent miracle can always be accounted for on a more probable hypothesis than that of the interference of a Being of whose very existence it is supposed to be the sole evidence. Thus far Hume's argument is conclusive. . . . Once, however, admit a God, and the production by his direct volition of an effect which in any case owed its origin to his creative will is no longer a purely arbitrary hypothesis to account for the fact, but must be reckoned with as a serious possibility.'[8]

There follows, accordingly, a discussion of the question from the Theist's point of view, and he remarks:

'We can see no reason on God's goodness why, if he deviated once from the ordinary system of his government in order to do good to man, he should not have done so on a hundred other occasions; nor why if the benefit aimed at by some given deviation, such as the revelation of Christianity, was transcendent and unique, that precious gift should only have been vouchsafed after the lapse of many ages, or why, when it was at last given, the evidence of it should have been left open to so much doubt and difficulty.'[9]

This consideration, taken in conjunction with the reflection

[8] P. 232.
[9] P. 235.

that the Christian miracles are 'attested by evidence not of a character to warrant belief in any facts in the smallest degree unusual or improbable,' leads him to the conclusion 'that miracles have no claim whatever to the character of historical facts, and are wholly invalid as evidences of any revelation.'[10]

While Mr. Mill is only in accord with an increasing number of Christian believers in thus holding that there is no legitimate thoroughfare to religious conviction by way of external miracles, his theory of the human mind closes for him that avenue of internal evidence which they find to be the most direct path to satisfying truth, so that he is necessarily left with the teleological argument as his only remaining chance of escape from utter scepticism. His manifest anxiety to allow to this argument all possible strength, is another conspicuous indication of his desire to find a logical passage to supersensual realities. It can hardly be doubted that the vast majority of the members of Mr. Mill's school of thought would heartily endorse the sentiment of the accomplished editor of the Fortnightly Review, and say of this argument from Design, that if it has not already received its death-blow at the hands of the Darwinian theory, it is at least for the nonce in that state of suspended animation which utterly disqualifies it for playing its former role in theological controversy.[11] Indeed, what is more natural than that the devotees of the Religion of Humanity should eagerly embrace the plausible idea that the doctrine of Natural Selection has effectually demolished the only remaining bridge over which the scientific inquirer might still be tempted to stray into the shadowy land of metaphysical illusions and spiritual dreams? So far, however, is Mr. Mill, in this his last essay, from exulting in or even admitting this supposed victory of Darwinism over Design, that he lucidly re-states Paley's argument, seeks to fortify it against unfair criticism, and, while admitting that the adaptations in nature are not such as to supply complete demonstration, thinks 'it must be allowed that, in the present state of our knowledge, they afford a large balance of probability in favour of creation

---

[10] P. 239.

[11] Fortnightly Review, January, 1875.

by intelligence.'¹² In reference to the true logical worth of this argument, he says:

'The Design argument is not drawn from mere resemblances in Nature to the works of human intelligence, but from the special character of those resemblances. The circumstances in which it is alleged that the world resembles the works of man are not circumstances taken at random, but are particular instances of a circumstance which experience shows to have a real connection with an intelligent origin, the fact of conspiring to an end. The argument therefore is not one of mere analogy. As mere analogy it has its weight, but it is more than analogy. It surpasses analogy exactly as induction surpasses it. It is an inductive argument.'¹³

He then takes the case of the structure of the eye, as one of the most impressive instances in which we discern not only likeness to the intelligent action of man, but also such an apparent converging of many means to one end, namely, the production of sight, that we are compelled to recognize the presence of final as well as of efficient causation, and therefore to ascribe the production to the energy of an intelligent will.

'But,' he adds, 'I regret to say that this latter half of the argument is not so inexpugnable as the former half. Creative forethought is not absolutely the only link by which the origin of the wonderful mechanism of the eye may be connected with the fact of sight. There is another connecting link on which attention has been greatly fixed by recent speculations, and the reality of which cannot be called in question, though its adequacy to account for such truly admirable combinations as some of those in Nature is still, and will probably long remain, problematical. This is the principle of "the survival of the fittest." ... Of this theory, when pushed to its extreme point, all that can now be said is, that it is not so absurd as it looks, and that the analogies which have been discovered in experience, favourable to its possibility, far exceed what any one could have supposed beforehand. Whether it will ever be possible to say more than this is at present uncertain. The theory, if admitted,

---

[12] P. 174.

[13] P. 169.

would be in no way whatever inconsistent with creation. But it must be acknowledged that it would greatly attenuate the evidence for it.'[14]

Such an expression of *regret* that the theory of 'the survival of the fittest' may possibly weaken the force of the argument from Design, would have sounded strangely out of harmony with the context had it occurred in the first of these essays.

Equally remarkable, too, is the change of tone in his estimate of the moral character of Nature. We before quoted the striking passage in which he reviles her so bitterly, and cannot find epithets strong enough to express his detestation of the revolting acts, the violations of justice and mercy, which she is constantly committing. In passing to his treatment of the same subject in the essay we are now discussing, we find ourselves transported from an icy and a stormy clime, where dæmonic agencies seem to reign supreme, to a region where there is much of genial sunshine, and no few marks of the sway of benevolent intention. If by chance some chapters of Baron D'Holbach's 'Systeme de la Nature' should be bound up in the same volume with one of the Bridgewater Treatises, the incongruity would hardly be more startling than that which strikes us as we turn from the earlier to the later pages of Mr. Mill's book.

> 'Endeavouring,' he says, 'to look at the question without partiality or prejudice, and without allowing wishes to have any influence over judgement, it does appear that, granting the existence of design, there is a preponderance of evidence that the Creator desired the pleasure of his creatures. This is indicated by the fact that pleasure of one description or another is afforded by almost everything, the mere play of the faculties, physical and mental, being a never-ending source of pleasure, and even painful things giving pleasure by the satisfaction of curiosity and the agreeable sense of acquiring knowledge; and also that pleasure, when experienced, seems to result from the normal working of the machinery, while pain usually arises from some external interference with it,

---

[14] P. 172.

and resembles in each particular case the result of an accident.'[15]

When we pass on from the consideration of the attributes of the Creator to the kindred question of Immortality, we are again agreeably surprised to find that Mr. Mill, instead of being a direct opponent of the Theist in this controversy, is a neutral spectator, whose sympathies and hopes are decidedly on the Theistic side. Considering the strongly materialistic tone which increasingly prevails in the utterances of his *quondam* admirers, Mr. Mill's emphatic refusal to admit that there is any scientific presumption against the Christian belief may fairly, we think, be regarded as some evidence that this doctrine took a stronger hold upon his spirit than he was willing to allow. Adhering firmly to his old idealistic position, he declines to leave the vantage-ground of consciousness for that materialistic standpoint to which many of his followers have removed.

> 'Feeling and thought are not merely different from what we call inanimate matter, but are at the opposite pole of existence, and analogical inference has little or no validity from the one to the other.... Mind (or whatever name we give to what is implied in consciousness of a continued series of feelings) is in a philosophical point of view the only reality of which we have any evidence; and no analogy can be recognized or comparison made between it and other realities, because there are no other known realities to compare it with. This is quite consistent with its being perishable; but the question whether it is so or not is *res integra*, untouched by any of the results of human knowledge and experience.'[16]

In the preceding essay he had spoken of 'the imaginative hope of a futurity which, if there is nothing to prove, there is as little in our knowledge and experience to contradict.'[17] However, at that time he attached little or no value to such hope; for he adds that 'history, so far as we know it, bears out the opinion that mankind can perfectly well do without a belief in a

---

[15] P. 190.
[16] P. 202.
[17] P. 120.

heaven.' In the case of those choicer minds who most devoutly engage in that peculiar *cultus* called the Religion of Humanity, this hope of immortality will (if we may trust Mr. Mill's earlier prediction) wax fainter and fainter, and tend to its final extinction; for he closes his second essay in these words:

> 'It seems to me not only possible but probable, that in a higher, and above all a happier, condition of human life, not annihilation, but immortality, will be the burdensome idea; and that human nature, though pleased with the present, and by no means impatient to quit it, would find comfort and not sadness in the thought that it is not chained through eternity to a conscious existence which it cannot be assured that it will always wish to preserve.'[18]

When, however, we turn to the essay on Theism, that which is represented above as a 'burdensome idea' to the highly cultivated mind, is now recommended to our notice as an elevating hope which we shall do well to cherish.

> 'On these principles it appears to me that the indulgence of hope with regard to the government of the universe and the destiny of man after death, while we recognize as a clear truth that we have no ground for more than a hope, is legitimate and philosophically defensible. The beneficial effect of such a hope is far from trifling. It makes life and human nature a far greater thing to the feelings, and gives greater strength as well as greater solemnity to all the sentiments which are awakened in us by our fellow-creatures and by mankind at large. It allays the sense of that irony of Nature which is so painfully felt when we see the exertions and sacrifices of a life culminating in the formation of a wise and noble mind, only to disappear from the world when the time has just arrived at which the world seems about to begin reaping the benefit of it.'[19]

The change of front in regard to the chief doctrines of rational Christianity of which we cannot but become aware as we compare this last essay with the earlier ones, is far too marked to be at all adequately accounted for by Miss Taylor's expla-

---

[18] P. 122.

[19] P. 249.

nation, that the essay on Theism had not, like the other two, undergone the author's searching revision. The whole spirit and tone of this treatise force upon us the conviction that in the last few years of his life Mr. Mill discovered that the Religion of Humanity alone was profoundly unsatisfactory to his higher affections, and that he studied anew the evidences of Theism in the *hope* that he might therein find a basis for a firm belief in God and Immortality. If this be so, we need not wonder at the criticism which Mr. Morley regretfully passes upon this essay, namely, 'that, strange to say, it is on its most important side a qualified rehabilitation of supernatural hypotheses.'[20]

II. The Autobiography furnishes, we think, the true key to the spiritual change which appears to have come over the author's inner life. We learn that after the composition of the second essay he suffered an irreparable loss in the death of his much-beloved wife.

> 'Since then,' he says, 'I have sought for such alleviation as my state admitted of, by the mode of life which most enabled me to feel her still near me. I bought a cottage as close as possible to the place where she is buried, and there her daughter (my fellow-sufferer and now my chief comfort) and I live constantly during a great portion of the year. My objects in life are solely those which were hers; my pursuits and occupations those in which she shared or sympathized, and which are indissolubly associated with her. Her memory is to me a religion, and her approbation the standard by which, summing up as it does all worthiness, I endeavour to regulate my life.'[21]

May we not reasonably suppose that during the ten years which preceded the composition of the concluding essay, the religious side of the writer's nature had undergone growth and enrichment, that the divine hand of sorrow had removed to some extent the scales from his spiritual vision, and rendered him faintly cognizant of influences that did not seem to belong to this visible world? Were it not for the gloom of night, of what sublimity and range would physical science be bereft!

---

[20] Fortnightly Review, January, 1875.

[21] Autobiography, by J. S. Mill, p. 251.

And is it not also true that amid the gloom of bereavement the organ of spiritual discernment ofttimes perceives in far clearer outline those eternal verities which form the objects of religious faith? Both in biography, and on a larger scale in history, noteworthy instances at once present themselves as illustrative of the rise and growth of faith in God and Immortality amid the deep and protracted sadness of bereavement.

For the adequate attainment, however, of satisfying religious convictions, it is clear that emotional and intellectual factors must co-operate. All genuine religion has, we believe, its origin and sustenance in the feeling that a guiding and sympathizing Spiritual Energy is very near to the human soul, and that influences, the most precious and life-giving, emanate thence and diffuse themselves through the believer's heart and mind. He who feels these influences in special power and purity, becomes to his fellow-men a prophet, or revealer of the truths of the spirit. As such truths, based on feeling, assume an intellectual form and pass from mind to mind, a popular theology grows up, in which the vital spiritual element, always inadequately expressed in human thought, now undergoes in general much misrepresentation and distortion. In the rise and growth of devout sentiment and conviction in society, there is always present more or less of immediate acquaintance with spiritual reality, owing to the kindling of the diviner affections by the felt presence of the Eternal; and along with this, partly as the occasion and partly as the consequence of this first-hand perception, there will naturally be found also a sense of the divine authority and of the priceless worth of those recorded prophetic teachings which form the Bible of the age. This faith, accordingly, does not at all arise by way of inference from observed phenomena; but nevertheless it requires for its complete establishment and purification, constant adjustment with the conclusions of the understanding concerning nature and life. In uncultured minds, this adjustment is in general a simple matter. Neither scientific knowledge nor scientific prejudices exist to serve as barriers to the hearty and unqualified acceptance of the tidings of great joy. Such natures suffer more from moral impurities which dim the eye and dull the ear of the spirit, than from the imprisoning restraints of intellectual scepticism. Their gospel, no doubt, contains a large and noxious admixture of alloy; but, such as it is, its reception is retarded by few mental scruples; so that whenever among them a true awakenment of the religious life occurs, the divine contagion speeds from heart to heart, and freely moulds men's views of life and nature in harmony with the postulates of their religious faith. As culture advances, however, Reason begins to exert its rightful and beneficent prerogative, and thoughtful minds review the received theological dogmas in the light of the dominant scientific and literary culture of the age. The popular religion, both in ancient and in modern times, has usually shewn itself in many respects out of harmony with the established facts of physical and mental science. It contains elements which violate both the common sense and the moral sense of thoughtful men. Whatever be the validity of the spiritual faculty in its proper sphere, it is evident that the sentiments of reverence and devotion, if allowed to operate upon the judgment unchecked by critical intelligence, do in general give birth to rank growths of mischievous superstition. The truths of spiritual experience can then, and then only, attain to and preserve their wholesome purity, when they exist in conjunction with the due culture of man's entire nature, of his intellectual and moral no less than of his spiritual discernment.

But if our spiritual faculty is thus liable to serious abuse and error, it is most important to remember that the scientific faculty also, when too exclusively exercised, has a like tendency to interfere with the clear vision of the soul, by producing inability to perceive and appreciate the most important elements of truth and wisdom. Over and above that acquaintance with the laws of phenomena which properly constitutes science, there almost inevitably arise in minds that are engrossed with outward observation, and do not frequently or habitually direct their attention to the spiritual side of our being, certain *assumptions*, which, although they cannot be verified and are apparently at variance with the clear deliverance of consciousness, yet by the force of intellectual habit take a powerful hold upon the judgment, and seek to usurp the authority of axiomatic truths. Among these articles of faith, which those of our savants who study only phenomena dogmatically lay down and call upon us to accept on pain of having our views regarded as hopelessly 'unscientific,' the principal are, that man must regard himself as a mere series of ideas, feelings and volitions, and not as a substantive *ego*, which thinks, feels and wills, and that he must further believe that this succession of states of consciousness which collectively form himself, is evolved on that principle of uniform sequence which excludes the possibility of true personal causality, or that power of preferential choice between springs of action which we term man's moral freedom. These assumptions, if logically developed, necessarily transform all estimates of moral worth into considerations of use or beauty; human nature can no longer be a fitting object of approbation or reprobation, but must be viewed as a combination of qualities and actions which, as the case may be, are useful or mischievous, attractive or repulsive; and the business of the educator and the statesman simply is, to strive to render them more useful and beautiful by the judicious application of fresh motive-power in the form of fear or desire. While these gratuitous hypotheses thus undermine the sense of moral responsibility, they at the same time effectually close the door to spirituality or religion, – to all belief, that is, in the immediate action of the Eternal Spirit upon the human soul. If all our knowledge is ultimately traceable to our own sensations or to those of our ancestors, – if not only the consciousness that certain courses of action are more noble and beneficent than others, but also the sense of duty, the moral imperative which makes us feel the obligation to give these the preference, must be ascribed to no higher inspiration than this sensational experience, – then, as a matter of course, the affirmations of the saints and prophets of every age are prejudged and discredited; neither present nor past revelation has any foothold in fact; and prayer and spiritual communion are mere self-delusions, which must no longer be allowed to mislead the enlightened mind. The upholders of these unsubstantiated dogmas are aware that their criticism does not, like that of the Theist, merely prune and rectify the popular faith, while leaving untouched its true vitality; they know they destroy theology root and branch; but they think they furnish an adequate compensation for this wholesale clearance of the religious convictions of mankind, by announcing that now at length human nature and human history are perfectly open to 'scientific' investigation. But the theory of Automatism, however tempting, contravenes too decidedly the facts of consciousness to be accepted as a true solution of the mystery of personality; and the most extensive knowledge of phenomena would be a poor substitute for glad tidings of a Living and a Loving God. We see good reason to cherish an expectation (which the study of the essays before us strongly confirms) that, after this too ambitious attempt on the part of physical science to force its limitations on psychology and theology shall have spent its force, the culture of Europe will recover its confidence in the immutable facts of consciousness, will accept the verified truths of science while rejecting its unwarranted assumptions, and will seek for true ideas of Substance and Causation, not in the groups and sequences of visible nature (in which we see effects only, and not the Casual Reality), but in that invisible Energy which produces these phenomena, and which is discerned to have its only known counterpart in man's volitional and spiritual being. No soul is wholly blind to the presence of this creative and sustaining Energy. In intensity our vision may vary, from Mr. Spencer's assurance of an Unknowable Cause of all phenomena, and Mr. M. Arnold's recognition of a Power not ourselves that makes for righteousness, to Kant's perception of a moral Lawgiver, or Madame Guyon's and Fenelon's felt communion with a Spirit of unfathomable love; but never can the consciousness of man be wholly divested of the haunting sense of God. To every form of this belief, the scientific prejudices to which we have referred are constantly antagonistic; and though they cannot wholly stifle the faith in spiritual reality, they do produce a harassing scepticism, from the bondage to which only severe study of all the facts of our inner life, or, what is still more effective, some vivid awakening of the diviner affections, will avail to deliver the soul. In the case of Mr. James Mill, these mental disabilities, which impair religious insight, appear to have culminated in what seems the nearest possible approach to congenital spiritual blindness. Such natures, accordingly, hardly feel the want of the truths they fail to see, and he would probably have regarded with pity, if not with disdain, his son's anxiety to retain by the faint tenure of hope doctrines of which his philosophy allowed him no right of possession.

In considering the causes which concur in producing this extreme dulness of spiritual apprehension, we must not, however, direct our attention to the false assumptions of scientific dogmatism alone. Those whose business it is to study and expound the truths of the Spirit, have displayed in their view of Revelation a similar one-sidedness of perception; and the unwarranted assumptions of the theological dogmatist must be credited with a very large share of the scepticism from which our present culture is suffering. If our savants have questioned and rejected spiritual truths which lie beyond their province, theologians have in like manner invaded with their unfounded prejudices the spheres of science and of history. Indeed, Mr. James Mill's position was to a large extent the logical outcome of that false antithesis between inspired and uninspired Scripture with which the Protestant reaction early identified itself. This bibliolatry was probably a necessity of the time, and has assuredly not failed to do some good service in concentrating a prodigious amount of mental activity on the study of the most precious chapter in the world's literature, and in bringing the book itself into close and beneficial relations with the daily life of many in all classes of society. But we must set off against this advantage a very serious drawback of intellectual and mental damage. The influences detrimental to rational conviction which have flowed from this source form two main streams, and each of these streams took part in sweeping out of James Mill's mind the vestiges of religious faith. In the first place, it is obvious that, in setting up this impassable barrier between the Bible and other books, Protestantism implied that the Bible taught truths which are not normally related to man's faculties, and that consequently these faculties cannot be applied to the criticism of the contents of this sacred volume. The authority of the book itself is supposed to rest on miracle and the fulfilment of prophecy, and, their validity being once established, all that is elicited from the Bible by fair interpretation has an equal claim to be considered the utterance of God, and becomes a part of revealed truth. Hence the Protestant Church, no less than the Catholic, has throughout its history enjoined belief in propositions, some of which are at variance with logical necessity, others with scientific fact, others with the natural conscience, and others again with the claims of the affections and the affirmations of direct spiritual experience. It was Mr. James Mill's fate to encounter the full force of this unnatural development of theological doctrine, and, confounding as he did the spirit of the Christian faith with the dogmas of Scotch Presbyterianism, he came at length to the not unreasonable conclusion, 'that the *ne plus ultra* of wickedness is embodied in what is commonly presented to mankind as the creed of Christianity.'[22]

But this is not the only mischief which orthodox Protestantism has wrought. In denying present inspiration, it weakened healthy interest in all the higher ethical and spiritual features of man's consciousness, and led to a practical disregard of the all-important revelation therein contained. The mind in its search for wisdom was confined to either the study of external nature or the literal interpretation of the Hebrew and Greek Scriptures; and although Cudworth and the other Cambridge Platonists in the seventeenth, and Bishop Butler in the eighteenth century, endeavoured to rest religion to some extent on intuition as its natural basis, yet the prevailing Protestant philosophy became, as was only to be expected, more and more prevailingly materialistic in its tone. Nor was it professed Christians alone who suffered from this fatal defect in the Reformation theory. The whole intellectual atmosphere of this country became impregnated with the false idea that, if we are to learn of God, it is only in the book of Nature or in that of documentary Revelation that there is any possibility of meeting Him; so that when the Deist found the bridge of external evidence give way, he seldom dreamed of finding a more legitimate access to the fertile fields of prophetic teaching through the consciousness of a Divine Presence acting upon his own inner life. The students of mental science, diverted from the higher and nobler departments of their special realm, began to treat psychology as though it were a branch of physics, and, falling more or less under the sway of those scientific prejudices which we have before described, they confounded Causation with Antecedence, and thus imported into the study of volition and morals conceptions that are appropriate to the sphere of phenomena alone. The author of the 'Analysis of the Human Mind,' probably the most acute of that long line of associational psychologists who trace their descent from the philosopher of Malmesbury, discerned more fully than any of his predecessors the logical exigencies of this theory. The Deists had unconsciously introduced into their Natural Religion a large admixture of intuitional faith. They had really gone to the study of the external world with the

---

[22] Autobiography of J. S. Mill, p. 41.

preconceived idea of a perfectly just, wise and loving God, and finding much in Nature which confirmed that prepossession, they passed lightly over the formidable array of apparent exceptions. But Mr. James Mill had no such weakness. A man of remarkable acumen and mighty force of will, one in whom morality was in the smallest degree 'touched by emotion,' he determined that his belief should be in strict accordance with the principles of his philosophy. Accordingly he carefully sifted out the lurking intuitions that beguiled the Deistic mind, and discovering that in Sensationalism and Utilitarianism pure and simple there was no sufficient basis for the doctrines of Natural Religion, he, 'doubtless after many struggles, yielded to the conviction that concerning the origin of things nothing whatever can be known;' and that if any one theory has claims to precedence over another, 'it is the Manichæan theory of a Good and Evil Principle, struggling against each other for the government of the universe.'[23]

III. Such were the influences that moulded the mental character of the father of the eminent man whose last words form the subject of this paper. How sedulously that father sought to fashion his son after his own image, that son himself has most graphically described. We regard it therefore as no weak testimony to the truth of Theism, and to the natural affinity between it and a rich and full development of man's higher faculties, that, notwithstanding the extremely adverse educational influences that hemmed in Mr. J. S. Mill from his infancy till the time when his intellectual character was fully formed, he should towards the close of his life sympathize so intimately with the sentiments of liberal Christians, should yearn to believe what they believe, and, almost in defiance of his philosophical creed, should proclaim his right and privilege to cherish hopes for which that creed affords no ground or justification. There is a curious parallelism between his case and that of many orthodox Christians. They likewise find themselves in the meshes of a logical network from which they can see no escape; yet, if they are pure-minded, loving natures they are constantly devising kindly sophistries which may appear to harmonize the sentiments of their hearts and the requirements of their creed; and if at length they find they

---

[23] Autobiography, p. 40.

cannot possibly construe the unmanageable dogma in such a way as to satisfy their ideas of justice and love, they still ascribe the failure to their own ignorance, and console themselves with the hope that some means of escape, at present unsuspected, will open before the many excellent people whom the articles of faith seem to consign to eternal perdition. But when thoughtful persons in their best frame of mind earnestly hope that the facts are better than their theological or philosophical creeds appear to sanction, we may reasonably suspect that such hope is the incipient stage of dissent from the creed in question; for it generally means that a certain affirmation (based on moral and spiritual insight) is taking shape in the soul, an affirmation which will continue to speak in more emphatic tones till it persuades or constrains the judgment to side with it, and either modify the objectionable dogma, or, if need be, entirely cancel it. With good reason, then, does Mr. Morley express dissatisfaction and alarm at the important advance which Mr. Mill thus makes towards the point of view of the Theist:

> 'They [the believers in God and Immortality] will contrast the iron unfaith of James Mill, that more than Roman figure of the Autobiography, with the eagerness of his son and most important disciple to restore the domain of the supernatural, after it has been removed from the region of Belief, into the region of Hope. So long as this domain of the supernatural is left to them in one quarter or another, they will feel that nothing is lost. Concede to them the region of Hope, and they will count pretty surely on making the old growths thrive in it with all the old vigour of the region of Belief.'[24]

Nor will they lack some excuse for so doing, seeing that such hope is generally the early dawn of spiritual insight. In regard to religious questions, if the spiritual affections (which are the true eyes of the soul) cling spontaneously and persistently to some cherished idea, it can hardly be but that the intellect, however incredulous and refractory at first, will gradually revise its *prima philosophia*, till its principles fall into harmony with this object of divine desire. And this intellectual reformation, though a work of time, is yet quite feasible, since, as

---

[24] *Fortnightly Review*, Nov. 1874.

we have seen, the principles which require correction are, in general, not based on matters of fact, but simply inveterate assumptions. We shall presently see that this 'hope' had so far acted on Mr. Mill's own philosophical system at the time when the essay on Theism was being written, that the thin edge of the wedge was already inserted which must in time have completely rent asunder Necessarian and Experiential dogmas, and given free access to Intuitional ideas.

But it was not only in his later years, when he felt the want of a sympathizing God and of a heavenly Home, that his expanding sentiments proved too strong for his philosophy. His Autobiography and other writings conclusively prove that throughout his adult life his ripening personality was continually pressing against, and at times actually rupturing, the limitations of his creed.

The earliest important protest of his nature against the philosophy in which he had been reared, is recorded in the interesting chapter of the Autobiography entitled, 'A Crisis in my Mental History;' and, as we might expect from so clear a thinker, the consciousness of free-will was the first psychological fact which he found at variance with the creed with which his mind had been so thoroughly indoctrinated. His mode of escape from that dilemma, after the subject had long and painfully exercised his mind, is characteristic of the whole course of his future mental development; he practically let slip the essence of the Necessarian hypothesis, whilst anxiously endeavouring to retain its outward form.

> 'I saw' (he says) 'that though our character is formed by circumstances, our own desires can do much to shape those circumstances; and that what is really inspiriting and ennobling in the doctrine of free-will, is the conviction that *we have real power over the formation of our own character;* that our will, by influencing some of our circumstances, can modify our future habits or capacities of willing.'[25]

On this passage Dr. Carpenter remarks:

> 'Thus even John S. Mill, the most powerful advocate of Automatism, found himself brought by his own mental

[25] Autobiography, p. 169

experiences to what is virtually an acceptance of the independence of the will.'[26]

Another great intuitional impulse, which must have sorely tried his adhesion to the paternal creed, was occasioned by his intimacy with F. D. Maurice, John Sterling and other kindred spirits. It reached its climax in the essays on Bentham and Coleridge. In the criticism, which occurs in the latter of these essays of the 'Evidences of Religion' in vogue in the eighteenth century, there are several passages which bear no little affinity to the sentiments of recent liberal divines. He says, for instance:

> 'In forgetfulness of the most solemn warnings of the Author of Christianity, as well as of the Apostle who was the main diffuser of it through the world, belief in his religion was left to stand upon miracles – a species of evidence which, according to the universal belief of the early Christians themselves, was by no means peculiar to true religion: and it is melancholy to see on what frail reeds able defenders of Christianity preferred to rest, rather than upon that better evidence which alone gave to their so-called evidences any value as a collateral confirmation.'[27]

And a little further on:

> 'If there is any one requirement of Christianity less doubtful than another, it is that of being spiritually-minded; of loving and practising good from a pure love, simply because it is good. But one of the crotchets of the philosophy of the age was that all virtue is self-interest; and accordingly, in the text-book adopted by the Church (in one of its Universities) for instruction in moral philosophy, the reason for doing good is declared to be that God is stronger than we are, and is able to damn if we do not. This is no exaggeration of the sentiments of Paley, and hardly even of the crudity of his language.'[28]

With these spiritual ideas we may compare the statement in the essay on Theism:

---

[26] Principles of Mental Physiology: Preface, p. x.
[27] Dissertations and Discussions, Vol. I. p. 434.
[28] Ibid. p. 435.

## 158  Mill and Religion

'It would not be easy even for an unbeliever to find a better translation of the rule of virtue from the abstract into the concrete, than to endeavour so to live that Christ would approve our life.'[29]

Can there be much doubt that, had it not been for the shackles of early intellectual habit, which fettered his mind as effectually as if Kratos and Bia had clenched the rivets, we should have met in Mr. J. S. Mill a powerful expounder and defender of Christianity as it is set forth in the Sermon on the Mount; of that Christian Theism which is now reasserting itself in many earnest minds, and preparing to defend the cause of truth and religion against the decaying dogmatism of Orthodoxy on the one hand, and the growing dogmatism of Science on the other.

We have before pointed out that his philosophical prepossessions rendered him unable to acknowledge the force of any Theistic argument save the teleological one. When, however, we look closely into his theological ideas as set forth in this essay, we cannot but see how readily they would adapt themselves to a thoroughly Theistic philosophy. They are, it is true, prevented from falling into confessed accord with Theistic reasonings by the two chief articles of the associational creed, namely, that, in the first place, causation means only invariable antecedence, and, secondly, that all knowledge is ultimately derived from outward experience. But it is curious and interesting to note how these two all-important dogmas, which formed the basis of his life-long scepticism, and which in his earlier writings he treats as unquestionable certainties, now begin to relax their rigidity, and to shew that they are gradually, and almost unconsciously to himself, yielding to the silent but most potent strain of dawning faith and hope.

'If there be a Creator' (he says), 'his intention must have been that events should depend upon antecedents, and be produced according to fixed laws. But this being conceded, there is nothing in scientific experience inconsistent with the belief that those laws and sequences are themselves due to a Divine Will. Neither are we obliged to suppose that the Divine will exerted itself once for all, and, after putting a

[29] P. 255.

power into the system which enabled it to go on of itself, has ever since let it alone. Science contains nothing repugnant to the supposition that every event which takes place results from a specific volition of the presiding Power, provided that this Power adheres in its particular volitions to general laws laid down by itself.'[30]

Mr. Mill admits that there is at least considerable probability that such a Being exists. If, then, it be quite compatible with scientific culture to regard each item in the series of natural phenomena as having no other connection with its predecessor than they both owe their origin to an exertion of the same invisible Will, what is this but to remove Causation altogether from the sphere of visible things, and to locate it in a Spiritual Power, of whose energizing Nature is the ever fresh expression? We do not see how Mr. Mill can consistently reprove the Theistic doctrine which assigns all real Causality to Spirit, unless, indeed, he were prepared to maintain that each antecedent event *causes* God to will its consequent, – a theory which would make Nature as much the creator of the Divine Mind, as this Mind the creator of Nature. It is, no doubt, true that Mr. Mill would regard this conception of Causality, not as a satisfactory proof of God's existence, but as a legitimate explanation of the universe by one who had already accepted the basal idea of Theism. Still, when we consider his earlier admission that the primitive consciousness and intelligence of man always assigns the events of nature to causative Will, and his present admission that Theism (which he considers a probable doctrine) sanctions this aspect of Causation, it is not, we think, too much to say that Mr. Mill in the present essay exhibits a marked approximation to the point of view of those who consider that by psychological necessity man looks for the Cause of phenomena, not in antecedent phenomena, but in an originating Power, of which the senses can take no cognizance, and which must needs be conceived after the type of the only other creative power which we know, namely, the volitional energy of our own spirit.

But the most satisfying evidence of the being and character of God is derived, we think, from the felt revelation of His presence made to our moral and spiritual nature. This, too, like

---

[30] P. 136.

the Volitional argument, is set aside by Mr. Mill as irrelevant, because in his view there is nothing in the idea of duty, or in the religious experiences of devout minds, which may not be explained by subjective intellectual and emotional processes. Yet, strange to say, after he has laid down this general principle as applicable to humanity at large, he suddenly startles us by an insinuation utterly subversive of his whole philosophy. Speaking of the advent of Christianity, and of the comforting and ennobling views which it professed to bring to mankind, he declares that there are some features in the character and teachings of Christ which do not appear to have arisen in the natural course of social evolution, and which therefore demand some other explanation. His words are:

> 'When we consider further that a gift extremely precious came to us, which though facilitated *was not apparently necessitated* by what had gone before, but was due, as far as appearances go, to the peculiar mental and moral endowments of one man, and that man openly proclaimed that it did not come from himself, but from God through him, then we are entitled to say that there is nothing so inherently impossible or absolutely incredible in this supposition as to preclude any one from hoping that it may perhaps be true.'[31]

It is not surprising that the editor of the Fortnightly Review sees in the words we have italicised an astounding and, from his point of view, quite inexplicable concession to intuitional claims. A marvellous change indeed must have come over the inner life of the eminent expounder of the Logic of the Moral Sciences ere he could have thus allowed himself to indicate the questionable solidity of the foundation on which his elaborate superstructure rests. We are entirely at one with Mr. Morley when he says:

> 'I am unable to conceive how any one accepting the 6th Book of the System of Logic could admit the possibility of Christ's mission being special or express, any more readily than the possibility of the sun having stood still at the command of Joshua in the valley of Ajalon.'[32]

---

[31] P. 240

[32] Fortnightly Review, Jan. 1875.

Mr. Mill's words clearly involve the virtual surrender of the one great assumption which supports and animates all the researches of Positivists into the origin and development of mankind, and shew that their deceased chieftain had conceived and cherished a fatal doubt whether, after all, there are not elements in human nature which must ever prove inaccessible to so-called 'scientific' investigation. If God at certain seasons confers on man special gifts, which could not come to him as effects of causes open to our research, well may his former admirers exclaim, as they do, with amazement and regret, 'What, then, becomes of the theory of Evolution? What becomes of Sociology and the Science of History?' And when we further note that this great thinker not only allowed the possibility of such an intrusion of incalculable Divine influence as would utterly frustrate the leading aims of Positivism, but actually exhorted men to *hope* that this supposed interposition is a fact, we cannot avoid the conclusion that, as we before said, the chains of intellectual habit which bound our author's thought were at length yielding to the gentle but irresistible pressure of a newly-awakened spiritual life and insight; and that, ere his departure from this world, he was beginning to understand and appreciate in some rudimentary way the wondrous spirituality of that prophet of Nazareth whose sublime morality he had long reverenced. If we suppose that a faint dawn of spiritual love, and its consequent vision, beguiled him at times, almost in spite of his understanding, into the attitude of discipleship to Jesus, and that in the serene faith of the Beloved Son he found a healing balm for his stricken heart, we can quite account for the otherwise inexplicable depth of admiration and reverence which he expresses for the Founder of the Christian faith:

> 'About the life and sayings of Jesus there is a stamp of personal originality, combined with profundity of insight, which, if we abandon the idle expectation of finding scientific precision where something very different was aimed at, must place the Prophet of Nazareth, even in the estimation of those who have no belief in his inspiration, in the very first rank of the men of sublime genius of whom our species can boast. When this pre-eminent genius is combined with the qualities of probably the greatest moral reformer and martyr to that mission who ever existed upon earth, religion cannot

be said to have made a bad choice in pitching on this man as the ideal representative and guide of humanity.'[33]

Why does he thus place Jesus in the foremost position among men of sublime *genius?* Not assuredly for the breadth and accuracy of his philosophical views, for never was a teacher who placed more reliance on spiritual intuitions and expressed himself in stronger terms of certainty on matters concerning which Mr. Mill's ideal philosopher would never venture beyond faint hopes and slender probabilities. Nor would even the position of Jesus as a moral teacher justify, in Mr. Mill's view, this ascription to him of the highest genius. His moral maxims Mr. Mill admitted to be of the loftiest character; still they omitted 'many essential elements of the highest morality;'[34] and surely from a utilitarian point of view, Christ's ethical theory was anything but adequate or correct. We can only suppose, then, that this supremacy of genius was attributed to Jesus because Mr. Mill vaguely felt that there is a spiritual discernment intimately connected with the warmth and purity of the heart's best affections, and that in Jesus this divine vision existed in unique clearness and richness. The exigencies of the case compel us to the conclusion that Mr. Mill would never have spoken of him and his mission in such unmeasured terms of eulogy had he not to some extent *trusted*, as well as hoped, that the spiritual announcements of the gospel were not mere subjective fancies, but reliable revelations of objective reality. It must be granted that he speaks of this spiritual faculty as an exceptional gift made to Jesus alone; but it is evident that, if the passage between the human soul and the spiritual world be once opened, the case of Jesus would come to be regarded as typical of that of mankind at large, and intuitional faith would, slowly, perhaps, but yet certainly, supplant our author's philosophy. Just as the Experientialism and Utilitarianism of Hartley and Priestley, associated as they were with belief in a special revelation and with intense reverence for the personal character of Jesus, underwent of necessity a gradual transformation into the religious philosophy of Channing and Martineau, so we believe that Mr. Mill's admission of a possible communion between Christ and God would probably in

---

[33] P. 254.

[34] Treatise on Liberty, p. 91.

the course of time have expanded into a like admission in the case of every man, and that in this way his soul would have finally disengaged itself from the trammels of Sensationalism, and have become prepared to study and appreciate those internal evidences of the truths of Religion, in the light and warmth of which his faint probabilities would have ripened into satisfying faith, and his hope of immortality would have blossomed into a sweet and peaceful confidence that death is powerless to remove us from the undying love and sympathy of that Eternal One in whose everlasting arms the devout soul trustfully reposes.

# [FROM REVIEW OF] THREE ESSAYS ON RELIGION
[Wathen Mark Wilks Call]

... To Mr. Mill the evidence derived from the consideration of the facts of the universe appeared insufficient to establish the omnipotence of the Creator. Strictly speaking, Mr. Mill does not recognise creative but only constructive power. The two great element of the universe, Matter the passive, Force the active elements, are in his view eternal. The author of the collocations which adapt the world to the results which it exhibits, was not the creator of force or matter, or of any of their properties. Accepting the hypothesis of a *Designing Deity*, who had to fabricate a world out of pre-existing materials, we are justified in ascribing to him skill, contrivance, wisdom, an assumption which in itself implies a limitation of power. The limitation of power allows us to entertain the supposition of absolute knowledge; but ingenious and admirable as is the machinery of contrivance in nature, it affords no proof that the knowledge or skill of the Constructor is infinite. Possibly the refractoriness of the materials out of which the orderly world was composed, possibly the inherent deficiency of intelligence in the Divine Artificer, possibly a third and unknown alternative, may be the true explanation of the arrest of creative skill or the frustration of benevolent purpose. Random guesses being worthless, and even reasonable conjectures unattainable, we are compelled to admit that we do not know how the power of the Great Artificer is limited. Granting the existence of design, the normal character of the machinery for the production of physical and mental pleasure affords some ground, in Mr. Mill's view, for inferring that benevolence is an attribute of the Deity; but to conclude that the final cause of creation was the happiness of sentient beings, is a conclusion directly opposed to the evidence. The notion of a providential government, for the sole purpose of promoting human welfare, must be dismissed; other motives of action appear to influence the

Deity. Even of His continual existence we have only the guarantee afforded by the presumption that, as the conditions which produce the liability to death are of his own making, he cannot be subject to the fatal law which affects human beings.

Such is the speculative construction of Deity, that one of the most eminent thinkers of our time, swayed by a yearning desire to accept all the fair possibilities which reason does not exclude, offers us. 'Such is the Deity whom Natural Religion points to: and any idea of God more captivating than this comes only from human wishes, or from the teaching of either real or imaginary Revelation.' Mr. Mill thus literally constructs for us the Probable God of Carlyle's sarcastic deprecation; a Deity the probability of whose existence will be reduced to the lowest degree by the triumph of the principle, of which it seems little likely to afford us an affirmative illustration, the Survival of the Fittest. The limited Deity, thus called into being, reminds us of the Demiurgus of Gnostic speculation, the Maker but not the Father of the world. The mystery of origin remains unexplained; matter and force, with their properties, are at least co-eternal with the Divine Artificer; we have no explicit assurance of his self-existence; we have hardly satisfactory evidence of his eternal continuance; to explain the imperfections of his workmanship we arbitrarily limit his power; his wisdom, though superhuman, may possibly be limited too; and his benevolence, though probably a real and genuine attribute, is subordinated to motives which are called into activity by interests which lie beyond the sphere of human sorrows and of human joys.

The genius, the philosophical power, the logical acuteness, the religious aspiration, of Mr. Mill, have not, in our judgment, enabled him to rescue natural theology from the fate which appears likely to overtake it. Must not all such speculations be attended with ill success? The Substance of Spinoza, with its attributes of thought and extension; the Unknowable of Mr. Herbert Spencer; the Spirit of intellectual beauty and love celebrated in the musical verse of Shelley; the eternal Not-ourselves of Mr. Matthew Arnold; the personified reason of the deist Reimarus, are they not all Idola of the tribe and of the den? We believe that Mr. Mill has failed in his efforts to reconstruct the theology of nature, not from any intrinsic circumscriptions, but from the absolute impossibility of the task.

If the logic of the Finite Sphere can demonstrate the existence of a Deity at all, the Deity whose existence it demonstrates must be the Deity of Mr. Mill's essay.

Next to the belief in an objective Holy Ideal, the belief most dear to mankind is the belief in the immortality of the soul. From the days of Plato to the days of Mr. Mill no philosopher, no logician, no theologian has succeeded in converting into glorious assurance the desire, the hope of an eternal futurity. Wisely, then, respecting the inevitable limits of the argument, Mr. Mill has confined his efforts to what seemed practicable. He has satisfied himself with an attempt to remove the great obstacle to the admissibility of the doctrine, opposed by the presumption that the relation of thought to a material brain is a kind of metaphysical necessity. It is remotely possible, he represents, that thought, that feeling, may survive the dissolution of their companion organism. In his own idealistic language, the material brain itself is a set of human sensations, our states of consciousness a series of states which it is as easy to imagine without as with this physical accompaniment. A succession of thoughts connected by memories constitutes a thinking substance; and feeling and thought, the only known realities, may continue to exist after their visible and palpable accompaniment has ceased to be; the music may survive when the lute is broken, the splendour illuminate when the lamp is shattered, and, as in the beautiful abstraction of the poet, 'the spirit may lie in the western sky, when we *love* but *live* no more.' To one who finds cause for satisfaction or incentive to usefulness in the hope of a future, there is, Mr. Mill concludes, no hindrance to his indulging that hope, but on grounds of natural religion he gives us no assurance whatever of a life after death.

These speculations on a post human existence are followed by a discussion on the claims on our attention, not of the Christian, or of any other particular system of belief, but of Revelation generally. The evidences of revelation are commonly distinguished as external or internal. Accepting this classification, Mr. Mill maintains, that as the human faculties are capable of appreciating moral excellence, there is no ground for asserting their incompetency to discover it, and, consequently, that the divine origin of an alleged communication from a Supreme Being cannot be demonstrated by its ethical recommendations, however admirable. Internal evidence, then, being inconclusive, we must have recourse to external evidence; in other words, to the exhibition of supernatural facts. The existence of God cannot be proved by a miracle: the existence of an Omnipotent Creator is contradicted by the testimony of nature. But if the existence of a God of limited powers be conceded, a sufficient standing ground is secured for Revelation, the presence of imperfections in a revelation being rendered plausible by the presence of imperfections in nature. Butler's argument, Mr. Mill contends, is conclusive from its own point of view, for 'the belief of Christians is neither more absurd nor more immoral than the belief of Deists, who acknowledge an Omnipotent Creator.' Butler's error lay in the refusal to admit the hypothesis of limited power. Accepting, then, the demiurgic deity, whose existence is rendered probable by the indications of design in the order of the world, there is no antecedent improbability in the supposition that a message may have really been received from him. On this assumption a miracle is not incredible. A survey of the subject, in its concrete relations, however, leads to the conclusion that the verification of a particular miracle is practically impossible. With a singular candour, with an impartial consideration of the alleged vulnerable points in anti-supernaturalist statements, with an over-generous readiness to appreciate the mental condition of believers, by the force of a sympathetic imagination, Mr. Mill travels, with a rapid but steady footstep, and with an eye that inspects the entire horizon of probability, over the moving morass of Supernaturalism. As in apparent anxiety to leave 'a sister when she prays, her early heaven, her happy views,' in a long and involved sentence, in which the chain of hypotheses vibrates as we read, Mr. Mill arrives at the tremulous conclusion, that 'there is nothing so inherently impossible or absolutely incredible in this supposition (the reality of the Christian revelation) as to preclude any one from hoping that it may perhaps be true.' But that 'miracles have no claim whatever to the character of historical facts, and are wholly invalid as evidences of any revelation,' is his own openly avowed and ultimate verdict.

An explanation of this intellectual urbanity and morally beautiful attitude of forbearance and indulgence to illusions dear to men, is, we conceive, suggested by occasional passages of wise thought and noble feeling, scattered over the fine essay on the *Utility of Religion*, and embodied in the closing section, entitled *General Result*. We are in an age of weak beliefs, complains our author, in one of these passages, and describes, truly and sadly, the painful position to a conscientious and cultivated mind condemned to be drawn in contrary directions by the two noblest of all objects of pursuit, truth and the general good. We are paralysed by the apprehension, that freedom of speculation or enlargement of thought, by making men unbelievers might make men vicious and miserable; or we are averse to dry up the fountain of feelings which we imagine can emanate from no other source than religion. In his critical estimate of the influences of authority, early education, public opinion, Mr. Mill supplies a corrective to the morbid misgivings which incline many to the timid conservatism of a sceptical reticence. By showing that conviction is not inseparable from religious sanction, but is largely influenced by the general concurrence of mankind in questions of opinion; that the sense of moral duty, the sincerity, courage and self-devotion, which animate many excellent persons, are attributable to the impressions of early education rather than to the force of a dogmatic creed; that regard to the sentiment of our fellow creatures is a pervading motive in nearly all characters; that the theocratic religion of the Jews, with its presumed punctual incidence of reward and punishment, did not prevent disloyalty to their law, or check their frequent lapses into paganism; that the overpowering magnitude of the penalty with which offenders, under the Christian dispensation, are menaced, does not deter them from the commission of sin and crime; by a comprehensive analysis, in brief, of the motives which determine human conduct, Mr. Mill encourages us to entertain the hope that the welfare of mankind will be better served by a frank recognition of the inaccessibility of certain subjects to our faculties, and the cultivation of those sources of virtue and happiness which can dispense with the artificial support of supernatural beliefs and inducements. But, though knowledge of right and wrong, or motives to moral conduct, are not, in the present state of human progress, inseparable from the sanctions of supernaturalism, the mystery of human existence, the insufficiency of human life to satisfy human aspiration, will beget an unquenchable desire for forms of existence, modes of life, higher hopes than we know on earth. So long, says Mr. Mill, with pathetic piety, as earthly life is full of sufferings, so long will there be need of consolations, which the hope of heaven affords to the selfish, the love of God to the tender and grateful. The poetic religion of Shelley made a profound impression on the mind of the writer of this paper, while yet a boy; the struggle between the Spirits of Good and Evil, so splendidly depicted in the opening canto of the Revolt of Islam, seemed to him almost an historical reality; and a belief in the Intelligent Spirit of Love and Beauty which that greatest of the English poets of this century worshipped with musical adoration, took a temporary possession of his mind. Mr. Mill tells us that he has known at least one cultivated and conscientious person who regards Nature and Life not as the expression throughout of the moral character and purpose of the Deity, but as the product of a contriving goodness and an intractable material, as was believed by Plato, or a Principle of Evil, as was the doctrine of the Manichæans, and who accordingly was entitled to look on himself, as a fellow-labourer with the Highest, a fellow-combatant in the great strife, the ultimate issue of which would be the complete triumph of good over evil. It is evident from the concession which follows this sketch of his friend's creed, that Mr. Mill extended to the 'pleasing and encouraging thought' of this modern Manichæan, the indulgence which he extends to the modern Christian. Apart from all dogmatic belief, there is for those who need it an ample domain in the region of the imagination which may be planted with possibilities, with hypotheses which cannot be known to be false. The contemplation of these possibilities is, he contends, a legitimate indulgence. Distinctly, Mr. Mill asserts, that the whole domain of the supernatural is removed from the region of Belief into that of simple Hope. As distinctly does he say that the benefit consists less in the presence of any specific hope, than in the enlargement of the general scale of the feelings. Impressed, as we conceive, with an over-powering sense of the appalling evils which desolate our mortal life, Mr. Mill recommends the indulgence of hope, 'with regard to the government of the universe, and the destiny of man after death,' as a legitimate expedient for elevating and solemnizing life. The reason once secured in its rights, the imagination may be permitted to follow its own end and do its best to make life pleasant and lovely. We are not prepared to go quite so far as Mr. Mill; but, while inclining rather to the view to which he gives so touching an expression, that 'in a higher and above all a happier condition of human life, not annihilation but immortality may be the burthensome idea,' we assuredly have no wish to circumscribe the area of the cultivated imagination, or to prohibit the indulgence of a blind hope, if its exercise be healthy and its conception genuine. Groundless hopes, however, and fair possibilities, are not sufficiently substantial to sustain the invasion of a continuous scepticism, or to survive the gradual decline of poetic sensibility, or the yearnings of passionate affection. Rather would we seek consolation in the identification of our own life, with the life of the race, in Action, in Science, and in the elevated joy which has its source in the contemplation of lovely and sublime objects in nature, in life, and in art – in the inspiration of mighty poets, the enthusiasm of the great Masters of music.

A consistent conception of ideal goodness is invaluable to regulate conduct and inspire action; and the undoubting belief of the existence of a Being who realizes our own best ideas of perfection, has, as Mr. Mill points out, a remarkable efficacy in fortifying and sustaining our moral sentiments. On the other hand, this advantage, as Mr. Mill is equally ready to admit, is neutralized by the bewildering casuistry which vainly seeks a moral justification of the government of the world. If, as Coleridge contended, a demonstration of the existence of such an objective ideal is inaccessible to human faculties, is it not possible that with continued expansion of heart and intellect, with a wiser discipline of our emotional nature, with a growing correspondence of human life to human requirements, we may cease to demand objective reality for the divine thought which we create within, and limit ourselves to the contemplation of that Human ideal which is its imperfect embodiment, and of such concrete approximation to it as may be found in the 'everliving dead men' of all ages and countries, who inspire us with their example, enrich us with their spiritual wealth, and console us with their ideal sympathy?

One such representative and guide of humanity Mr. Mill recognises in the Prophet of Nazareth, and though we cannot allow even the possibility of the express commission from God, which he somewhat reluctantly concedes, we are not unwilling to regard Jesus as a unique figure, and to assent, though not without qualification, to our author's admiring estimate of his character. A reformer, a martyr, a man of profound insight, with the eloquence of an orator and the spirit of a poet, Jesus has had an influence which we cannot think wholly undeserved. In the new commandment of love; in the recognition that the greatest are those who serve; in the reverence for the weak and humble; in the lesson of the Good Samaritan; in the doctrine of the essential equality of men, we believe, with Mr. Mill, that Jesus carried goodness to a greater height than had ever been attained before. Gleams of tender and noble sentiment indeed shine forth from the pages of Plato, of Seneca, of Marcus Antoninus; but the influence of Christ, and of the Christian life which he helped to create, concentrated the scattered rays into one luminous orb, to warm and enlighten the world. A not dissimilar appreciation of the character of Christ was embodied by Strauss in the popular 'Life of Jesus;' and Shelley, in his fragmentary 'Essay on Christianity,' speaks of its founder in language not unlike that of Mr. Mill.

In addition to the powerful Arraignment of Nature, the striking confession of faith in the primeval character of the elements of Force and Matter, and the valuable thoughts on the utility of religion, may be found scattered here and there, through this last literary bequest of a fine intellect and noble heart, comments on human life, its joys, its sorrows, its objects, its discipline, with which we cordially sympathize. Glimpses there are in it of the affectional side of the author's nature, which we should be sorry not to have. If its publication will not throw fresh lustre on a fame already sufficiently brilliant; if, in some respects, we could have desired a treatise from Mr. Mill conceived in a different spirit, and executed with a steadier hand, we yet welcome it for its comprehensive and intelligible re-statement of old problems, for the courageous originality of its speculation, and for the charitable condescension of a philosophy which tolerates the mystical predominance of innocent and elevating possibilities.

The concessions which Mr. Mill offers will, in all probability, be turned to account by the despairing champions of Orthodoxy; but Truth is patient, and can smile composedly at temporary delays to her progress, or ineffectual efforts to arrest her triumph. And what, after all, do these concessions amount to? A Probable Deity: a hope of Immortality which cannot be disproved, but for which there is no warrant; a possible revelation, from which miracle is discarded, and which is discredited by flagrant moral difficulties and perversion; a revelation mutilated by the removal of atonement, redemption, original sin, and vicarious punishment. Are these concessions calculated to nerve the failing arm or revive the drooping energies of the Theological Giant Despair? Far from expressing an absolute approval of the attenuated Christianity to which he extends a reluctant toleration, Mr. Mill considers it, like all supernatural religions, to be morally compromised by the system of rewards and punishments which is a constituent of it, and through which it fosters the selfish part of our nature. The impressions which are derived from a faith or a hope in the possibility or reality of the divine mission of Christ, are principally valuable, it would seem, as impressions to fortify the purely human religion which we have already briefly portrayed. With Mr. Mill –

> 'The essence of religion is the strong and earnest direction of the emotions and desires towards an ideal object recognised as of the highest excellence, and as rightfully paramount over all selfish objects of desire. This condition is fulfilled by the Religion of Humanity in as eminent a degree, and in as high a sense, as by the supernatural religions even in their best manifestations, and far more so than in any of their others.'

# [FROM] LEAVING US AN EXAMPLE: IS IT LIVING – AND WHY?
## Anonymous

... Such then is the conclusion at which the French sceptical writer [Renan] and the English sceptical philosopher [Mill] alike arrive. Probably no two men could be more unlike in their habits of thought; yet they are agreed in assigning to Him [Christ] the first place among the great and the good. Their estimate of Him may fairly be cited as representing the conclusions of modern free thought on this point. It is the view taken by the ablest of those who reject the supernatural element in His history. And as such it forms a safe basis on which to found an argument concerning the nature of His work.

But this is not all. For it is further allowed that Christ is preeminent not more by his superiority to all others than by the lasting influence which His example has exercised upon the world. From whatever cause it may arise it is certainly a fact that His example has still all the force of a living example. When those who, like M. Renan, reject the supernatural element in His life, confess notwithstanding that 'cette sublime Person chaque jour preside encore au destin du monde,' they do but acknowledge a fact which is a matter of history and of present experience. Whatever view may be taken of Him or of His religion, this at any rate cannot be denied – that to thousands of persons now living, as well as to countless numbers in the past, His Example has been and is a living Example....

In this survey of the Character of Christ we take our stand for the time at that point of view which Mr. Mill tells us that the rational sceptic must always be prepared to allow as possibly the true point of view, and regard Christ, not as God, but as 'a Man charged with a special, express, and unique commission from God to lead mankind to truth and virtue.' We cannot be wrong in considering His character from this point of view; since this is common ground to those who believe and those who deny His Divinity. Whatever else He was, that He was truly man – that His earthly life was a real human life – all are agreed. It is as Man that we shall now consider His character.

In accepting this position for the time, we do not, however, concede the question of the miracles, which cannot be disposed of in the summary manner in which Mr. Mill has dealt with them.[1] The writer of *Ecce Homo* puts the case as it really stands – 'On the whole, miracles play so important a part in the scheme of Christ, that any theory which would represent them as due entirely to the imagination of His followers, or of a later age, destroys the credibility of the documents, not partially but wholly, and leaves Christ a personage as mythical as Hercules.'[2] We may add that if the Divine mission of Christ be admitted, the reason for His miraculous power becomes at once apparent.

This is not the place to enter into the question of miracles, but we may remark in passing that it is possible to believe fully all that the Evangelists record as to the miracles of Christ without considering them as violations of the laws of nature. They may have been worked in accordance with natural laws unknown, or only partially known to us.

But we do wrong to speak of the laws of nature: strictly speaking, we ought to say the *forces*, not the laws of nature. Nature is a collection of forces, and there is but one law which rules these forces – viz., the law that the weaker force should give way before the stronger. This is the only order of nature. And this being so, it is incorrect to speak of a miracle as a violation of the laws of nature; since it is in strict accordance with *the order of nature* that the stronger force should subdue the weaker. A miracle is the result of the action of a force or forces new to our experience and superior to the forces with which we are conversant in nature. The real question at issue between those who deny and those who affirm the possibility

---

[1] This will be clear to any one who will observe the manner in which M. Renan deals with this subject. He supposes them to have been 'pious frauds' arranged by the disciples of Jesus and permitted by Him, or at any rate not disallowed by Him. It has been well said that this view is fatal to the perfect sincerity of Christ. (See Liddon's *Bampton Lectures*, pp. 161, 201, 202; and Bishop of St. David's *Charge*, pp. 34, 35. 1863. Rivingtons.)

[2] *Ecce Homo*, p. 4.

of miracles is – *Is it possible that any such force or forces exist in the universe?* If this be possible, miracles are possible. . . .

A Christian is one who is striving with all his might to follow a perfect Example. In the light which this truth sheds upon religion, new life is imparted to words which had well-nigh lost their meaning; faith, conversion, the new birth, all become realities. We have seen what faith is; and what is conversion, if it be not a turning into the path of Christ's footsteps? What is the new birth but the first commencement of our re-creation after His image? Conformity to the likeness of Christ; this is the Alpha and Omega of Christianity. It is because this truth is not realised that so much genuine religious feeling is wasted, and comes to nothing for want of *aim*; it evaporates like steam let off instead of being condensed; the power which might renovate the whole man is wasted, and worse than wasted. If those who now waste all their religious fervour in emotion, or in misdirected energy, would but realise the mighty truth, that their whole religion is to become like Christ, then, at last, that life and death would bear abundant fruits; it would be found that the Spirit of Christ is still a living power mighty to heal the moral diseases of society; then the self-sacrifice of the cross would kill the selfishness of men. When the religious world realises this – when it leaves off cleaving to the shadow, fighting for the shadow, worshipping the shadow, and puts the substance in its place – then the religion of Christ will cease to be a matter of mere feelings, and notions, and odious party watchwords; it will become a reality, a mighty engine for good; *it will convert the world!*

Is not this the Gospel for the nineteenth century? Does it not harmonise with all that is good in that new religion which has taken such hold of some of the most thoughtful minds of our age? – does it not supply all that is wanting in the '*Religion of Humanity?*' We cannot better describe the leading features of the new religion than in the words of one of the most profound among its disciples.

In his essay on 'Theism,' from which we have already quoted, Mr. Mill describes this 'real, though purely human religion' as 'being the cultivation of a religious devotion to the welfare of our fellow-creatures, as an obligatory limit to every selfish aim and end, for the promotion of which no sacrifice can be too great.' 'This principle of action is disinterested; it carries the thoughts and feelings out of self, and fixes them in an unselfish object, wooed and pursued as an end for its own sake.' This object is, in short, the universal good of man . . . .

Such, then, is the religion of humanity. Now, Christianity, if our estimate of it be the true one, has this in common with this 'purely human religion,' that it is *'the strong and earnest direction of the affections towards an ideal object, recognised as of the highest excellence, and as rightly paramount over all selfish objects of desire.'* That which the religion of humanity has not in common with Christianity is the ideal made actual. It must construct the ideal for itself. It feels the need of an ideal of human perfection as an object of intense veneration amounting to worship, in order to keep alive the 'religious devotion to the welfare of our fellow-creatures, for the direct promotion of which no sacrifice can be too great;' and, seeing this need, it seeks to create a purely imaginary ideal for the worship of its disciples. Will not He supply this want of whom the author we have quoted has so truly said – ' When this pre-eminent genius is combined with the qualities of probably the greatest moral reformer and martyr to that mission who ever existed upon earth, religion cannot be said to have made a bad choice in pitching on this man as the ideal representative and guide of humanity; nor even now would it be easy, even for an unbeliever, to find a better translation of the rule of virtue, from the abstract to the concrete, than to endeavour so to live that Christ would approve our life?' In striving to follow such an Example we must surely be aiming at nothing less than the universal good.

But Christ not only supplies us with an Ideal; He also supplies us with motives for the imitation of this Ideal. This meets another want in the religion of humanity – the want of motive. This want must strike every one who reads the foregoing extracts. Pure disinterested devotion to the universal good, such as this religion demands, is only to be looked for in the very highest natures. What amount of secular training can make the selfish unselfish? There is, indeed, one kind of training which can effect this object. The religion of Christ, while it takes men as they are, and appeals in the first instance to such motives as have power with human nature generally, issues in the purest and most disinterested devotion to an Ideal of perfect Self-sacrifice. *'It carries the thoughts and feelings out of self, and fixes them on an unselfish object, loved and pursued for its own sake.'* What Mr. Mill says of the effect of the promises and threats of a future life as tending to foster the selfish element of our nature is not true in regard to those whose hearts are given to the great Example; devotion to an ideal of self-sacrifice can never tend to make men selfish. This is one of the most striking of the adaptations of Christianity to man's moral nature; it draws him to Christ by an appeal to motives of self-interest, and having brought him there it teaches him to forget self – to die to self. In offering to men His yoke Christ appeals to self-interest; but the yoke which they are thus led to take upon them is the yoke of love, of the purest and most disinterested Self-sacrifice.

No doubt there is truth in Mr. Mill's remark, that 'in its effect on common minds, what now goes by the name of religion operates mainly through the feelings of self-interest.' But the cause of this is to be found, not in the religion itself, but in the miserably defective way in which it is frequently taught. The remedy for this is found in the truth which we have here endeavoured to set forth. It needs but to place this great central truth of the Gospel in its right place, and every lower motive will be lost in the endeavour to follow the great Example. Surely here is a meeting-point for the new religion and the old! That which the religion of humanity wants is nothing else than THE SON OF MAN: the Gospel for the nineteenth century is simply the Gospel of the first.

# [FROM] IS THEISM IMMORAL? AN EXAMINATION OF MR. J. S. MILL'S ARGUMENTS AGAINST MANSEL'S VIEW OF RELIGION
Anonymous

Mr. J. S. Mill in his Autobiography represents himself as having been confirmed in his imprudent purpose of writing a book on the Philosophy of Sir William Hamilton by the fact, as he declares it to be, that the peculiar doctrines of that philosophy had been made by Mr. Mansel the justification of a 'profoundly immoral view of religion;' the view, namely, 'that it is our duty to bow down in worship before a Being whose moral attributes are affirmed to be unknowable by us, and, perhaps, extremely different from those which, when speaking of our fellow creatures, we call by the same name.'[1] It is scarcely necessary to say that such a view of religion was not held by Mansel, and could not be held by any Christian. It is true that Mansel, like Sir W. Hamilton, Mr. Mill himself, and many others, maintained that we cannot know God 'as absolute,' and cannot consequently know anything of His essential attributes, *a priori*, or antecedently to experience. But Mansel, far from holding that it is our duty to worship God 'as absolute,' held, on the contrary, that it is impossible for us to do so; that we can only worship Him because we can only know Him as He has been pleased to reveal Himself in nature and in Christ; and it is of this view of religion, and not of that represented by Mr. Mill, that he made Hamilton's philosophical doctrines a justification. It is true, also, that Mansel, like all Christians, affirmed that the various mysterious phenomena exhibited in the course of natural providence 'are, no doubt, reconcileable, we know not how, with the infinite goodness of God,' and that Mr. Mill asserts, though he makes no attempt whatever to prove, that to say this is, 'in other words, to say that the

[1] Autobiography, p. 275.

infinite goodness ascribed to God is not the goodness we know and love in our fellow creatures, but is another quality altogether.'[2] But Mansel, as Mr. Mill himself admits, disavows the nonsensical doctrine thus attributed to him; and it is one of the least respectable of all the artifices known to the craft of controversy, though, unfortunately, it is one to which Mr. Mill too often resorts, to attempt to discredit an opponent, not by refuting what he says, but by imputing to him something which he does not say.

The view of religion which Mr. Mill regarded as profoundly immoral, is, as we shall hereafter see, that commonly known as Theism – the opinion that, notwithstanding the existence of evil in the world, its Almighty maker is infinitely good. Mr. Mill admitted, of course, that the doctrine of the infinite goodness of God has been, and is, professed by multitudes, but he maintained that it has really been believed by none; and holding this view he consistently regarded the profession of it as immoral, the 'assertion in words of what is not thought in meaning;' the flattery of a Being supposed to be all powerful, but not believed to be really good, by the application to Him of 'epithets which we fancy He likes to hear, in the hope of winning Him over to our own objects.'[3] And, doubtless, if the fact be as Mr. Mill imagined, the religion of Theists is immoral enough.

The doctrine of the immorality of Theism – the belief that it is 'depraving' to worship God – is one into which Mr. Mill was trained from a child. Frequent discourses having for their purpose his confirmation in this peculiar creed, seem to have constituted the sole religious instruction, if such it can be called, of his early years. It was, as he tells us,[4] his father's persuasion, that all religions, with the exception, perhaps, of that of the ancient Persians, were morally bad, and the Christian religion, as generally understood, the worst of all, the special enormity in the case of the latter being that it inculcated the worship of an 'Omnipotent Author of hell.' If this had been the only difficulty in the way of his acceptance of Christianity it might not have been insuperable. The foun-

---

[2] Examination of Hamilton, p. 121 (3rd Edition).

[3] Examination of Hamilton, p. 125.

[4] Autobiography, pp. 39, 40.

dation article of the catholic faith is a belief in the 'Father Almighty, maker (not of hell, but) of heaven and earth;' and not a few who were unquestionably Christians, have declined to profess more than this. At any rate Deism, at least, is certainly possible without a belief in the existence of hell. But Mr. James Mill could not accept Deism any more than Christianity: his quarrel was not simply with the omnipotent author of hell, as it is, or was supposed by some to be, but also with the omnipotent author of earth as it actually is. 'He found it impossible,' his son tells us, 'to believe that a world so full of evil as ours, was the work of a Being combining infinite power with perfect goodness and righteousness. His intellect spurned the subtleties by which men have attempted to blind themselves to this open contradiction. The Sabæan or Manichæan theory – the theory of a good and evil principle struggling against each other for the government of the universe – he would, probably, not have equally condemned; he would have ascribed to it no depraving influence;' but as for 'religion in the sense usually attached to the term,' that is, a religion based on, or including Theism, 'he regarded it with the feelings due not to a mere mental delusion, but to a great moral evil.'[5] This view of religion he taught his son, warning him, however, that it was one of which it would not be prudent to make a public profession. And the son embraced it heartily, and held it firmly to the end. The worship of Almighty God, the belief in a Being combining infinite power with perfect goodness, and ruling the world in righteousness – a faith and a worship which, one would have thought, experience had abundantly proved to be consistent with the sublimest intellectual endowments, and conducive to the highest spiritual excellence – he regarded as a gross mental delusion, a great moral evil, one of the main hindrances to the perfection of the individual and the regeneration of the race; and it is no wonder, that so regarding it, he should have laboured hard to subvert it, and to discredit all philosophical doctrines which seemed to countenance or were employed to justify it.... [Mill's own argument] justifies us in believing, on the testimony of One who gave sufficient evidence that He came from God, and had an immediate knowledge of God, that, in spite of all the imperfections of earth, our Father who is in heaven is PERFECT.

[5] Autobiography, pp. 39, 40.

Incredible as the statement may appear *a priori*, inconsistent as it may be with the conception of Mr. Mill's character as a logician which some of my readers may have formed from their relative knowledge of his writings, it is yet one which they are "not at liberty to disbelieve" on the ground of such inconsistency, but which they are bound to accept, because it is proved by evidence, that the passage last quoted from Mr. Mill is the only pretence at an attempt which he anywhere makes to establish the charge of absurdity and immorality which he brings against Mansel's conclusion. He has simply proved the absurdity or the immorality of his own attack upon it. He has shown that it does not follow from the fact that human knowledge is relative that we are bound to believe everything we hear concerning God. If he really supposed that Mansel contended that such a conclusion does follow, that he taught that because our knowledge of God is relative, we are 'not at liberty to disbelieve' that Mahomet is His prophet, that He inspired the Book of Mormon, that the contradictory assertions of Christian theologians respecting Him are all equally true, that, in short, He has done everything that everybody has ever said He has done – if he really supposed that this was Mansel's practical conclusion, in that case I admit, and in that case only, his answer was honest, but his confusion of thought was wonderful. If he did not believe this himself, but only wished his readers to believe it, his want of candour was lamentable. In any case, Mansel's real conclusion from the relativity of human knowledge, namely, that we are disqualified from judging *a priori* what God can and what He cannot do, and that the only mode by which we can discover what He could do is by examining the external evidence which proves what He has done; this conclusion is not touched, is not so much as threatened, either by Mr. Mill's reasoning or by his rhetoric.

I have said that Mr. Mill, while denouncing Mansel's conclusion as morally pernicious, and warning his readers against adopting it, adopted it unhesitatingly and acted upon it invariably himself. Let us look for a moment at the main articles of his theological creed. He says that the world is crowded with suffering and deformed with injustice, and that to permit injustice and suffering is unworthy of a good being. He concludes from this that, if the world was made, and is governed by God, God cannot be absolutely good, and man ought not to worship Him. If, indeed, we choose to believe that the author of the world is *not* God, but a being of 'extremely limited power'[6] – of power so limited (for this is necessarily implied in his argument) that of all the evil which has existed from the beginning he could not in the slightest degree lessen the *sum* – then we may lawfully call him good, because, upon this hypothesis, he would not have *permitted* evil, it would have come into existence and continued to exist, simply because he could not help it. But if we believe that He is all-powerful, or sufficiently powerful to have prevented the existence of evil, or diminished its total amount, if He had pleased, then, not having done so, He cannot be perfectly good, and He is not a fit object for human worship. Many persons, 'whose belief is far short of Deism' (and I suppose no reader of Mr. Mill's autobiography can doubt that he was himself one of these), have consequently refused to worship the Maker of the world, and have formed for themselves a subjective divinity 'to which they habitually refer as a guide of their conscience;' and 'this ideal of God is usually far nearer to perfection than the objective Deity of those who think themselves obliged to find absolute goodness in the Author of a world so crowded with suffering and so deformed with injustice as ours.'[7] The world being what it is, we cannot without idolatry worship the Creator; and every man who would have a 'God' whom he may lawfully worship must create one for himself....

If any Theist, accepting to the fullest extent Hamilton's principles and Mansel's conclusion, should be asked the question, What is the goodness of God? does any one suppose that he would give the nonsensical answer which Mr. Mill attributes to Mansel? Would he say, It is a goodness which human beings know nothing about, except indeed that it has no resemblance to that which human beings mean by goodness? His answer would be very different. He would say: It is that in God which causes Him to desire and to provide for the pleasure of His sentient, and the improvement and perfection of His rational and moral creatures. It is true (he would say) I know nothing of God immediately and intuitively, and therefore in the absence of external evidence I could not know that He possesses this attribute. But then, external evidence is *not* absent;

---

[6] Essays on Religion, p. 40.

[7] Autobiography, p. 46.

and I see in the world around me sufficient proof that He does possess it. 'This is indicated by the fact that pleasure of one description or another is afforded by almost everything, the mere play of the faculties, physical and mental, being a never-ending source of pleasure, and even painful things giving pleasure by the satisfaction of curiosity and the agreeable sense of acquiring knowledge.'[8] As Mr. Mill, 'endeavouring to look at the question without partiality or prejudice, and without allowing wishes to have any influence over judgement,' found sufficient evidence of this, so do I. If Mr. Mill's Rationalists were entitled to ascribe this attribute to God because they 'considered it as proved, not absolutely by an intuition of God, but phænomenally by His action in creation as known through their senses and rational faculty,'[9] so am I. I have senses and a rational faculty as well as Mr. Mill and his Rationalists, though I do not profess – as they do not profess – to have faculties competent to an intuition of the Absolute. I know further, as a fact which is also, as I consider, proved by evidence, that God has provided a system of supernatural means, having for its purpose and its effect the training of His moral creatures to higher and higher stages of spiritual perfection and blessedness. As I give the name of 'goodness' to that in man which prompts him to acts in some measure resembling these, so I give the same name to the corresponding attribute in God. If Mr. Mill, speaking on behalf of the Rationalists, had a right to call this attribute 'goodness,' so have I, though I do not profess, as they do not profess, to be able to solve the mystery of evil. If you ask me what the divine attribute is in its absolute *essence* I tell you I do not know – I know nothing about absolute essences: but I know very well what it is in its relative manifestations, and that is enough for me – quite enough for veneration, quite enough for worship, quite enough to justify me in reasoning from my conception of goodness to the goodness of God, and refusing to accept, without strong external evidence, any statement concerning Him which I cannot reconcile with that conception, though not quite enough to entitle me to set up my finite conception as an absolute criterion of the infinite goodness of God, by virtue of which

---

[8] Mill's *Essays on Religion*, p. 191.

[9] *Examination*, p. 120.

alone, and without reference to evidence, I can decide infallibly what statements concerning Him are and what are not intrinsically inadmissible – what He can and what He cannot do.

Is there anything in this which a Theist, agreeing completely with every word of Mansel, cannot say with perfect truth and perfect consistency? If not, on what new principle of logic or morality is he compelled to think, or bound to affirm, that he 'knows nothing about' a goodness about which he really knows all this?

It is true that Mansel asserts that we cannot know God 'as Absolute and Infinite' (being careful, as Mr. Mill remarks, thus to qualify the assertion); and if he had also asserted that it is our duty to worship God 'as Absolute and Infinite,' Mr. Mill's denunciations would have had some sense and reason in them. But it is notorious that Mansel does nothing of the kind, that he does in fact the precise contrary. One of the main points which he sought to establish by his argument is that we *cannot* worship God as Absolute and Infinite: that we can only worship Him, because we can only know Him, as He is revealed in Nature and in Scripture and in Christ, and that those who – like the philosophical Rationalists of Germany – are not content with this, but aspire to know the Absolute and Infinite Being in Himself, attempt the impossible, fall inevitably into Pantheism, and become involved in endless contradictions. Accordingly he argues against the attempt in serious prose and satirizes it in sparkling verse.[10] But because we cannot know

---

[10] As in the 'Hymn to the Infinite' of the Cloudy Professors, in *Phrontisterion*: –

'With deep intuition and mystic rite
We worship the Absolute-Infinite,
The Universe-Ego, the Plenary-Void;
The Subject-Object identified;
The great Nothing-Something, the Being-Thought,
That mouldeth the mass of Chaotic Naught,
Whose beginning unended, and end unbegun,
Is the One that is All and the All that is One.

Great Non-Existence passing into Being,
　Thou two-fold Pole of the Electric One,
Thou Lawless Law, thou Seer all Unseeing,
　Thou Process ever doing, never done!
　Thou Positive-Negation!
　Negative-Affirmation!
Thou great Totality of everything
That never is but ever doth become,
　Thee do we sing
　The Pantheist's King.'

God as He exists absolutely in Himself that is no reason why we cannot know Him as He exists relatively to us. The contradictions which follow the attempt to conceive a Being aloof from all relation, are no obstacles to our knowing that Being as revealed in relation – as the Creator who has endowed us with faculties which are a never-ending source of pleasure, and as the Father of spirits, who has provided effectual means for our never-ending progress towards moral perfection. Because we can know nothing of the divine attributes by an intuition of their essence, it by no means follows that we cannot know something of them by experience of their effects. How then can it be said that to assert that we cannot know God as Absolute and Infinite is to assert that we cannot know Him at all?

There is only one way out of the difficulty, and Mr. Mill adopts it. He must say – if he would maintain his indictment of Mansel's doctrine – that that doctrine is not merely that we can know nothing of God as He exists absolutely, but that we can know nothing of Him as He exists relatively. Accordingly he does say so. He says that Mansel asserts that 'the relative qualities of an Absolute Being (meaning God) are unknowable.'[11] . . .

---

[11] Examination, p. 120.

# [FROM] THEISM AND CHRISTIANITY
## George Hill

Theism includes the naturalism and deism of the past, and in its modern aspect, adds thereto the moral and ethical teachings of Christianity. It rejects the supernatural, but accepts its practical side, its noble example and generous humanity. It maintains that the law of Christ is written in the heart, while all else of the New Testament is incredible and of no authority.

While theism may contain subjectively all the essentials of religion, producing good fruits in the lives of its intelligent believers, still we believe it to be defective, in that it makes no account of the spiritual power of Christ as a teacher sent from God. It lacks the helpful grace of his Gospel, and apparently denies the affectionate parental relationship of God to man. It denies God's ability and disposition to do anything outside the realm and method of prescribed and fixed law. It even goes so far with some of its advocates, as to limit God in his power and wisdom.

J. S. Mill in his essays on religion says, 'The net results of natural theology on the question of the divine attributes are: a Being of great, but limited power, of great and perhaps unlimited intelligence, who pays some regard to the happiness of his creatures, but whose purpose, in our quarter of the universe, at least, is an ignominious failure.' 'There is no shadow of justice in the general arrangements of nature.' The universe is so 'imperfect,' and its contrivance 'so clumsy,' as to teach that his power is not merely finite, but 'extremely limited.' 'Such is the Deity whom natural religion points to; and any idea of God, more captivating than this, comes only from human wishes, or the teaching of a real or imaginary revelation.' Again he says, 'It is impossible that any one, who habitually thinks, and who is unable to blunt his inquiring intellect by sophistry, should be able without misgiving, to go on ascribing absolute perfection to the author and ruler of so clumsily made and capriciously governed a creation as this planet, and the life of its inhabitants.'

In these essays he is speaking of the God of Nature, and he does not hesitate to impugn his wisdom, his power, his goodness and intelligence, leaving us, if his criticisms are well founded, no God at all, simply because Mr. Mill either fails to see, or seeing fails to give credit to, the ultimate purpose of God in subjecting man to vanity, and in leaving his natural handiwork imperfect. He seems to pass judgment upon God and his work, as though the material creation was completed, when man was introduced to it. He does not admit, in connection with the above charges, that God may be doing and completing his work, in and through man, as an agent. Is God imperfect and unkind because he has surrounded us by pressure, compulsory motives, and every inducement to labor, struggle, subdue, and improve the earth, thereby making ourselves strong in body, wise in intellect, and pure in heart? Mr. Mill does see this aspect of the case, but he does not admit it in the right place; but seeing it at all should have precluded his irreverent criticism of the character and attributes of the God of Nature. He says, 'One elevated feeling may be admitted, the feeling of helping God, of requiting the good he has given, by a voluntary co-operation, which he, not being omnipotent, really needs, and by which a somewhat nearer approach may be made to the fulfilment of his purposes.' He does not base this possible co-laborship on the ground of man's good, and therefore growing out of God's goodness, but on the ground of God's limit of omnipotence, growing out of man's goodness and desire to help his creator. Theism with Mr. Mill comes nearer to Atheism than anything else. But so long as he admits of a powerful, though not omnipotent God, and that man may finish up his incomplete work out of pity for his weak and clumsy contrivance; so long as he admits that human intelligence is the complement of physical nature, why, on the same principle, may not the religion of Jesus Christ be the complement of man's defective nature; and if so theism falls as an inadequate religion. Christianity comes to man in his imperfect, undeveloped condition, where nature leaves him, and by the grace and truth of the Son of God, makes him a full-grown man, after the pattern of a perfect man. It adds something to what nature and his own wisdom are able to do for him. It not only quickens slumbering powers, but guides them to the formation of a better self and a higher experience. The wisest of the wise men of antiquity admitted that man could not save man. No one was sufficiently righteous, sufficiently complete in love, wisdom and self-sacrifice, to draw all men unto him as an example of the way of life, making them righteous by his positive and vital influence over their hearts and lives.

This same defect inheres in the theistic religion of this age. By denying the divine element of Christianity, it leaves man shorn of the power, either to know the possibilities of his nature, or to attain to the measure of his completeness of moral and spiritual stature. Theism does not contain Christianity, but the reverse is true. The latter meets the natural aspirations and desires of the heart, with the answering truth and love of God, bringing man into such spiritual connection with God, as to raise him up from the plane of his natural self-hood to what the Apostle Paul terms, 'heavenly conditions in Christ Jesus.'

But still naturalism rejects the Christ and revelation of the Scriptures, more from a misapprehension of what they teach, than from hatred of what is actually taught. The hostility of skepticism is shown towards the false Christ, and false theology, of the churches. Christ, as the Supreme Deity, slain upon Calvary to appease his own wrath, and save his children from his own eternal vengeance; Christ as a God-man professing to be a teacher and example to a race of imperfect mortals, between whom and himself there could be no possible bond of likeness or sympathy; Christ as the friend of sinners in this world, and their inexorable judge and grim executioner in the world to come, any religion which includes human reason is compelled to reject; and such a Christ is found nowhere but in the Gospel according to Calvin. But in casting away the spurious coin of false theology, theism has committed the error of rejecting the golden image of truth itself. It has not discriminated between the traditions of men, and the commandments of God. Read almost any work on free religion or theism, and you will find the author making war upon the Christianity of the popular churches, the errors of theology, rather than making an attack upon the pure and undefiled religion of Christ. It leaves out the Christ of Ecclesiasticism, while retaining the Christ-idea and doctrines of the Christ of the New Testament. One of the most earnest theists of the present time, Miss Frances P. Cobb, labors through a whole volume to construct a religion suitable to human needs, outside of Christ, dealing many hard blows against the Christ of modern theology; and then after demolishing a man of straw, lays down as the basis of the true religion, the three following principles: 'the absolute goodness of God,' 'the final salvation of every soul,' 'the divine authority of conscience;' a very good platform; but what are these principles, but the teachings of the Gospel of Christ, as they have long been known and held, by liberal Christians? And Mr. Mill comes very near making a similar mistake when he says in his essay on Religion, pp. 113–114; 'The recognition, for example, in the Christianity of the Gospels, of the object of highest worship is a being who could make a Hell; and who could create countless generations of human beings with the certain foreknowledge that he was creating them for this fate. Is there any moral enormity which might not be justified by imitation of such a deity? And is it possible to adore such a one, without a frightful distortion of the standard of right and wrong?' 'It may be doubted,' he says further on, 'whether Christianity is really responsible for atonement and redemption, original sin, and vicarious punishment, and belief in the divine mission of Christ as a necessary condition of salvation,' although in 'the ordinary interpretation,' these doctrines are all found in the 'Christianity of the Gospels.' But Mr. Mill had heard of a better interpretation, and hence was careful not to draw his indictment too loosely. But the whole tone of his essay is keyed in opposition to the theological Christianity of England. And he allows these erroneous and immoral dogmas, built upon the ordinary interpretation, to outweigh 'all the beauty and benignity and moral greatness which so eminently distinguish the sayings and character of Christ,' found in the right interpretation of Christianity. Naturalists and theists protest against Christianity taken at its popular interpretation, whereas if they understood the Christianity of Christ, they would leave the false and cleave to the true, finding in it, the very object of their search presented much better than they can present it, and under the sanction of a person and authority, the divinest that ever lived.

It is difficult to get completely outside the atmosphere and lines of Christian thought and spirit. If men build anything good and lovely, it must be of Christian materials. The real Christianity is so identical with God's thought in nature, and his purpose towards man, that it cannot be eliminated from any correct theory of the moral constitution of the universe. It is in the heart of man, it includes the teachings of natural religion; it reaches up to God, it includes all moral and spiritual duties.

The need of Christ in the religious culture of man and the work of salvation is by no one more eloquently or truly expressed than by Martineau. He attributes to Christ, in addition to his revelation of the character and will of God by his life, teachings and miracles, the hardly less important revelation of that living power in man, by which human nature knows the law, and is capable of being wrought into the likeness of Christ. This fact is not acknowledged in the religion of naturalism. Since Christ, man's moral and spiritual nature has attained a new growth, and arrived at a higher degree of divine knowledge. 'This power,' says Martineau, 'had been there no doubt in all men and all times; the germinating life of an inward spirit of involuntary good had never been a stranger to man; it had always pushed with gentle pressure against the limits of narrow minds and narrow hearts and of positive evil, not indeed with the keen and piercing thrusts of divine judgment, but with spontaneous movement of a better life, striving to cast off the scale of long worn habit. But now this power was not only felt, but its origin was revealed. It was that same divine human nature which had been embodied in the earthly Christ, that was stirring in the hearts of all men. It was he whose life had been so strange and brief a miracle of beauty, to whom they might trust to mould afresh the twisted shapes of human interpretation, to push forward the growth of the good seed, and the eradication of the tares within them. Here then was a revelation, not simply of the absolute nature of God, but of the formative power of Christ, that is at work to cancel distorted growths, and the natural deficiency in every human heart. Nay, it did more, it took away sin itself from those who could bring themselves to trust their hearts freely to his influence to reveal to them the great divine law written in the heart. This was the revelation of the true nature in man; a nature that not only, as the Gentilo nations felt, asserted the primitive truth and goodness belonging to every human creature, but that is capable of restoring that truth and goodness, cancelling the sinful habit, melting the rigid heart, emancipating the sullen temper, by the mere exertion of its spontaneous fascination over any spirit which once surrenders to its control.'

No clearer statement of the inner life wrought by Christ could be made. And how the theist or naturalist can deny Christ, when he, like other men, is so deeply indebted to him for the correct interpretation of himself, and the world he inhabits, it is difficult to conceive. Christianity thus asserts its superiority and authority over all other systems of religion; and the various theories of human invention only serve to show more fully the world's need of Christ and his divine sonship over the world of life and immortality.

# JOHN STUART MILL AND THE DESTRUCTION OF THEISM
Daniel Seelye Gregory

Two intimately related movements of religious or anti-religious thought have been going forward for a quarter of a century and more in the English word – one having as its aim the destruction of theism, and the other the construction of an imposing and comprehensive system of anti-theism, or atheism. In the former, John Stuart Mill has been the leading spirit; in the latter, Herbert Spencer; and to these two men, more than to all others combined, the present atheistic trend of English thought in the more pretentious circles is, in the opinion of the best judges, to be ascribed. The fact that they have done their work in the name of science and philosophy has doubtless added very largely to their influence.

Five years ago Mr. Mill ruled with absolute despotism a large proportion of the so-called educated and thinking men in Great Britain. Indiscriminate laudation of his logic, his philosophy, his candor, his high motives, etc., was the order of the day to such an extent that it was safer to find fault with the sun itself than with this great philosophic light. His agnostic conclusions were widely accepted without question; his flings at theism were voted worth more than solid arguments in favor of it; his reticence in the statement of his atheistic views, though it had alienated Comte, had made such an impression of reserve force upon his worshippers, that faith in Mill seemed with them to have already superseded faith in God. But English thought, so far as Mr. Mill is its subject, has undergone a most remarkable change since his death. It is interesting to trace the growing sense of fear on the one side and of freedom on the other.

Immediately after his death, one of his most enthusiastic admirers, Miss Edith Simcox, a lady who holds a prominent place in the present English rationalistic literature for reasons similar to those which have given Mr. Mill his influence, came before the public with what she was pleased to style

> 'an attempt to show not only that Mr. Mill's influence on the ordinary thought of the day is still undiminished, but also that it would indeed be a national calamity for that influence to become either weakened, warped, or forgotten.'

After the publication of the *Autobiography*, Lord Blachford, an able writer of an opposite school, ventured to express his opinion with some degree of confidence, as follows:

> 'If the intellect of our universities (as I understand to be the case) is being moulded into accordance with this philosophy, it appears to me that we may expect some startling conclusions from the rising generation. Whether these conclusions will be long maintained, either by the thinking or by the unthinking part of the world outside, is another matter.'

Upon the publication of the *Three Essays*, the *Pall Mall Budget* declared that Mill's followers in England received them 'with mingled feelings of surprise, disappointment and of something closely bordering on irritation.'

The truth was evidently beginning to drawn on the minds of some of the 'thinkers' and 'philosophers.' Three years more have now passed, and the growing sense of light and freedom has so increased that Professor W. Stanley Jevons, of University College, London, the man perhaps best fitted to dissect Mr. Mill and his logic, has risen to protest against the despotism which has compelled him for twenty years to use Mill's works as text-books in his college instruction. So intricate is the sophistry of these works, that ten years of study passed before he 'began to detect their fundamental unsoundness.' But during the last ten years the conviction has been growing upon his mind, 'that Mill's authority is doing immense injury to the cause of philosophy and good intellectual training in England.' Professor Jevons, in the opening essay of a series in review of special points in Mill's logic and philosophy, writes:

> 'But for my part, I will no longer consent to live silently under the incubus of bad logic and bad philosophy which Mill's works have laid upon us. On almost every subject of social importance – religion, morals, political philosophy,

political economy, metaphysics, logic – he has expressed unhesitating opinions, and his sayings are quoted by his admirers as if they were the oracles of a perfectly wise and logical mind. Nobody questions, or at least ought to question, the force of Mill's style, the persuasive power of his words, the candor of his discussions, and the perfect goodness of his motives. If to all his other great qualities had been happily added logical accurateness, his writings would indeed have been a source of light for generations to come. But in one way or another Mill's intellect was wrecked. The cause of injury may have been the ruthless training imposed upon him in tender years; it may have been Mill's own lifelong attempt to reconcile a false empirical philosophy with conflicting truth. But, however it arose. Mill's mind was essentially illogical.'

These plain words clearly indicate a radical revolution in the mind of Professor Jevons. That he does not at all *underestimate* Mr. Mill's logical acumen will be made to appear from a careful examination of that logician's criticism and supposed refutation of the theistic argument for a First Cause, found in the essay on *Theism,* one of his latest productions, professedly written in the name of exact science. It is far from clear, however, that Professor Jevons does not *overestimate* Mr. Mill's 'candor' as well as the 'goodness of his motives.'

Mill's argument is undoubtedly one of the most dangerous ever constructed in opposition to Theism. There are those of his own party who are inclined to underestimate its strength, but until they furnish a stronger it may fairly be considered as the best that can be done from the destructive side. Moreover, it cannot justly be claimed that it omits any considerations of essential importance on the anti-theistic side. It even takes in, by anticipation, the latest conclusion of Professor Huxley and Tyndall, that man is a mere *automaton,* a machine run by necessary forces, so that the last vestige of the old anthropomorphic basis for argument to a First Cause is apparently swept away.

But the danger from the argument does not lie in the strength so much as in the marvellous combination of intricate sophistry and utter confusion of thought, with an extraordinary show of candor and fairness, and a tone of supreme confidence such as is ordinarily begotten only by a certain and infallible grasp of truth. It is this element in Mill's writings that enabled them for ten years to dazzle so clear an eye as that of the distinguished Professor in University College, and it is this that enables them to pass for little less than philosophic inspiration with multitudes of less discerning minds. As soon as this feature can be clearly exposed, Mill's works will cease to be dangerous....

The final effort of Mr. Mill is directed to the task of ridding the universe of an Eternal Mind, by accounting for the existence of mind by matter and force. The argument is again remanded to the region of experience, which term is here covertly used in the third sense, or for experience plus all the logical feats of the 'bubble companies.' The great logician proceeds to dissect and expose the fallacy of the assumption, that 'it is self-evident that only mind can produce mind.' He finds at the basis of the assumption the notion 'that no causes can give rise to products of a more precious or elevated kind than themselves.' Now no man of sound sense, be he scientist or theologian, would for one moment accept Mill's perversion of the principle of causation as a basis for argument. The master of logic, however, proceeds to show that this principle, in this perverted form of statement, is at variance with the known analogies of nature. In showing this, he finally rests the case against a First Cause on three logical supports.

The first is an illustration of a general fact drawn from nature, and contradicting the principle that lower cannot produce higher. We give him the benefit of his own form of statement:

> 'How vastly nobler and more precious, for instance, are the higher vegetables and animals than the soil and manure out of which and by the properties of which they are raised up!'

So plants and animals and man are nothing but 'soil and manure'! What of vegetable life, animal life, rational life, and all the rest? The lion's skin lifts and we see – evolution!

The second support is evolution pure and simple. All higher has come from the lower:

> 'The tendency of all recent speculation is towards the opinion that the development of inferior orders of existence into superior, the substitution of greater elaboration and higher organization for lower, is the general rule of nature.'

It has already been shown that the competent physicists unanimously reject materialistic evolution, pronouncing it a 'puerile hypothesis,' at variance with all true scientific conclusions. Taking only the special propositions of evolution here involved, competent scientists have demonstrated their unscientific character. *'That the earliest organisms were the natural product of the interactions of ordinary organic matter and force,'* is not true. Neither observation, experiment, nor reason gives any testimony in favor of such a view. Life has been in all cases due either to antecedent life, or to a power or force from without that was not identical nor correlated with the ordinary physical forces. *'That all the forms of animal and vegetable life, including man himself, have been successively and gradually developed from the earliest and simplest organisms,'* has not a shadow of truth. Such a scheme of progression has no existence in nature. There is no evidence of it in existing forms of life; there is no indication of it in fossil remains; and there is no possibility of such a progression, even as a matter of theory, in accordance with the recognized laws of morphology.'[1] What then becomes of this main support of Mill's argument for the origin of mind from matter?

The third and last support is certainly an extraordinary one for a master of logic and analysis to present. It is to serve if the others fail:

> 'Whether it be so or not (that is, this hypothesis of evolution), there are at least in nature a multitude of facts bearing that character, and this is sufficient for the argument.'

What facts? Those of evolution? Or, those of man as the product of 'soil and manure'? Plainly, it is evolution again – evolution first, midst, and last! So we have at length found the tortoise which supports the logical elephant on which Mill's world of atheistic ontology rests. It is *evolution!* EVOLUTION! EVOLUTION! And that is all that atheism can adduce to support its irrational assumption of the non-existence of an eternal First Cause.

No one can lay down the argument of the great destroyer of theism, after a careful study of it, without mingled feelings of humiliation and indignation – humiliation, that so many of

---

[1] Elam, 'Automatism and Evolution.'

the so-called thinking and educated men of the age should be so incapable of clear thought as to be imposed upon and moulded by such so-called thought; indignation, that men in high places, who ought to know better, are constantly assuming substantially the same views and urging them upon mankind as an addition to, or substitute for, a Christian theism. It does not fall within the range of our purpose to present the positive arguments for a First Cause or for a personal God; but we are convinced that thorough discussion and popular presentation of this branch of the evidences of Christianity is one of the great theological and practical necessities of the present age. Since the days of Kant's famous 'Critique,' as Ulrici remarks, arguments for the existence of God have fallen into disrepute. Since that, the wide-spread opinion of believers and unbelievers has been that the being of God does not admit of proof. Theologians have fallen in with this view, forgetting that the *proofs* of the divine existence are identical with the *reasons* for the *belief* in God, and that belief without reasons is essentially irrational and absurd. Modern theology, in so readily giving up the arguments for the divine being, not only surrenders there-with its claim to be a science, but also virtually annihilates the very faith and religion of which it is a theology.[2] One requisite for the return to the old faith in theism is the strong and clear presentation of the proofs that there is a God, together with a merciless exposure of the intricate sophistries of atheism and anti-theism.

---

[2] Ulrici, 'Gott und die Natur,' Introduction.

# [FROM] THE HOPES OF THE HUMAN RACE, HEREAFTER AND HERE: ESSAYS ON THE LIFE AFTER DEATH
Frances Power Cobbe

In the following Essay I have stated to the best of my ability the grounds on which I think an affirmative answer to the great enigma may be given by all those who believe in a *Righteous* as well as an *Intelligent* Ruler of the world. I have no desire to blink the fact that it is on the moral attributes of God that the whole question appears to me to hinge; and that, without the help of Religion, (of a real religion, which takes for its corner-stone that God is good and just, not a philosophy which merely admits the hypothesis of an intelligent Force behind Nature,) the reasons for denial seem to me to preponderate altogether over those in favour of affirmation....

If God be really so feeble a Being as Mr. Mill suggests, if His contrivances be so 'clumsy' (p. 30), and even His own immortality open to doubt (p. 243), it is idle to argue any further concerning His goodness, for He may be sincerely desirous of giving to us eternal joy hereafter, and yet fail to do so as completely as He has failed to give us perfect happiness here. This world being the bungle it is reported to be, it is hopeless to count on what the sequel of it may prove.

If God's wisdom be really 'limited,' and His contrivances 'clumsy,' there is in nature a very singular anomaly, for it appears that He has made a being more clever than Himself, and able to point out where He has failed, if not exactly how to do better. The intelligence of man is the highest work of God with which we are acquainted (though nothing hinders us from supposing He may have made indefinitely nobler intelligent inhabitants of other worlds); but to suppose that this *chef d'oeuvre* of the human brain is endowed with such similar but superior powers to its Maker as to be qualified to criticise and discriminate the clever from the clumsy among them, would be astonishing indeed. I do not mean this remark in the sense of the 'brow-beating' of the human intellect to which divines are so prone. There can be no audacity in exercising any faculties with which we are gifted. I only desire to observe that there is, on the face of the matter, something very like absurdity in supposing that we, who, on the hypothesis, are, ourselves, God's handiwork, could find the end of His knowledge or wisdom. Practically, when we reflect on any one branch of the Divine Art, on the architecture of the starry heavens, on the chemistry of the ever-shifting gases and fluids and solids in which creation every hour is born and dies, on the mechanism of the frame of an animalcule, or of our own bodies – say, of the Hand alone, as exemplified in Sir Charles Bell's splendid treatise – it seems indeed monstrous for us to open our lips regarding the Wisdom of the Creator.

Where the limits of His Power may lie, is another question, of which it seems impossible we should ever guess the answer. Undoubtedly Christian theologians have written much folly about 'Omnipotence,' having first invented a purely metaphysical term, and then argued back from it to facts, as if it were a specific datum within our measurement, like the horse-power of a steam-engine or an hydraulic-press. A more sober and reverent mode of regarding the stupendous Power above us, may, as I have long hoped and argued, become a 'Note' of Theism; and in the full admission that there must be *some* limits even to supreme Might (limits existing in the very nature of things, which cannot at once be and not be, or unite contradictory properties, such as those of a circle and a triangle), we may find some help in contemplating such evils as those which seem to follow inevitably on the grant of moral freedom to a finite being such as man.

But such limitations of the Divine Power as Mr. Mill seems to contemplate, would narrow it (if I understand him rightly) far beyond this mere negation of contradictions; and if we are to admit them into our philosophy, it ought surely to be on the ground that there are marks of such limits in nature; places where the creative energy seems to have fallen short, or the obvious design has aborted. Now it is possible that some evils in nature – some forms of disease, for example – may seem to possess this character; but unquestionably the greater mass of evil bears no such marks. It is, as I have just said, woven into the very tissue of life on the planet, and seems just as much a part of the great plan as all the rest. All the terrible things in the world – the ruthless beak, the poisoned fang, the rending claw – are as much an integral part of the work as the downy breast of the bird or the milk of the mother-brute. Further, there is a very curious parallel, which I do not think has received sufficient attention, between the exceptional *ugliness* in a Beautiful world and the exceptional *evil* in a Good one, which apparently alike demand some other solution than that of a limitation of the Maker's Power. ...

What view can we take, then, of this mystery of Ugliness, since it would seem that any hypothesis which may account for it may very possibly fit that yet greater and more dreadful mystery of Suffering? Putting it thus before us, it seems absurd to say that perhaps the Divine Power was not equal to the task of harmonizing the macaw's colour or the peacock's voice, or of reducing to proportion and grace the unwieldy rhinoceros or the revolting spider. That His power should act freely in constructing the lion and the horse, the eagle and the ibis, the lark and the butterfly, and yet should be unaccountably thwarted and trammelled when He made the animals so strangely contrasted with them, is almost ridiculous to suppose. It seems, then, as impossible to frame an hypothesis which shall fit this æsthetic anomaly of nature, as one which shall meet the moral anomaly of Pain.

Thus, in short, it appears that every one of the theories on the origin of Evil which have been put forth from the days of the Pentateuch to the appearance of these Essays on Religion, are more or less unsatisfactory and incomplete; and we may, with only too great probability, resign the hope that we shall ever hear of a better, or that any Œdipus will arise in the ages to come to resolve 'the riddle of the painful earth,' and relieve us from its direful pressure.

Two things only, I conceive, remain for us to do in the matter. The first is, to define somewhat more closely than, while oppressed by the declamations of pessimists, we are generally able to do, *what it is* in Nature which the human moral sense recognizes as Evil. Secondly, to convince ourselves what is the testimony to the goodness of the Creator to be set over against it, which may enable us – not by any means to honour Him on the balance, but – to give Him our heart-whole love and allegiance, and treat the mystery of Evil as we should treat the inexplicable conduct of a revered Father. ...

Brought to its actual limits, then, I conceive the problem of

Evil stands before us as a vast, but not an *immense* exception, in a rule of Good. A certain large share of it we can recognize as having great moral purposes fully justifying its existence, and even elevating it into the rank of beneficence; such are the sufferings (of rational beings) which punish and repress sin, and those through whose fires the noblest and the purest virtues have ever passed to perfection. That there is some wondrous power in Suffering thus to bring out of human souls qualities immeasurably nobler than are ever developed without its aid, is a fact equally plain to those who have watched the almost divine transformation it sometimes effects upon characters hitherto hard, selfish or commonplace; and to those who have noted how thin-natured and unsympathetic, if not selfish, are at the best those men and women who have lived from youth to age in the unbroken sunshine of prosperity. Even among very ordinary characters, and where the lesson of suffering has not been deep, there are very few of us, I believe, who after the lapse of a little while would wish that we could unlearn it, or return to be the slighter, feebler, shallower-hearted beings we were before it came. Rather do we recognize the truth of the poet's words:

'The energies too stern for mirth,
The reach of thought, the strength of will,
'Mid cloud and tempest have their birth,
Through blight and blast their course fulfil.'

Another share of evil may be attributed to – though not altogether explained by – the beneficent purpose of securing preponderating physical advantage to the sufferer; as, for example, the pains which guard the integrity of the bodies of animals. But beyond all these, we are compelled mournfully to conclude that there exists, both in human life and in the life of the brutes, a large mass of evil, which can by no such hypotheses be accounted for consistently with the benevolence of the Creator; and which utterly baffles now, and will probably for ever baffle, the ingenuity of mortal man so to explain.

What is it that shall help us to look this great residuum of inexplicable evil in the face? Where shall we find ground of faith whereon we may take our stand and confront it with unshaken hearts?

Strange it is indeed to say, that I have hopes that the publication of the Essays on Nature, the Utility of Religion and

Theism, which will give such bitter pain to all believing hearts, such double sadness to those who, like myself, regard their author with undying honour and gratitude, may even prove the turning-point of this controversy – may set us at last on the right track for the solution of the problem. For what have we in these powerful, limpidly clear, bravely outspoken words? We have, for the first time perhaps in human history, revealed sharply and distinctly what that element in human nature must be which to the majority of mankind is the origin and organ of Religion, and which it is so transparently evident that Mr. Mill *had not*.[1] Hitherto we have seen it in its highest development in the saints, and had opportunity to learn what it *positively* is. But so natural does it seem to man, so much does it, in ordinary men and women, harmonize with and shade off into the moral, affectional and ratiocinative faculties, that it was easy to mistake their action for its own. Now it seems possible to learn more of it by the aid of the complete self-revelation of a very noble mind, wherein, owing to almost unique circumstances, the whole element has been eliminated; and we are left to mark what are the tracts of human nature which it normally covers, and which are found to lie bare like the sea-shore when that mighty tide has flowed away back to its bed. We behold one of the keenest intellects of this or any century, and, on the human side, one of the tenderest and most

---

[1] Let it be understood that, in speaking of the Religious Sentiment as deficient in Mr. Mill's nature, I use the term expressly in the sense of *that spiritual organ whereby man obtains direct perception of the Living God.* In the broader meaning of the word, implying general reverence and tenderness towards all things noble and holy, – a sense of the mystery surrounding human life, and a fervent devotion to the ideal of Duty, – Mr. Mill was assuredly an eminently religious man. How it came to pass that such a soul could by any mortal hand be debarred from the happiness of direct recognition of God, is one of the riddles wherewith the spiritual as well as the physical world is full. As he himself says, 'it is possible to starve an instinct;' and, as Mr. Upton has well explained in his profound paper on the 'Experience Philosophy and Religious Belief,' beside all other conditions on which spiritual knowledge is obtained, it is needful 'that the understanding should be freed from all tyrannous misconceptions which preclude or distort the intellectual cognizance of spiritual truth.' Nothing short of such a Divine *blow* as smote St. Paul would have been strong enough to overthrow the 'tyrannous misconceptions' wherewith Mr. Mill's education must have fenced his mind. I need scarcely add that, in my view, the absence of *conscious recognition* of the relations between God and the soul is very far indeed from implying the non-existence of such relations, or the loss of some of the richest blessings which they bestow.

capacious of hearts – a man whose moral sense (whatever were his theories of its nature) quivered with intensest life, and was true as needle to the pole of the loftiest justice to man, to woman and to brute, who yet, great philosopher as he was, when he comes to deal with a subject on which the rude tinker of Bedford has instructed the world, writes like a blind man discoursing of colours, or a deaf man criticising the contortions of a violonist wasted on the delusion of music. When he speaks of the Utility of Religion, he confounds, as if they were identical, those realms of human nature which public opinion or human authority may sway; and those which, in the solemn hours of visitation from the Divine Spirit, fall under the inner law of Conscience and of Love. And when he writes of the Consciousness of God, all he has to say of it, is to refer to the metaphysical subtleties of Cousin about the laws of perception ....

[A]s we did not first gain our knowledge of God from the external world, so we shall never obtain our truest and most reliable idea of Him from the inductions which Science may help us to draw from it. Spiritual things *must* be spiritually discerned, or we must be content never to discern them truly at all. In man's soul alone, so far as we may yet discover, is the moral nature of his Maker revealed, as the sun is mirrored in a mountain lake....

The fact that we *want* a Perfect God does not of course prove that any such Being exists, but it leaves such a Deity as Mr. Mill has propounded for our *quasi*-belief altogether outside the *religious* question. If the Intellect or the Fancy may be contented with a Probable God, provisionally accepted as Benevolent, it is certain that the Religious Sentiment can no more attach itself to such a Deity than a man can embrace a cloud. A balance of probabilities may properly determine our choice of an investment for a sum of money; but when it comes to the gift of our heart's allegiance, we need a different kind of assurance. No man can stand by patiently while arguments *pro* and *con*. are carefully weighed, and begin to love when the scale turns by a hair on the side of Benevolence, and drop on his knees in reverence as Justice begins to preponderate, and adore when the balance of Good appears finally by some degrees heavier than that of Evil. If this be so, then it follows that the Inductive Method is for ever inapplicable to the solution of the greater problems of theology, because under the most favourable circumstances it can only give us a balance of more or less probability – a *General*, not an *Universal* proposition. We are compelled to seek in some other modes of thought an assurance of quite another kind. . . .

But I quit the ungracious, and, in my case, most ungrateful, task of offering my feeble protest against the last words given to us of a man so good and great, that even his mistakes and deficiencies (as I needs must deem them) are more instructive to us than a million platitudes and truisms of teachers whom his transcendent intellectual honesty should put to the blush, and whose souls never kindled with a spark of the generous ardour for the welfare of his race which flamed in his noble heart and animated his entire career.

# [FROM] JOHN STUART MILL. A CRITICISM: WITH PERSONAL RECOLLECTIONS
## Alexander Bain

... The posthumous *Essays on Religion* do not correspond with what we should have expected from him on that subject. Never, so far as I know, did he give any hint of wishing or attempting to re-construct a system of theism on a scientific basis. In one sentence in the *Hamilton* he spoke approvingly of the argument from Design, but laid more stress on its persuasiveness than on its soundness. The *Autobiography* represented his attitude towards Religion as pure negation, or nescience, just as his father's had been.

The Essay on *Nature* paints the world black enough, and from that he was not likely to rise to a flattering estimate of Nature's God. I think he should have widened his survey considerably, before pronouncing as he does. For, although there are good grounds for many of his statements of fact, the case is by no means complete. By his own showing in other places, many happy lives have been passed in the world as we find it, and he looked forward to a time when happiness might be the rule instead of the exception. I should have expected him to push the analysis of the causes of evil a step farther; namely, first, to the inadequacy of man's intellectual force to cope with the obscurities of nature, and next to the want of ability to counteract known causes of mischief. A remark that he once made regarding his own temperament, is a part of the case in considering nature: he said, in answer to some gloomy utterance of Grote's, that with himself the difficulty was not so much to realize pleasure as to keep off pain; and it is the fact that there are many pleasurable resources in the world, if we could only submerge the attendant miseries. His exposure of the insufficiency of Nature as a *guide* is pure logic, and in that he was not likely to be wanting. The so-called Light of Nature is mere darkness; while we are often notoriously incapable of following the light we have. We are only just beginning to tract the secrets of disease; including the forms of pestilence that from time to time commit wholesale ravages alike upon man and beast.

The Essay on the *Utility of Religion* is a farther illustration of his old theme (in the *Utilitarianism*) as to the sufficiency of the sanctions and motives of the present life for sustaining, not only the inferior moral virtues, but also the elevated sentiments of mankind. He here puts forward a sort of Religion of Humanity, constructed on the basis of men's amiable feelings towards one another. To this he had been led, I have no doubt, in the first instance, by Comte, although the filling-up is his own.

But by far the most laboured of the Essays is the last – uniting a destructive and a constructive *Theism*. The destructive part is in accordance with all his antecedents; it is the constructive part that we were not prepared for. It was indeed quite compatible with his warm human sympathies, and with his long-standing doctrine that every creed is likely to contain some portion of truth, that he should try to ascertain what there was in religion to commend it to the best minds among its adherents: our doubt would have been whether, after painting the world in such gloomy hues, he could set up a Deity that would replace, in the hearts of men, the one that he undertook to destroy. Religion, we know, is exceedingly variable; but there are some things in it not easy to dispense with. Until the advent of the modern sentimental Theism, it has usually contained the idea of authority and subjection – the prescription of duties with rewards and punishments attached to them. Men's deities in all early ages had to be propitiated as powers capable of evil at least, if not also of good. In pure Monotheism, the unbounded beneficence of the Deity has been an indispensable attribute, in spite of the difficulties attending it. Plato insisted that this belief should be supported by state penalties; and we know how essential it is regarded in the present day by those of the Theists that do not accept revelation. All these points of support Mill dispensed with; while working upon the idea, so repugnant to the religious worshipper, of putting a logical limitation and restriction on the great object of worship. A Being that would not interfere to do us either harm or good can scarcely excite in us any strong regards; at least until we have undergone a new education. The supposed limitations of his power, besides being strangely at variance with the undeniable vastness and complex adjustment of the world, would seem fatal to his ascendency in our minds.

The speculation is equally precarious as regards a future life. Mill hardly does justice to the natural difficulties of reproducing human existence, after death, for an eternal duration; and yet casts doubts on the omnipotence of the Power that is to perform the miracle.

Seeing that the only argument for Theism that Mill put any value upon, was the argument from Design, it is unfortunate that he should have considered nine pages sufficient for its discussion. The handling is not only short, but extremely unsatisfactory. It is what we might suppose to be the first of the three redactions that all his writings went through; a mere rough note, to be worked up in one or two subsequent elaborations. His attempt to show that the argument rises above Analogy into the sphere of Induction is not, as I conceive, a logical success; at least, it stands in need of a much more detailed justification. He ought manifestly to have disposed of the objections advanced by Hume and Kant respectively: in so doing, he would have made his own position clearer, if not stronger. He very properly introduces into the case the canons of Induction, strictly so called, and the conditions (first distinctly stated by himself) of proof from Analogy; he ought farther to have brought into play his doctrine of what constitutes a logical Hypothesis, and have shown the bearings of this upon the supposed Anthropomorphic origin of the Universe.

Both his Theism and his estimate of Christianity as founded on the character of Christ, are concessions to the existing Theology; and, as is usual in such cases, the inch has been stretched to an ell. . . .

It seems, at first glance, a bold proceeding to take to pieces the Christ of Christianity, and to appropriate just so much of him as suits a 'rational criticism'. Something of this kind has already been tried by the Unitarians, but with small success, if that is to be measured by the extent of popular reception. It would seem, in this as in other parts of religion, that what the rationalist disapproves of most, the multitude like best.

We are, of course, at liberty to dissent from the prevailing view, which makes Christ a divine person. But to reduce a Deity to the human level, to rank him simply as a great man, and to hold ideal intercourse with him in that capacity, is, to say the least of it, an incongruity. Historians and moralists have been accustomed to treat with condemnation those monarchs that, after being dethroned, have accepted in full the position of subjects. Either to die, or else to withdraw into dignified isolation, has been accounted the only fitting termination to the loss of royal power. So, a Deity dethroned should retire altogether from playing a part in human affairs, and remain simply as an historic name.

The point of congruity or propriety is not, as I conceive, the worst objection to Mill's proposal. The doctrines, prescriptions, or sayings of one believed to be a God, must all have a religious bearing; they are properly adapted to men in their religious capacity. They may often refer to matters of mere worldly conduct, but the religious side is still a vital part of them. If religion were done away with, to the extent that Mill would have it, those sayings of Christ must lose their suitability to human life as so transformed. 'Forgive that ye may be forgiven (by God)' – is no longer applicable. The best guidance, under such altered circumstances, would be that furnished by the wisest of purely secular teachers. The same applies to Christ as an example. He is so to those that accept him in his own proper character, and who view the world as he viewed it. In a purely secular scheme of life, the ideal that he holds forth must seem greatly over-strained.

Mill was, doubtless, able to state and to give reasons for his own view of the plan of the universe. He was also highly qualified to discuss particular portions of the groundwork of the prevailing creeds. I think, however, that he was too little versed in the writings of Theologians, to attack their doctrines with any effect. He absented himself during his whole life, except as a mere child, from religious services. He scarcely ever read a Theological book. He could not help knowing the main positions of Theology from our general literature. That, however, was scarcely enough for basing an attack upon Christianity along the whole line. Just about the time when the Essays on Religion appeared, Strauss's last book, called 'The Old Faith and the New,' was published in this country. Anyone reading it would, I think, be struck with its immense superiority to Mill's work, in all but the logic and metaphysics. Strauss speaks like a man thoroughly at home with his subject. He knows both sides as a life-study can enable one to know them. Mill, even supposing him to be in the right, would not be convincing. He may puzzle opponents, he may compel them to change front; still, he does not meet their difficulties, nor take account of what they feel to be their strength. He is not even well read in the sceptics that preceded him. If he had studied the whole cycle of Hume's argumentative treatises, so lucidly condensed by Mr. Leslie Stephen, he might have put his case on the negative side much better, while he would have been led to modify his constructive Theism.

It has been said by his opponents, with some show of plausibility, that Mill was at bottom a religious man. Setting aside special dogmas, and looking only to the cheering influence of religion on its most favourable side – an influence that may be exerted in a variety of ways – we may call his aspirations and hopes for a bright future to the race, a religion of humanity. To hold up an ideal that involves no contradictions to our knowledge, to inspire and elate the mind, oppressed by the dulness and the hardships of the present life, – will be accepted by many as comfort of the spiritual kind, the real analogue of religion. And something of this effect is undoubtedly produced by Mill's later writings. With all this, however, the fact remains, that in everything characteristic of the creed of Christendom, he was a thorough-going negationist. He admitted neither its truth nor its utility. His estimate of its best side is given in the remark to a friend under domestic sorrow – 'To my mind the only permanent value of religion is in lightening the feeling of total separation which is so dreadful in a real grief'.

# [FROM] MOVEMENTS OF RELIGIOUS THOUGHT IN BRITAIN DURING THE NINETEENTH CENTURY
John Tulloch

[Mill Speaks of] the 'invariableness' of the order of Nature. But 'invariableness' first of all is not the true note of Causation. This note is origination and not order, invariable or otherwise, as he constantly makes it. The word retains to the last the traces of its origin, and when men speak of a cause they do not mean the mere antecedent of a phenomenon, but the original power which called it into being. Secondly, 'invariableness' can only be predicated, even of the order of Nature, by assuming that there is nothing behind this order, and that our experience of its uniformity has never been broken and never can be broken. But no experience can justify a conclusion of this kind. It may justify a presumption; it cannot generate an absolute and necessary truth; and especially in the face of the suggestion of a Power behind phenomena that lies within the very idea of Cause from the first. We cannot, without inverting the order of knowledge, convert the external uniformity of Nature into an iron necessity, which *de facto* excludes the fact through which alone we have been able to rise to the apprehension of Causation or uniformity in Nature at all.

When we look at this great question from the moral side, Mr. Mill's cardinal doctrine becomes still more untenable. As even science may be said to begin with will, so all morality and religion not only begin, but end with the same central fact of human life. The moral law has no meaning, save as applied to that self-consciousness within us which is ever the same amidst all the changes of our external life, and the modifications of our moral growth. The commands which it lays upon us are commands addressed to our wills – in other words, to ourselves – ever the same in virtue of the mysterious gift of personality. It is only thus we become responsible, and in contrast with all other creatures enter within the circle of moral and religious aspiration. If the will be a fiction, a mere cluster of hereditary instincts indissolubly bound together by the law of association, and the growth throughout, therefore, of circumstance, it seems unintelligible how the ideas of right and wrong should cling to us as they do – how in short what we mean by conscience should arise. The sense of right and wrong rests on an absolute feeling that we are free to choose the good and avoid the evil. Moral ideas are no doubt largely developed by association and circumstance, but moral acts come from our own free choice in such a sense at least as that the deepest misery may spring from wrong action. It seems impossible to explain this save by recognising Will as an original power within us, and conscience as its Divine guide. If Will be the growth of circumstance, conscience can only be a calculation of chances. And how in such a case should it ever accuse and condemn us? We can never really act otherwise than we do. And yet that we can so act, and have frequently failed so to act, is the experience of every higher nature. The sting of a lost good is that we ourselves lost it. The misery of a present evil is that we ourselves did it. Once admit the thought that the good was never in our power, and the evil a necessary sequence in our life, and the whole fabric, both of religion and morality, disappears. Responsibility in any true sense vanishes. Nay, self-conciousness becomes a dream. For the very essence of this consciousness is that it erects itself against the law of causality, which is supposed to bind all being in order, and to explain all. It refuses this explanation. It says, 'I am not bound. I am free to choose the evil or the good. I am more than nature, or any product of nature. I may be crushed by its laws, but I am more than any of its laws. I have that within me which no mere circumstance has given. I have will and conscience, and divine reason. I am the child of God, and the inspiration of the Almighty hath given me understanding.'

All true morality and religion, therefore, imply in man a breach of Mill's law of natural causation. In other words, the experience-philosophy, of which he was the great teacher, is a philosophy inadequate to grasp the realities of human nature and life. There is more in man than is dreamt of in this philosophy; and the whole course of its expositor's own intellectual development was so far an evidence of this. He maintained to the last that character, like all natural phenomena, is born of circumstance; but he allowed for what he called the action of the will upon circumstances, and seemed to himself in this way to discriminate between his doctrine of necessity and the common interpretation of that doctrine as fatalism. But his reserves were merely sentimental; they were forced upon him by the urgency of facts to which he could not shut his eyes. They did not spring from any change in his point of departure; and his system was really fatalistic, whatever he thought of it. He held it with less clearness and firmness the longer he lived. He had neither the hardihood nor the coarseness of *the true faith* which animated his father and his father's unhesitating followers. This really argued that he had higher elements of character and more comprehension of thought than they had, although they did not think so. His very hesitations in the full acceptance of his father's creed were tributes to a more expansive philosophy, and although he never reached the clear heaven of such a philosophy, he left behind him enough to confound the partisans of that narrow no-faith which have made such a boast of his name.

This brings us to the consideration of his special view of religion, as explained in his posthumous essays. It is evident from these essays that the subject of religion fascinated him, studiously as he had been trained without any knowledge of it. Not only so, but he came to realise – with all his loyalty to his father's main teaching – that religion was a far more important factor in human life than he had been led to believe. All the same the savour of his hereditary teaching remained, and mixed itself with all his thought. His father's pessimism, for example, intensified by a vein of intellectual pride, partly inherited and partly his own, appears prominently in the first essay on 'Nature.' James Mill thought very little of the world. It was to him upon the whole a bad world. Human life was 'a poor thing at the best.' The son turned the father's thought – which was also his own – into a sort of philosophy. It is difficult to say whether Christianity was more obnoxious to him than 'the optimistic Deism or worship of the order of Nature,' to which modern scepticism has so much inclined, and more than ever since his time. A 'natural religion' like that recently expounded under this name, would have seemed to him essentially unreasonable. Nature, so far from being to him an object of admiration, as it was to Wordsworth and the author of *Natural Religion*, was, on the contrary, a cruel and mischievous power. 'All the things which men are hanged or imprisoned for doing to one another, are,' in his opinion, 'Nature's everyday performances.' No writer of sane mental comprehension has ever drawn such an indictment against nature. He does not even give it the credit of that 'order' of which he elsewhere speaks so much. Disorder is rather 'a counterpart of Nature's ways,' he says. 'Anarchy and the Reign of Terror are overmatched in injustice, even as death, by a hurricane and a pestilence.'

This tone of superiority to the world, – as if it might have been better if they had had the making of it, – is a remarkable feature in the intellectual character of both the Mills. They seem to have been unconscious of the strange intellectual presumption it implied, and its essential inconsistency with the fundamental principle of their own philosophy. For if Nature be supreme in its facts and laws, and there be nothing but a development of Nature, it seems, to say the least, to be an unreasonable philosophical attitude to indulge in abuse of it or its manifestations. Mill not only does this, but in the most elaborate of his essays – that on Theism – he may be said to construct a Theistic theory on his recognition of the imperfections of the world. It was this essay which, more than the others, proved a stumbling-block to the school which looked to him as its chief apostle. It is a tribute so far to the candour and openness of mind which characterised him beyond all the other members of his school, but it is in some respects the least successful of all his writings. In his treatment of the argument for a First Cause, he recurs to the old thought which pervades the chapter on Causation in the *Logic*, and which we may be excused therefore from still further glancing at. 'All the power that Will possesses over phenomena,' he contends, 'is shared by other and far more powerful agents,' such as heat and electricity, which evolve motion on a far larger scale than human volition. And what right have we therefore, he virtually asks, just as Hume did, to conceive of intelligent will or mind as the original cause of all things? 'what peculiar privilege has this little agitation of the brain which we call thought, that we must make it the model of the universe?' None at all, we admit, on a mere phenomenal basis. But once suppose that there is more in heaven and earth than we can gather from the knowledge of phenomena – that man is more than matter – that mind is more than any combination of matter, and all analogy between mental force and other forms of force disappears. Does it not even disappear when the facts are looked at in themselves? All forms of material force are obviously in themselves mere transformations. They operate unconsciously; they are merely *changes* – transferences. We recognise force in them because we have experience of force in ourselves; but they do not themselves yield the idea of force. We could never get the idea from them; and therefore Comte, the most consistent of all phenomenalists, would have the term disused as misleading – as implying something of which we have no knowledge. The idea of force is only given in the action of mind; it is the product of self-consciousness – of nothing else. And does not this separate conscious Will from all other facts in Nature? It is confessedly intranslatable. No process of merely natural change can generate it. Does it not, therefore, by its very character, stand apart from the category of matter, and compel us to recognise its distinction? Does not, in short, the purely scientific view of mind, as something in experience absolutely apart from all other motor forces in the world, lead us up to the theological view that mind, as self-conscious, is a singular power – an efflux from a higher Source than matter?

It may be impossible to prove Mind to be what the Christian heart believes it to be, and so to infer that the Primal Force or First Cause of the Universe must be a Supreme Mind – and nothing less. Facts are so far in favour of the theistic hypothesis. So far as experience extends, Mind cannot be generated from any other or inferior force, or any combination of Matter and Force. On this ground the Theist holds it to be *sui generis* – a Divine particle implying a Divine Author. But even if this cannot be proved, it seems evident that a Divine Author or Creative Mind can only be argued on the basis that Mind is something more than any mere function of matter. What otherwise comes of the principle of Design? – with which Mr. Mill, no less than the Theist, largely works. He is greatly in favour of Design in Creation. Repudiating all other evidences of Theism, he thinks that the argument from marks of Design in Nature is 'of a really scientific character.' He does not allow the argument to the extent of the Christian Theist. The 'marks of Design' appear to him to imply an Evil as well as a Good Power, or at least an imperfect Power. There is evidence of benevolent Design, but it is also evident he thinks that benevolent Design has been hemmed in and hindered by lack of adequate power or intractableness of material. But leaving aside the character of his conclusion, of which we have already said enough, is there not a radical weakness at the root of any Design argument in his hands? for if mind be a mere quality or outcome of matter, we may certainly ask, with Hume, why should it be made 'the model of the universe'? What right have we to transfer it to natural phenomena at all as their explanation? Design is only intelligible as the purposeful operation of an intelligent will. It is essentially the expression of such a will. And is this not already to own an intelligence behind the order of Nature? Does not Theism of any kind, in short, even such Theism as Mr. Mill's, imply a metaphysical basis – an intelligent will operating behind the changes of experience; while a philosophy like Mr. Mill's, which *ab initio* denies that there is anything at all behind experience, and makes the will itself merely a phenomenon, really leaves no room for Will in Nature at all. No analogy of mere experience can enable us to find in Nature what we do not recognise in ourselves. The whole fabric of Mr. Mill's Theism therefore tumbles to the ground. It is the old story again of *Nullus spiritus in Microcosmo, nullus Deus in Macrocosmo*. Blot out the Divine in Man, and no Divine can be found in Nature. Soul and God are essentially co-relative, and if soul is denied, God, or a Creative Mind, can nowhere be found.

It is remarkable how far Mr. Mill is disposed to recognise Design in Nature – as in the formation of the eye for example. Sight not being precedent, but subsequent to the organic structure of the eye, this structure can only be explained by an antecedent idea as the efficient cause. 'And this at once marks the organ as proceeding from an intelligent Will.' But is not the idea of an intelligent Will essentially metaphysical? It has no meaning as a mere educt of experience. Intelligence may be predicated on a mere basis of observation, but an intelligent Will – Mind as a creative or original agent – is something deeper than any mere experience, and lies at the background of all experience. We cannot play with words in this manner; we cannot use 'Design' and speak of 'an intelligent will,' and yet maintain a merely phenomenal basis. The distinction of the two systems of thought is radical, and there is no binding the two together. Atheism is the consistent result of Phenomenalism, and by its very premisses shuts out the Divine both in

Man and Nature. It holds all life throughout in its everlasting grasp, and there is no getting behind it. Because, *ex hypothesi*, there is nothing behind, – there is no metaphysic.

There can hardly be a doubt therefore that what were supposed to be Mill's earlier views were the true logical outcome of his mode of thought, far more than the pallid Theism propounded by him in his posthumous essay, which recognised a Creator, but denied to Him either full benevolence, or the power to carry his benevolent purposes into effect. A God thus limited – whose hand is shortened that it can not save, is no God at all, and no religion worth speaking of could rest on such a basis.

It may be asked, then, What is the value of Mr. Mill's thinking upon religion? Is it not purely negative? Even if it were so, it would claim our attention. The advocates of a thesis can never overlook the anti-thesis, and those who defend it. The very breadth of Mr. Mill's negations and the negations of his school has been of service to religious thought. The thoroughness of his logical analysis on one side has led to a more thorough analysis on the other side. The ideas of Order, of Miracle, of Free Will, have all come forth from his searching logic more clear and intelligible. They have been set in a higher light, and Christian reason has come to see how unworthy were some of its old conceptions on such subjects.

But Mr. J. S. Mill has not merely done this negative work in religious thought. He has done much more. The effect of his thoroughgoing criticism has been to make clearer than before the roots of the great opposing lines of thought, on which all higher speculation rests. In the end, on either side, a postulate stares us in the face. Man is either divine from the first – a free spiritual being standing apart from all nature, – or he is essentially material. On the latter basis, no religion in the old sense can be based. All attempts to find spirit in matter, if spirit is not already presupposed as prior to matter, is a mere futile imagination. All attempts to reach God through Nature, the Unseen through the seen, must necessarily fail. We can never gain from natural law anything but some product of that law. Once bring man within the chain of causation binding the life of nature, and there is no rational outlet towards the Divine. The Divine may be held by faith as an hypothesis running parallel with the natural; but it cannot in such a case be established on any grounds of reason. This result was apparent enough long ago, when Hume delighted to emphasise the absolute separation between faith and reason; but it has been scientifically exhibited by Mill. He shrank from the downright atheism to which his principles inevitably lead; but the real drift of these principles is nowhere obscure. Determinism in philosophy lands in the negation of all religion. Religion may be tacked on by faith or superstition to a Determinist Philosophy or Doctrine of Necessity; but it cannot be rationally evolved from it. And thinkers like Baden Powell in our own time, or Chalmers and Jonathan Edwards in former times, who attempted to combine Determinism with Christianity, have all failed, with whatever power of argument. They started from a wrong beginning. The marches between the great lines of thought have been thoroughly cleared by help of Mill's logic and other books of the same school. They are not likely to be obscured again; and this of itself is to have done a great service to religious thought.

But yet, again, Mill has done service in vindicating everywhere the moral side of religion. It was in fact his tendency in all his writings to confound morality with religion. Setting aside, as he did, the Divine as an imaginary sphere, and yet recognising so strongly the moral and social bonds that make so large a part of religion, it was inevitable that he should exalt these human aspects of the subject. They were estimated not unduly in themselves, but disproportionately in comparison with others. But the very emphasis with which our philosopher dwelt on moral attributes in relation to the Divine Being, as well as to human society, was of great value. If it tended to bring down religion from heaven to earth, it also tended to purge the Heavenly Ideal of all grosser taint. Nothing could be further from the truth than the picture of the Christian God given by both the Mills; but it is not to be denied that there lies in all religious systems an inclination to conceive of God more or less after an arbitrary manner, as dealing with mankind on other principles than those of pure Morality, notwithstanding that this moral conception of the Divine is everywhere supreme in the Gospels. This is a perilous inclination, and not undeserving the indignation it excited in their minds. The famous passage in the *Examination* of Hamilton's Philosophy, which sent a thrill through many Christian hearts, had a tinge in it of that intellectual pride of which we have already spoken; but it also breathed a fine moral intensity.[1] Nothing but degradation can come to religion from lowering the Divine Ideal beneath the Ideal of the highest good that we can ourselves conceive. The true ideal of Christian thought is not only more real, but more perfect and beautiful than any human ideal whatever.

---

[1] 'If, instead of the "glad tidings" that there exists a Being in whom all the excellencies which the highest human mind can ever conceive exist in a degree inconceivable to us, I am informed that the world is ruled by a Being whose attributes are infinite, but what they are we cannot learn, nor what are the principles of his government, except that the highest human morality, which we are capable of conceiving, does not sanction them, convince me of it, and I will bear my fate as I may. But when I am told that I must believe this, and, at the same time, call this Being by all the names which express and affirm the highest human morality, I say in plain terms that I will not. Whatever power such a Being may have over me, there is one thing which he shall not do. He shall not compel me to worship him. I will call no Being good who is not what I mean when I apply that epithet to my fellow-creatures; and if such a Being can sentence me to Hell for not so calling him, to Hell I will go.' – *Exam. of Sir William Hamilton's Philosophy*, pp. 123–4.

# WHAT WAS CHRIST?
# A REPLY TO JOHN STUART MILL
George William Foote

There are many passages in John Stuart Mill's *Three Essays on Religion* which the apologists of Christianity very prudently ignore. Orthodoxy naturally shrinks from the description of a God who could make a Hell as a 'dreadful idealisation of wickedness.' Nor is it pleasant to read that 'Not even on the most distorted and contracted theory of good which ever was framed by religious or philosophical fanaticism, can the government of nature be made to resemble the work of a being at once good and omnipotent.'

But Christian lecturers are never tired of quoting the panegyric on their blessed Savior, which occurs in another part of the same volume. They never mention the fact that the Essay which contains this eulogium was not revised by the author for publication, while the other two essays were finally prepared for the press. It is enough for them that the passage is found in a volume of Mill's. Whether it harmonises with the rest of the volume, or whether the author might have considerably modified it in revision, are questions with which they have no concern. 'Here is Mill's testimony to Christ,' they cry, 'and we fling it like a bombshell into the Freethought camp.' We propose to pick up this bombshell, to dissect and analyse it, and to show that it is perfectly harmless.

Mill's panegyric on Christ, as Professor Newman says, 'caused surprise.'[1] Professor Bain, who was one of Mill's most intimate friends, and has written his biography,[2] uses the very same expression. The whole of the Essay on Theism 'was a surprise to his friends,' not for its attacks on orthodoxy, but for its concessions to 'modern sentimental Theism.' Professor Bain observes that these concessions have been made the most

---

[1] 'Christianity in its Cradle,' p. 57.

[2] 'John Stuart Mill: A Criticism; with Personal Recollections.'

of, 'and, as is usual in such cases, the inch has been stretched to an ell.' Speaking with all the authority of his position, Professor Bain adds that the 'fact remains that in everything characteristic of the creed of Christendom, he was a thoroughgoing negationist. He admitted neither its truth nor its utility.'

How, then, did Mill come to write those passages of his Three Essays which caused such surprise to his intimate friends? The answer is simple. 'Who is the woman?' asked Talleyrand, when two friends wished him to settle a dispute. There was a woman in Mill's case. Mrs. Taylor, afterwards his wife, and the object of his adoring love, disturbed his judgment in life and perverted it in death. He buried her at Avignon, and resided near her grave until he could lie beside her in the eternal sleep. No doubt the long vigil at his wife's tomb shows the depth of his love, but it necessarily tended to make his brain the victim of his heart. There can be no worse offence against the laws of logic than to argue from our feelings; and when Mill began to talk about 'indulging the hope' of immortality, he had set his feet, however hesitatingly, on the high road of sentimentalism and superstition. How different was his attitude in the vigor of manhood, when his intellect was unclouded by personal sorrow! In closing his splendid Essay on *The Utility of Religion*, he wrote:

> 'It seems to me not only possible, but probable, that in a higher, and, above all, a happier condition of human life, not annihilation, but immortality, may be the burdensome idea; and that human nature, though pleased with the present, and by no means impatient to quit it, would find comfort and not sadness in the thought that it is not chained through eternity to a conscious existence which it cannot be assured that it will always wish to preserve.'

How great is the range of egoism, even with the best of us! Writing before his own great loss, Mill sees no argument for immortality in the yearning of bereaved hearts for reunion with the beloved dead; but when he himself craves 'the touch of a vanished hand and the sound of a voice that is still,' he perceives room for hope. His own passion of grief lights a beacon in the darkness, which his sympathy with the grief of others had never kindled.

We can easily understand how Mill's profound love for his wife affected his intellect after her death, when we see how it deluded him while she lived. In his *Autobiography* he describes her as a beauty and a wit. Mr. Maccall says that she was not brilliant in conversation, and decidedly plain-looking; and the same objection appears to be hinted by Professor Bain. Carlyle refers to her several times in his *Reminiscences*, always as a light gossamery creature. It is notorious that the Grotes regarded Mill's attachment to her as an infatuation. And certainly he did a great deal to justify their opinion. In the dedication of his Essay on Liberty, he refers to her 'great thoughts and noble feelings,' and her 'all but unrivalled wisdom.' This eulogium a little astonished those who had read her Essay in the *Westminster Review*, reprinted by Mill in his *Dissertations and Discussions*, which revealed no very wonderful ability, and assuredly did not place her beside Harriet Martineau or George Eliot. But in his *Autobiography* this panegyric was completely eclipsed. Mill informs the world in that volume that her mind 'included Carlyle's and infinitely more,' and that in comparison with her Shelley was but a child. Apparently seeing, however, that sceptics might inquire why a woman of such profound and original genius did not leave some memorable work, Mill confidently tells us that she was content to inspire other minds rather than express herself through the channels of literature. In other words, she played second fiddle in preference to first, which is exactly what men and women of original genius will never do. But *whom* did she inspire? We know of none but Mill, and on examining his works chronologically we find that all his greatest books were composed before he fell under her influence. Mr. Gladstone explains Mill's 'ludicrous estimate of his wife's powers,' by saying that she was a quick receptive woman, who gave him back the echo of his own thoughts, which he took for the independent oracles of truth.

Over the tomb of this idolised wife, whom his fancy clothed with fictitious or exaggerated attributes, Mill wrote his Essay on Theism. Miss Helen Taylor says it shows 'the carefully-balanced results of the deliberations of a life-time.' But she allows that –

> 'On the other hand, there had not been time for it to undergo the revision to which from time to time he subjected most of his writings before making them public. Not only, therefore, is the style less polished than of any other of his

published works, but even the matter itself, at least in the exact shape it here assumes, has never undergone the repeated examination which it certainly would have passed through before he would himself have given it to the world.'

If Mill had lived, he would perhaps have made many improvements and excisions in this unfortunate essay. As it stands it is singularly feeble in comparison with the two former Essays. He 'hopes' for immortality, and 'regrets to say' that the Design Argument is not inexpugnable, as though this were the language of a philosopher or a logician. After writing several pages on the 'Marks of Design in Nature,' he passingly notices the Darwinian Theory and admits that, if established, it 'would greatly attenuate the evidence' for Creation. Yet he drops this great hypothesis in the next paragraph, and talks about 'the large balance of probability in favor of creation by intelligence *in the present state of our knowledge*'. What he meant was, *in the present state of our ignorance*. Mill neither understood nor felt the force of Darwinism. We shall find, in examining his panegyric on Christ, that he understood that subject just as little, and that, where his knowledge did apply, he flatly contradicted what he had written before.

Let us now ascertain what were Mill's qualifications for the task of estimating the teachings and personality of Christ. He had a subtle logical mind, strong though restricted sympathies, a singular power of mastering an opponent's case, and remarkable candor in stating it. But his intellect was of the purely speculative order. He possessed a 'rich storage of principles, doctrines, generalities of every degree, over several wide departments of knowledge,' as Professor Bain says; but he 'had not much memory for detail of any kind,' although 'by express study and frequent reference he had amassed a store of facts bearing on political or sociological doctrines.' In short, 'he had an intellect for the abstract and the logical out of all proportion to his hold of the concrete and the poetical.' He was cut out for a metaphysician, a political speculator and a sociologist. But he never could have become an historian or a man of letters. He had little sense of style, no faculty of literary criticism, a dislike of picturesque expression, a scanty knowledge of human nature, and an extremely feeble imagination. He was a great philosopher, but perhaps less an artist than any other thinker of the same eminence that ever lived.

Now the faculties required in dealing with the origin of Christianity, including the character of its founder, are obviously those of the literary critic and the historian, in which Mill was deficient. He was, therefore, not equipped by nature for the task.

Had he even the necessary knowledge? Certainly not. There is not the slightest evidence that he had studied the relation of Christianity to previous systems, the growth of its literature, the formation of its canon, and the development of its ethics and its dogmas. He probably knew next to nothing of the oriental religions, and was only acquainted with the name of Buddhism. Nay, if we may trust Professor Bain (his friend, his biographer, and his eulogist), he knew very little of Christianity itself. He 'scarcely ever read a theological book,' and he only knew 'the main positions of theology from our general literature.' Just when Mill's *Three Essays on Religion* appeared, Strauss's *Old Faith and the New* was published in England, and Professor Bain justly remarks that 'Anyone reading it would, I think, be struck with its immense superiority to Mill's work, in all but the logic and metaphysics. Strauss speaks like a man thoroughly at home with his subject.' Mill does indeed say, in his *Autobiography*, that his father made him, at a very early age, 'a reader of ecclesiastical history': but he does not tell us that he continued so in his after life, and even if he did, ecclesiastical history begins just where the problem of the origin of Christianity ends.

Another thing must be said. Professor Bain states, and we can well believe him, that Mill was 'not even well read in the sceptics that preceded him.' He was really ignorant on both sides of the controversy. His idea of Christ was formed from a selection of the best things in the New Testament. A most uncritical process, and in fact an impossible one; for the New Testament is not history, but an arbitrary selection from a mass of early Christian tracts, of uncertain authorship, different dates, and various value. The literature on this subject, even from the pens of eminent writers, is vast enough to show its immense complication. Unless it is read in a *child-like* spirit, which in grown men and women is *childish*, the New Testament needs to be explained; and when the process has fairly begun, you find all the familiar features shifting like the pieces in a kaleidoscope, until at last they reassume an organic, but a different, form and color. Twenty Christs may be elicited from the New Testament as it stands. Mill deduced one, but the nineteen others are just as valid.

Strictly speaking, our task is completed. It would logically suffice to say that Mill's panegyric on Christ is a mere piece of fancy. Like other men of genius, he had his special aptitudes and special knowledge, and his authority only extends as far as they carry him. Mr. Swinburne's opinion of Newton is of no particular importance, and Newton's famous ineptitude about *Paradise Lost* in no way affects our estimate of Milton.

Let us go further, however, and examine Mill's panegyric on Christ in detail. In justice to him, as well as to the subject, it should be quoted in full:

> 'Above all, the most valuable part of the effect on the character which Christianity has produced by holding up in a Divine Person a standard of excellence and a model for imitation, is available even to the absolute unbeliever and can never more be lost to humanity. For it is Christ, rather than God, whom Christianity has held up to believers as the pattern of perfection for humanity. It is the God incarnate, more than the God of the Jews or of Nature, who being idealised, has taken so great and salutary a hold on the modern mind. And whatever else may be taken away from us by rational criticism, Christ is still left; a unique figure, not more unlike all his precursors than all his followers, even those who had the direct benefit of his personal teaching. It is of no use to say that Christ as exhibited in the Gospels is not historical and that we know not how much of what is admirable has been superadded by the tradition of his followers. The tradition of followers suffices to insert any number of marvels, and may have inserted all the miracles which he is reputed to have wrought. But who among his disciples or among their proselytes was capable of inventing the sayings ascribed to Jesus or of imagining the life and character revealed in the Gospels? Certainly not the fishermen of Galilee; as certainly not St. Paul, whose character and idiosyncracies were of a totally different sort; still less the early Christian writers in whom nothing is more evident than that the good which was in them was all derived, as they always professed that it was derived, from a higher source. What *could* be added and interpolated by a disciple we may see in the mystical parts of the Gospel of

St. John, matter imported from Philo and the Alexandrian Platonists and put into the mouth of the Savior in long speeches about himself such as the other Gospels contain not the slightest vestige of, though pretended to have been delivered on occasions of the deepest interest and when his principal followers were all present; most prominently at the last supper. The East was full of men who could have stolen any quantity of this poor stuff, as the multitudinous Oriental sects of Gnostics afterwards did. But about the life and sayings of Jesus there is a stamp of personal originality combined with profundity of insight, which if we abandon the idle expectation of finding scientific precision where something very different was aimed at, must place the Prophet of Nazareth, even in the estimation of those who have no belief in his inspiration, in the very first rank of the men of sublime genius of whom our species can boast. When this pre-eminent genius is combined with the qualities of probably the greatest moral reformer, and martyr to that mission, who ever existed upon earth, religion cannot be said to have made a bad choice in pitching on this man as the ideal representative and guide of humanity; nor even now, would it be easy, even for an unbeliever, to find a better translation of the rule of virtue from the abstract into the concrete, than to endeavor so to live that Christ would approve our life.'

Our first complaint is that the whole passage is too vague and rhetorical. What is the meaning of 'the absolute unbeliever' in the first sentence? If it means a person who rejects *all* the pretensions of Christ, the sentence is absurd. If it means a person who rejects his divinity, it is practically untrue; for, as a matter of fact, those who have thought themselves out of Christianity (which Mill did not, as he was never in it) very seldom do take Christ as 'a standard of excellence and a model for imitation,' much less as 'the pattern of perfection for humanity.' When the supernatural glamor is dispelled, we see that Christ is no example whatever. He is simply a preacher, and his personal conduct fails to illustrate a single public or private virtue, or assist us in any of our practical difficulties as husbands, fathers, sons, or citizens. Mill has himself shown that even Christians do not attempt to imitate their Savior; and we are puzzled to understand how he could speak of

Christ's having 'taken so *great* and salutary hold on the modern mind' after telling us, in his *Essay on Liberty*, that he has done nothing of the kind. He there says:

> 'By Christianity, I here mean what is accounted such by all churches and sects, the maxims and precepts contained in the New Testament. These are considered sacred, and accepted as laws by all professing Christians. Yet it is scarcely too much to say that not one Christian in a thousand guides or tests his individual conduct by reference to those laws. . . . Whenever conduct is concerned, they look round for Mr. A and B to direct them how far to go in obeying Christ.'

Had Mill forgotten this passage when he wrote the Essay on Theism, or had Christendom changed in the interval? Scarcely the latter. John Bright has justly said that the lower classes in England care as little for the dogmas of Christianity as the upper classes care about its practice.

Until Christians follow their Savior's teachings, it is idle to expect unbelievers to do so. Yet it is perhaps as well they do not, for there are many things recorded in the Gospels which are far from redounding to his credit. It is a great pity that Mill, before eulogising Christ, could not read the chapter on 'Jesus of Nazareth' in Professor Newman's last work. Why did Jesus consort with Publicans (or Roman tax-gatherers), the very sight of whom was hateful to every patriotic Jew? Why did he herd with Sinners, who so far despised ceremony as to dip in the dish with dirty fingers? Why did he avoid all who were able to criticise him? Why did he exclaim, 'Ye hypocrites, why put ye me to proof?' when the Jews sought to test his claims, and to act on his own advice to 'Beware of false prophets'? Why did he rudely repel educated inquirers, and then solemnly thank God that 'he had hidden these things from the wise and prudent, and revealed them unto babes'? Why did he denounce inhabitants of cities he could not convince, and prophesy that they would fare worse in the Day of Judgment than the filthy inhabitants of Sodom and Gomorrah? Why did he assail his religious rivals with invectives which, as Professor Newman says, 'outdo Tacitus and Suetonius in malignity, and seem to convict themselves of falsehood and bitter slander?' Why, in short, did he so constantly display the vanity and passion of a spoilt child? Surely these are not characteristics we should emulate, but glaring blots in a 'pattern of perfection.' When the arrogance of Christ is countenanced by a writer like Mill, these defects must be insisted on. Professor Newman rightly says that

> 'If honor were claimed for Jesus as for Socrates, for Seneca, for Hillel, for Epictetus, we might apologise for his weak points as either incident to his era and country or to human nature itself – weakness to be forgiven and forgotten. But the unremitting assumption of super-human wisdom, not only made for him by the moderns, but breathing through every utterance attributed to him, changes the whole scene, and ought to change our treatment of it. Unless his prodigious claim of divine superiority is made good in fact, it betrays an arrogance difficult to excuse, eminently mischievous and eminently ignominious.'

But this prodigious claim cannot be made good. As Professor Newman says: 'It is hard to point to anything in the teaching of Jesus at once *new* to Hebrew and Greek sages, and likewise in general estimate *true*.' The same view was expressed by Buckle, with more vigor if less urbanity. 'Whoever,' he said, 'asserts that Christianity revealed to the world truths with which it was previously unacquainted, is guilty either of gross ignorance or of wilful fraud.'

Mill had himself, in the *Essay on Liberty*, shown the evil of taking Christ, or any other man, as 'the ideal representative and guide of humanity.' He there charged Christianity with possessing a negative rather than a positive ideal; abstinence from evil rather than energetic pursuit of good constituting its essence, in which 'thou shalt not' unduly predominated over 'thou shalt.' He accused it of making an idol of asceticism, of holding out 'the hope of heaven and the threat of hell as the appointed and appropriate motives to a virtuous life,' and of thus 'giving to human morality an essentially selfish character.' And he added that –

> 'What little recognition the idea of obligation to the public obtains in modern morality, is derived from Greek and Roman sources, not from Christian; as, even in the morality of private life, whatever exists of magnanimity, high-mindedness, personal dignity, even the sense of honor, is derived from the purely human, not the religious, part of our education, and never could have grown out of a standard of

ethics in which the only worth, professedly recognised, is that of obedience.'

Mill does indeed throw a sop to orthodoxy by allowing that Christ and Christianity are different things; but he is obliged to add that the Founder of Christianity failed to provide for 'many essential elements of the highest morality.' He maintains that 'other ethics than *any* which can be evolved from exclusively Christian sources must exist side by side with Christian ethics to produce the moral regeneration of mankind.' And he deprecates the policy of 'forming the mind and feelings on an exclusively religious type.' Surely these arguments are quite inconsistent with Mill's later notion of taking Christ as our ideal, and living so that he would approve our life.

Besides, as Professor Bain points out, the morality of Christ belongs to this exclusively religious type. Its sanctions are all religious, and if religion is dispensed with they 'must lose their suitability to human life.' Professor Bain very justly observes that 'the best guidance, under such altered circumstances, would be that furnished by the wisest of purely secular teachers.'

That Christ was 'probably the greatest moral reformer' that ever lived is a statement easy to make and difficult to prove. When Mill, in the *Essay on Liberty*, twits the Christians with professing doctrines they never practise, he furnishes a catalogue of the duties they neglect.

> 'All Christians believe that the blessed are the poor and humble, and those who are ill-used by the world; that it is easier for a camel to pass through the eye of a needle than for a rich man to enter the kingdom of heaven; that they should judge not lest they should be judged; that they should swear not at all; that they should love their neighbors as themselves; that if one take their cloak, they should give him their coat also; that they should take no thought for the morrow; that if they would be perfect they should sell all they have and give it to the poor.'

Surely Mill was aware that all these absurd and impracticable maxims were taught by Christ. How, then, except on the theory we have advanced, could he call him the greatest moral reformer in history?

The 'rational criticism' by means of which Mill obtains the

'unique figure' of Christ is a purely arbitrary process. George Eliot, who knew the subject far better, said in one of her letters that the materials for any biography of Jesus do not exist. The Unitarians have tried Mill's process with small success; and, as Professor Bain maliciously observes, 'It would seem in this, as in other parts of religion, that what the rationalist disapproves of most the multitude likes best.' Professor Bain's remarks on Mill's construction of his 'unique figure' from the Gospels are so pertinent and happy that we venture to give them in full:

> 'We are, of course, at liberty to dissent from the prevailing view, which makes Christ a divine person. But to reduce a Deity to the human level, to rank him simply as a great man, and to hold ideal intercourse with him in that capacity is, to say the least of it, an incongruity. Historians and moralists have been accustomed to treat with condemnation those monarchs that, after being dethroned, have accepted in full the position of subjects. Either to die, or else to withdraw into dignified isolation, has been accounted the only fitting termination to the loss of royal power. So, a Deity dethroned should retire altogether from playing a part in human affairs, and remain simply as an historic name.'

Mill finds in Christ 'sublime genius' and 'profundity of insight.' Surely it did not require any very sublime genius to teach those peculiar doctrines which Mill catalogued for backsliding Christians, nor any very great profundity of insight to see that none but paupers and lunatics could ever practise them. Many of the best sayings ascribed to Jesus were the common possession of the East before his birth; but many of the worst seem more his own. 'Leave all and follow me' is a vain and foolish command. 'Give to everyone that asketh' is an excellent rule for pauperising society. 'That industry is a human duty,' says Professor Newman, 'cannot be gathered from his doctrine: how could it, when he kept twelve religious mendicants around him?' 'Resist not evil' is a premium on tyranny. 'Blessed be ye poor' and 'Woe unto you rich' are the exclamations of a vulgar demagogue, a cunning agent of privilege, or an irresponsible maniac. 'By shovelling away wealth,' says Professor Newman, 'we are to buy treasures in heaven. Unless our narrators belie him, Jesus never warns hearers that to give without a heart of charity does *not* prepare a soul for heaven nor "earn salvation"; and that selfish pre-speculation turns virtue into despicable marketing. To forgive that we may be forgiven, to avoid judging lest we be judged, to do good that we may get extrinsic reward, to affect humility that we may be promoted, to lose life that we may gain it with advantage, are precepts not needing a lofty prophet.' It is also from the words of Christ alone, according to the New Testament, that the doctrine of Eternal Punishment can be established; and he is responsible for the intellectual crime of identifying Credulity with Faith, which has been a fatal rottenness at the very core of Christianity.

As for the 'personal originality' of Mill's 'unique figure,' he might be safely challenged to demonstrate it from the Gospels. We shall have something more to say about the originality of Christ's teaching presently; we confine ourselves now to his personal character. Take away from the Gospel story the pathetic legend of Calvary, which throws around him a glamor of suffering, and what is there in his whole life of a positive heroic quality? He is a tame, effeminate, shrinking figure, beside hundreds of men who have not been made the object of a superstitious cultus. His brief, ineffective career, so soon closed by his own madness or ambition, will not bear a moment's comparison with the long and glorious life of Buddha. It pales into insignificance before the mighty genius of Muhammed. Doctrine apart, the Nazarene is to the Meccan as a pallid moon to a fiery sun. With the single exception of Cromwell, who was a more original character than twenty Christs rolled into one, where shall we find Muhammed's equal in history? As Eliot Warburton well said, he stands almost alone in 'the sustained and almost superhuman energy with which he carried out his views, in defiance, as it would seem, of God and man.' Christ quails in his Gethsemane. Muhammed struggles through his seven years' ordeal of obloquy and danger like a resolute swimmer, who scorns to turn back, and will reach the other shore or die. When his followers faint under the burning desert sun, he tells them that 'Hell is hotter,' and silences their murmurs. Christ cries in an agony of despair, 'My God, my God, why hast thou forsaken me?' When Muhammed's assassination is resolved on at Mecca, each of the tribes devoting a sword to drink his blood, and Abubekar, the companion of his flight, says 'We are but two,' the indomitable prophet answers 'We are three, for God is with us.' Christ implores 'O my father, if it be possible, let this cup pass from me.' When Muhammed is threatened by the Koreishites, so that his most devoted followers remonstrate against his projects, he makes the sublime answer, 'If they should place the sun on my right hand, and the moon on my left, they should not divert me from my course.' Within a century after the Hegira, the empire of Islam had spread from Arabia eastward to Delhi and westward to Granada. Oh, it is said, Muhammed used the sword. True, but not before it was drawn against him. The man who rode to Jerusalem, and called himself King of the Jews, would have used the sword too had he dared. 'The sword indeed,' snorts Carlyle at this rubbish, 'but where will you get your sword? Every new opinion, at its starting, is precisely in a *minority of one*. In one man's head alone there it dwells as yet. That *he* take a sword and try to propagate with that will do little for him. You must first get your sword. On the whole, a thing will propagate itself as it can. We do not find, of the Christian religion either, that it always disdained the sword, when once it had got one.' True, thou sarcastic old sage of Chelsea, and the sting is in the tail. From Constantine downwards, Christianity has not been imposed on mankind without, as Sir James Stephen remarks, exhausting all the terrors of this life as well as the next.

Mill tells us that Christ was a 'martyr' to his 'mission' as a 'moral reformer.' We should like to know how he discovered the fact. Certainly not from the Gospels. It was not the Sermon on the Mount, but his vagaries at Jerusalem, that led to the crucifixion. Christ deliberately chose *twelve* disciples, the legendary number of the tribes of Israel, and told them that when he came into his kingdom they should sit on twelve thrones as judges. Professor Newman answers those who call this language figurative with the just remark that 'we should call a teacher mad who used such words to simple men, and did not expect them to understand him literally.' When the disciples ask him, 'Lord, wilt thou at this time restore the kingdom unto Israel?' he does not rebuke them (although it is after his resurrection), but simply says that the time is a secret. His triumphal entry into Jerusalem can only be considered as a declaration of sovereignty, and his countenancing the shout of *Hosanna!* (the war cry of previous insurrections, and an appeal to Jehovah against the foe) could only be construed as rebellion against Rome. His conduct inside Jerusalem was that of a man intoxicated with vanity and ambition, without judgment, policy, or purpose. The very inscription on the cross shows that he was believed to aim at earthly royalty. Pontius Pilate tried to save Jesus, acting wisely and humanely as the representative of an empire that was always tolerant in matters of religion. He would not receive a charge of blasphemy, but he could not overlook a charge of sedition. Yet he still gave Jesus an opportunity of escaping. 'Come now,' he seems to say, 'your enemies want your blood. Your blasphemy is no business of mine, and I shall not decide a squabble between your rabid sects. But I must try you if they accuse you of sedition. You are young, and cannot wish to die. Plead "not guilty." Deny the charge. Say you are not the King of the Jews and do not contemplate rebellion. One word, and I save you from death. You shall go free though all the rabbis in Jerusalem howled like mad dogs. Rome shall stand between bigotry and blood.' But Jesus actually admits the indictment and afterwards remains contumaciously silent. Pilate had no alternative: he sentenced Jesus to execution; but amid all the absurd fictions of the narrative, the fact shines out clearly that he did so with the utmost reluctance. To call the death of Christ in these circumstances, martyrdom, is to degrade the name. He died for no principle. The truth would have saved him, and he would not utter it. Either he was in a stupor of despair, or so crazed with the Messianic delusion that he still trusted to the legion of angels or his rescue. In any case it was an act of insanity. He courted his doom. It was not a martyrdom but a suicide.

We may also observe that, if a cultus had not been formed around it, and men's imaginations suborned in its favor from the cradle, the 'martyrdom' of Christ would be obviously less severe than that of many persecuted reformers. Giordano Bruno's Gethsemane was an Inquisition dungeon, where he languished in solitude for seven years, and was tortured no one knows how often. What was Christ's few hours' agony of weakness before death compared with this? Bruno died by fire, the most cruel form of murder, whilst Christ suffered the milder doom of crucifixion. Christ was watched by weeping women, whose sympathy must have alleviated his pain; and it was not until the hand of death touched his very heart that he despaired of assistance from heaven. Bruno stood alone against the world, without any sources of courage but his own quenchless heroism. Christ quailed before the inevitable. Bruno met with a serene smile, for he had that within him which only death could extinguish – a daring fiery spirit, that nothing could quell, that outsoared the malice of men, and outshone the flames of the stake.

Mill's remarks on the originality of Christ's teaching betray his utter ignorance of the subject. It is of no use, he says, to assert that the Christ of the Gospels is not historical. Begging his pardon, that is the most important factor in the problem. If the Gospels are what we allege (and no scholar would dispute it), George Eliot is right in saying that the materials for a biography of Jesus do not exist, and Mill's 'rational criticism' is a purely fantastic process. But the reason he assigns for his position is still more absurd. Who, he asks, could have invented the sayings ascribed to Jesus? Certainly, he says, not St. Paul: a sentence which alone stamps him as an incompetent critic. No man who understood the subject would ever have thought of anticipating such a preposterous objection. 'Certainly not the fishermen of Galilee,' is equally futile, for no student of the origin of Christianity supposes that the Gospels were written by the first disciples. They are of much later date. But except for that fact, why might not the 'fishermen of Galilee' have been able to invent the *logia* of the Gospels as well as Jesus? He was only a carpenter, and there is no reason in the nature of things why fishermen should not equal carpenters as prophets, preachers, and moralists. Mill is altogether on the wrong scent. There was no need for Christ or his disciples to invent the sayings ascribed to him. As we have already remarked, they were the common possession of the East before his birth. The Lord's Prayer is merely a *cento* from the Talmud, and, as Emanuel Deutsch showed, every catchword of Christ's was a household word of Talmudic Judaism before he began his ministry. There is not a single maxim, however good or bad, however sensible or silly, in the whole of Christ's discourses that cannot be found in the writings of Pagan moralists and poets or Jewish doctors who flourished before him; and his best sayings, if they may be called his, were all anticipated by Buddha several centuries before he was born. It is also well known that the Golden Rule, as it is called, was taught by Confucius long before the time of Christ, without any of the absurdities with which the Nazarene surrounded it. 'Love your enemies,' says Christ, as though it were wise or possible to do so. Confucius corrected this exaggeration. 'No,' he said, 'if I love my enemies, what shall I give to my friends? To my friends I give my love, and to my enemies – justice!'

We think we have said enough to show that Mill's panegyric on Christ is utterly valueless. Mr. Matthew Arnold is far more subtle and dexterous in his eulogy; but he knows the subject as well as Mill knew it badly. If the apologists of Christianity are prudent, they will cease to make use of Mill's tribute to their Blessed Savior, or at least employ it only before people who are in that blissful ignorance which fancies it folly to be wise.

# [FROM] LIFE OF JOHN STUART MILL
## William Leonard Courtney

... The *Autobiography*, part of which had been written in 1861, and part after 1870, came out after his death, and enabled all men to understand how serious and simple had been the life of the man who had died so calmly. The other posthumous work, *Essays on Religion*, caused more commotion, and renewed many of the controversies which had existed during his lifetime as to his real convictions. To some the book came as a disappointment, to others as a relief, to all as a surprise. But while it renders still more difficult the task of reconciling the various items of Mill's creed, it must be remembered that the third essay, at all events, is only a first draft, and had not the benefit of that careful revision which Mill was in the habit of giving to all that he published on his own authority.

'The two first of these three essays,' says Miss Helen Taylor in her introductory notice, 'were written between the years 1850 and 1858, during the period which intervened between the publication of the *Principles of Political Economy* and that of the work on *Liberty*. The last essay belongs to a different epoch. It was written between the years 1868 and 1870, but it was not designed as a sequel to the two essays which now appear along with it, nor were they intended to appear all together.' It is important to remember these facts, for they serve to explain in some measure the divergence in view between the earlier and later portions of the volume – a divergence which we may take for granted, since so enthusiastic a disciple of Mill as Mr. Morley has taken pains to accentuate it in the articles which he wrote in the *Fortnightly Review*.[1] The first essay has as its subject the various interpretations which may be given of the term Nature. *Its purpose is* to show that if 'Nature' be taken as a guide either in religion or in morals, it

---

[1] *Fortnightly Review*, 1874, 1875.

is a term equally ambiguous and defective. We can neither construct an ethical theory on the ground of 'conformity to Nature,' as, for instance, the Stoics attempted, nor have we any justification for basing a religious creed on a consideration of natural processes. For the fact is, according to Mill, that Nature, as distinct from human activity and foresight, exhibits specimens of reckless violence and brutality which would be universally condemned according to any human standard. In a passage of great rhetorical energy Mill describes Nature as Tennyson describes her in his *In Memoriam*: 'red in tooth and claw with ravine.' All the good that has been done to the world and to humanity has been effected by human powers in limiting, controlling, and overpowering the blind and senseless havoc of natural forces. How, then, can a so-called 'natural religion' be defensible? To argue from the signs and evidences of the natural world to its Creator, is to ascribe what is immeasurably below man to that which is, in the language of religious fervour, asserted to be infinitely above man. One of the hardest tasks which is assigned to the human race is the duty of reforming religion itself. The conclusion which Mill reaches is thus expressed[2] – 'The only admissible moral theory of Creation is that the principle of good cannot at once and altogether subdue the powers of evil, either physical or moral; could not place mankind free from the necessity of an incessant struggle with the maleficent powers, or make them always victorious in that struggle, but could and did make them capable of carrying on the fight with vigour and with progressively increasing success. Of all the religious explanations of the order of nature, this alone is neither contradictory to itself nor to the facts for which it attempts to account.' It must be admitted, however, that the value of the essay is much lessened by the fact that at the time at which it was composed, Darwin's newer view of nature was not fully before the world. Here, as elsewhere in Mill, we are to regard Nature on the ground of a conception based on individual experiences. Mill takes, as Mr. Morley terms it, merely the surface or horizontal view of Nature. The works of Darwin and Herbert Spencer enable us to substitute for this what may be called a transverse section of natural phenomena, whereby we can observe the successive layers of a historical development. One result of the latter view

[2] *Essays on Religion*, p. 39.

is effectually to reduce that power which Mill attributed to man, of altering or transforming the course of nature for his own and other's good: for man is shown to be swept along the current of natural forces, and to be himself a part of nature. This may or may not affect the general conclusions of the essay; it obviously interferes with some of the arguments in detail.[3]

The second essay may be passed over with only a slight reference. It is on the Utility of Religion, and is, in Mr. Morley's summary, an attempt to answer the following questions: – Is religion of direct service to temporal interests, a direct instrument of social good? Is it useful in improving and ennobling individual human nature? If its utility in either of these two ways be allowed, must the form of religion be necessarily supernatural, involving a journey beyond the boundaries of the world which we inhabit, and beyond anything which could be supplied by the idealisation of our earthly life? In dealing with these questions, Mill's general contention is that religion is of considerable utility, but it need not be supernatural, nor deal with problems beyond the reach of human ken. But as we found that Mill's *Utilitarianism* was considerably embarrassed by the want of any clear conception of what happiness is, so his discussion of the present subject is hampered by a similar obscurity in his conception of religion. Religion is apparently a yearning to know whether our ideal and imaginative conceptions have realities answering to them in other words than ours. But the conclusion of the essay is that the Positivist religion of Humanity, or as Mill prefers to call it, the religion of Social Duty, has all the value of the popular religion, as well as greater scientific certainty. Now, a religion of Humanity has clearly nothing to do with other worlds than ours. Hence some part, at all events, of the essence of religion is missed in that which Mill proposes to give as an entirely adequate substitute.

His object is, as we have said, to replace what is ordinarily termed Religion by the Positivist conception of a religion of Humanity. But the value and expediency of this substitution is rendered more than doubtful in the third essay. In the *Essay*

---

[3] The reader may be referred for an able polemic in favour of the religious view as against some of the inferences from Darwinism to Dr. James Martineau's *Study of Religion*, esp. vol. ii, pp. 270–397.

on Theism there is sometimes the suggestion, sometimes the clear recognition, that what is valuable in religion (or, at all events, that which renders it valuable to the majority of mankind) is the element of wonder and mystery which encircles the problems with which it deals. With regard to three leading ideas – the idea of God as cause of the world, the idea of Christ as a divinely-appointed teacher, and the idea of immortality – Mill has considerations to offer which render them not indeed dogmas to be intellectually accepted, but hypotheses of some little probability, which may be defended on even scientific grounds. The ideas are not, it is true, such as they would be represented by the religious consciousness, but they are put forward in a sketchy, tentative fashion, as though most of the destructive portions of the two first essays had never been written. It is this playing with probabilities, this deliberate attempt to live in a twilight land of semi-faith, which caused so much consternation among those of Mill's disciples who had fed themselves on his earlier work. God is declared to be, though not omnipotent, yet always benevolent; albeit that the main object of the Essay on Nature was to show that natural operations were replete with unreasoning cruelty. There is a shadow of chance that the soul may be immortal, because the physical part of our thinking frame is only a concomitant, not the cause of our mental life.[4] Lastly, if we select all those sayings of Christ which strike us as of the highest value, and reject all those which appear to be merely on the level or below the level of the morality of his age, we are left with a character which is apparently inexplicable on natural and historical grounds. Yet if there was one thing more than another which the sixth book of Mill's *Logic* was designed to teach, it was the notion of a science of social development, in which there could be no breaks, no want of continuity in the natural order. A science of historical sociology could not admit that, at a given period in the world's development, a character arose which had no relation to the past, and no roots in the existing social conditions. Yet here in the last of Mill's writings there is the suggestion that Christ was charged with 'a special, express, and unique commission from God to lead mankind to truth and

---

[4] This consideration would, of course, only lead up to metempsychosis, not personal immortality.

virtue.'⁵ The passage in which these words occur has often been quoted, but it is worth while to quote it once more. If it proves nothing else, it proves how ready Mill was to find some sympathetic alliance with those whose feelings he had so obviously outraged in the earlier essays. On the strength of this passage it has been suggested that Mill was at bottom a religious man. Such a notion is clearly in direct contradiction to the facts of his life. But he was, as we have had many opportunities of seeing, a man of uncommon warmth and intensity of feeling; and it is in the light rather of his emotional than of his religious character that the following words should be regarded: –

> 'Whatever else may be taken away from us by rational criticism, *Christ is still left*; a unique figure not more unlike all his precursors than all his followers, even those who had the direct benefit of his personal teaching....'

This is a striking paragraph on many grounds, and perhaps it is no wonder that Mr. Morley, in reviewing the essay, should have felt that the Mill he knew and admired was slipping from his grasp. But it need cause no wonder to those who accept that conception of Mill's character which it has been the object of these pages to enforce. Let us remind ourselves that Mill had acknowledged as his chief office in the realm of thought to see the truth in the views of opponents, and to put the adversary's case, as was said of him in the House, better than the adversary himself could have put it. The sentences in the *Autobiography* are quite decisive on this point: – 'I thought myself much superior to most of my contemporaries in willingness and ability to learn from anybody; as I found hardly anyone who made such a point of examining what was said in defence of all opinions, however new or however old, in the conviction that even if they were errors there might be a substratum of truth underneath them, and that, in any case, the discovery of what it was that made them plausible would be a benefit to truth.' ... 'Goethe's device, "many-sidedness," was one which I would most willingly have taken for mine.'⁶ A man who takes such a view of his duties would be likely enough to astonish his more dogmatic and more logical friends.

---

⁵ *Essays on Religion*, p. 255.
⁶ *Autobiography*, pp. 163, 242, 243.

In truth, Mill's character was eminently receptive of all the influences to which it was subjected. In his youth the prevailing influence is Bentham and James Mill; then comes the time when Sterling and Carlyle gain a large share of his sympathies; to that succeeds the influence of Mrs. Taylor; and after his wife's death, his views (as in the Essay on Theism, which was composed after his bereavement) seem to swing back on some of the older lines from which her ascendency over his mind had diverted them. It is his mental receptivity which constitutes, perhaps, his chief charm; it is that which explains his aims of reconciliation and mediatorship. But it is this also which gives that *vacillation* which here and there we have noticed in his grasp of doctrines, and leaves us with the final verdict that he belongs to a transitional period of thought. No one but a 'transitional' thinker could, for instance, have written the following sentence in his Essay on Theism – 'It is perfectly conceivable that religion may be morally useful without being intellectually sustainable.' Such a phrase reminds us of the allegorical devices within which the less audacious spirits took refuge in their criticism of early mythology. It is like the Legal Fictions, which serve as a compromise for those who desire to retain the letter while they change the spirit of old institutions. But it is not written in the temper either of the clear-eyed iconoclast, or the constructive reformer. It belongs to the middle period between two eras, when men's thoughts are swaying ἐν μεταιχμιγ σκοτον, in the battle-ground of darkness.

# [FROM] JOHN STUART MILL AND CHRISTIANITY, II
## James Orr

... If there is much in Mr. Mill's teaching that attracts our sympathy, there is necessarily much also which can only be regarded as antagonistic to the complete Christian view. And though, as formerly remarked, Mr. Mill's influence in recent years seems greatly on the wane, his positions are still sufficiently typical to entitle them to serious consideration. Here, first of all, the remark must be hazarded that, with all his distinction as an expounder of logical theory, Mr. Mill cannot be looked upon as pre-eminently a logical thinker. The inconsistencies between his various standpoints and doctrines are, to any one who cares to judge them strictly, enormous. His philosophy is full of paradoxes. Even on subjects non-metaphysical, the contradictions and anomalies into which he falls fill one with astonishment. A few examples of this

### ILLOGICALNESS

may prepare us for judging better of the value of his dicta in some of his arguments against Christianity. As a philosopher, Mr. Mill's position was not essentially different from Hume's, and had he carried his principles out as that thinker did, he would have been a sceptic as Hume was, and not an earnest Positivist. His doctrine was one which theoretically resolved all reality into sensations and association of sensations. Independent entities, whether of mind or of matter, had no place in his system. Logically carried out, this view strikes at the root of all knowledge beyond that of the immediate experience, and lands us, as Hume showed, in philosophical scepticism. It removes from us God, self, and freedom, and in so doing destroys the foundations both of morals and of religion. Yet we have seen Mill, in his three posthumous essays, gravely discussing the question of theism, and arriving at certain positive conclusions in regard to it. We find him arguing for the permanency and separate existence of the soul – 'the thinking and conscious principle' – not only during life, but after death. We find him setting up Matter and Force as self-existent entities outside of the Deity, though, on his own principles, Matter has no existence apart from the minds apprehending it, and Force has no real existence of any kind, causation being resolved by him into simple antecedence and consequence, and the existence of any casual nexus being denied. The idea of some more intimate connection, of some peculiar tie, or mysterious constraint exercised by the antecedent over the consequent is, he tells us in the *Logic*,[1] a delusion which the reason repudiates. There is no such compulsion exercised; causes do not draw their effects after them by a mystical tie. Yet here, in the essay on 'Theism,' we find, as we have seen, Force reappearing – nay, hypostatized, and exhibited as a separate existence, co-eternal with God. These philosophical premises of Mr. Mill come into conflict with his remaining positions in a myriad of other ways. This writer, who has no choice but to be a Necessitarian, is yet an enthusiastic advocate of 'Liberty.' In his essay on that subject he claims for every man the right to think and act for himself, uninfluenced by authority or the opinions of others; while in the essay on 'The Utility of Religion' his thesis is that the benefits at present got from religion might all be secured by a system of rules, if only sufficiently reinforced by authority, education, and social opinion. In the sphere of morals, Mr. Mill's inconsistencies of opinion are not less perplexing. Happiness is the end of action – the test and criterion of what constitutes virtue – yet happiness must not be made the end, but virtue is to be loved and followed after for its own sake; nor are we at liberty to seek our own happiness, but only the happiness of others. Pleasure is the criterion, yet a Socrates dissatisfied is better than a fool satisfied; and so paramount and indefeasible are the claims of virtue, that Mr. Mill conceives it would be his duty to go to the place of woe rather than submit to what his moral sense declared to be wrong. In another essay – that on 'Nature' – Mr. Mill maintains that no intelligible sense can be attached to the phrase 'follow Nature' as a guide in morals; yet in his *Utilitarianism* he says: 'No reason can be given why the general happiness is desirable, except that each person, so

---

[1] Bk. III, Chap. v.

far as he believes it to be attainable, desires his own happiness,'[2] which is surely but another way of saying that he adopts this end, because it is the end that Nature dictates. As a last example, we may refer to his view that Nature – in which in this connection must be included the course of history – affords no evidence of moral attributes, save only of benevolence, in the Creator; while in nearly the last words of his essay he proclaims that Good is gradually gaining ground over Evil, 'yet gaining it so visibly at considerable intervals as to promise the very distant but not uncertain final victory of Good.'[3]

Reverting again to those positions of Mr. Mill which bear directly on Christianity, we have to touch critically on his views of Theism, of the evidences of Revelation, and of the claims of Christ. Mr. Mill's

## THEISTIC POSITIONS

were outlined with sufficient distinctness in the last paper. The only argument to which he allows any weight in proof of the existence of God is the argument from design in Nature, and this, he grants, yields a balance of probability in favour of creation by intelligence. But this is accompanied by the view that the Creator's power cannot be regarded as unlimited, and that Matter and Force are in all probability independently existing realities, with the intractableness of which the Creator had to contend in the execution of His purposes. Only on this supposition, he thinks, can the evil and imperfection of the world be reconciled with the goodness of the Creator – either that, or there is defect also in his knowledge.

There are two questions here: first, Is it so clear that the existing arrangements of the universe are irreconcilable with infinite power, wisdom, and goodness in its Author? and second, Is the counter-hypothesis of Mr. Mill – one which is tending to be revived by others besides him – philosophically tenable? On what ground, we ask first, does Mr. Mill deny omnipotence to the Creator? One argument which he uses is so extraordinary of its kind that we almost hesitate to delay upon it. The very existence of design, he holds, proves limitation of power. To use means to attain an end implies absence

[2] P. 52.
[3] *Three Essays*, p. 256.

of omnipotence, for omnipotence is able to attain its ends without means. Was ever such reasoning heard before? It is practically equivalent to saying that omnipotence could not create a finite world at all; for if a finite world is to be created, there must be adaptation of means to ends in its arrangements. 'Infinite power and wisdom,' as an able writer has pointed out, 'must necessarily work under limitations when they originate and control finite things; but the limitations are not in the infinite power and wisdom themselves, they are in their operations and effects.'[4] The limitation asserted, therefore, must be proved, if provable at all, from the character of the effects; and here Mr. Mill offers us the alternative that either the Creator is limited in power, or He is limited in benevolence and justice; for the evils of the world are such, he thinks, that only the most unblushing jesuitry can reconcile their existence with the assumption of a Being *at once* all powerful and all-good. We admit the difficulty which Mr. Mill urges. The existence of natural and moral evil is a problem which it is difficult to find a solution for on the assumption of an all-wise, all-good God. It is one thing, however, to say that we cannot see fully how certain things are to be reconciled with the character and government of God, and an immense step beyond to say that they *cannot* be reconciled. Even without taking into account what Mr. Mill ignores – that much physical pain and evil in the world have relation to a state of sin – it seems a very daring thing to say that in the far-reaching plans of an infinite mind there can be no justification of such a fact as physical suffering, for it is this aspect that Mr. Mill chiefly insists on. To our mind, it is the existence of moral evil which constitutes by far the greater difficulty. If all the pain and sorrow which have their origin directly or indirectly in human sin, or imprudence, or folly could be eliminated from the world, the problem would be reduced to manageable dimensions indeed. Mr. Mill may then ask, Why does God permit sin? That question we cannot answer, and do not need to answer. Sin originates in the will of the creature, and God's relation to it is that of permission and subsequent control – in the case of humanity, of gracious interposition in redemption – and this with a view to ends which, as infinite wisdom beheld

---

[4] Flint, on *Theism*.

them, made this particular plan of government the wisest and the best. Is Mr. Mill in a position to criticize it? Would he not require to be in the position of the infinite intelligence that devised it before he could do so satisfactorily?

In his zeal to prove that Nature exhibits no trace or shadow of moral attributes in the Creator, save only, in a limited degree, of benevolence, Mr. Mill must be held guilty of gross exaggeration. Verily, the prophets and teachers of our race have been widely astray, if there are not discernible any traces of a moral government of the world. We had thought it was a commonplace that a life of vice entailed upon the transgressor physical penalties, not to speak of mental, moral, and social penalties; we had thought there was truth in the statement that righteousness exalteth a nation, and that vice as invariably corrupts and destroys it; we had believed Butler when he taught that 'in the natural course of things, virtue as such is actually rewarded, and vice as such is punished,'[5] and Matthew Arnold when he assured us that the one thing 'verifiable' in nature and history is that there is 'a Power not ourselves that makes for righteousness.' This is what human beings as yet generally believe, and we are not convinced that Mr. Mill has shown any good reasons to the contrary.

Mr. Mill, however, while holding that we have no positive grounds for attributing moral perfection to the Creator, yet thinks, as we formerly saw, that we do well to cherish belief in His infinite wisdom and goodness. What men do believe in, he imagines, is the idea of excellence in their own minds, which, despite appearances, they persist in regarding as embodied in the Divine Being. But the question arises regarding this ideal, Whence came it? Is it a mere fancy, a subjective creation, the factitious product of association and custom, having no authority beyond what association and custom give it? If so, by what right does Mr. Mill apply it as a standard to the Divine Being, and presume to judge Him by it at all? If, on the other hand, this ethical ideal represents something absolute and unconditioned, something valid for all moral beings, therefore for Deity Himself, then, plainly, we cannot refuse to accept the testimony which comes from it to the character of Deity. However its origin is conceived, it must be recognized that

---

[5] *Analogy*, Part I., Chap. iii.

man has been so constituted by his Creator as to arrive at the knowledge of it, and to approve of it when he does know it. How, then, can the conclusion be avoided that the Creator also entertains this ideal of excellence, and regulates His action according to its laws? And this, in another form, is simply the moral argument, which Mr. Mill rejects. The truth is, that great as is the difficulty of the existence of moral and natural evil on the assumption of an infinitely wise and good Creator, the problem would not be lightened, but would be unspeakably darker and more difficult, if we could not believe that there was perfect wisdom and goodness behind, and could not trust in it for an ultimate solution. Nor is the issue uncertain. Mr. Mill, as we have seen, is firm in his conviction that Good is gaining ground over Evil – gaining it so visibly as 'to promise the very distant but not uncertain final victory of Good.' Yet he thinks there is no evidence of moral government!

A few words may suffice to dispose of Mr. Mill's counter-hypothesis

### OF DUALISM

Matter and Force, he thinks, are eternally subsisting, independent realities, by which the Creator is conditioned and hampered in His work. Hence the imperfections of the visible universe. This is not quite the old Platonic or Aristotelian dualism, for there Matter was simply a formless substratum, a naked *hyle*, without qualities or properties of any kind. In Mr. Mill's view, both Matter and Force have eternally existed, with all the properties and laws which at present belong to them, 'working together and fitting into each other.' Such a supposition is philosophically so untenable that it is difficult to understand how a mind of the acuteness of Mr. Mill's could for a moment entertain it. Not to speak of the objection which may be taken to all dualism, that it supposes two absolutes in the universe, perfectly unrelated to each other, yet capable of entering into relation; it may be pointed out that Mill's theory supposes the existence, not of the two absolutes alone, but of millions and millions of absolutes; for every separate atom of matter is a distinct absolute; yet somehow these absolutes all exist in relation to each other, have properties which have reference to each other, and are capable of 'working together, and of fitting into each other' – a fact of which no explanation is afforded. But there is a yet more conclusive answer to this hypothesis on Mr. Mill's own principles. What, on the face of it, could be more crude than the idea of a creator working from without on a material already endowed with all manner of laws and properties – a determinate, definite material – which yet he had no hand in producing? Mill grants the existence of design in Nature. He infers intelligence from the existence of order and final cause. But is not this definite constitution of matter – these orderly relations which subsist between the elements, these laws of number, proportion, measure, size, weight, which belong to them, their reciprocal actions and adaptations, themselves so many proofs of an intelligible constitution of things? Strip matter of all that the Aristotelian would call 'form,' and what remains that is thinkable? Clothe it with laws and properties, and you attribute to it that which it needs intelligence to account for. How, for instance, are we to account for the precise similarity of all atoms belonging to the same class? Here we have incalculable myriads of simple bodies, each of which in size, structure, and properties is an exact copy of the rest. Must we not fall back on Herschell's principle that 'when we see a great number of things precisely alike, we do not believe this similarity to have originated, except from a common principle independent of them'; and must we not assent to his conclusion, 'The discoveries alluded to effectually destroy the idea of one eternal, self-existent matter, by giving to each of its atoms the essential characters at once of a manufactured article and a subordinate agent'?[6] To account for the existence of such matter and force as we know, without the assumption of a presiding creative mind, is a mystery greater than any other which Mr. Mill has enumerated.

If these Theistic speculations of Mr. Mill have been dwelt on at what may seem undue length, the reason is that it is these Theistic views which really govern all his remaining religious opinions. They determine, for example, his theoretical position on the question of immortality, the common arguments for which, he admits, might be valid if we could believe in the perfect power and perfect goodness of the Creator. They affect also his views on the

---

[6] Quoted, with approval, by Clerk Maxwell, Tait, &c.

## EVIDENCES OF REVELATION

a subject on which we shall now offer a few words. That Mr. Mill does not absolutely reject revelation is evident from a remarkable sentence already quoted. 'To the conception of the rational sceptic,' he says, 'it remains a possibility that Christ actually was what He supposed Himself to be... a man charged with a special, express, and unique commission from God, to lead mankind to truth and virtue.'[7] Here is an admission of the possibility of revelation, of the possibility even of the truth of the Christian revelation, yet it is held that no clear proof exists which can raise this possibility to a certainty. We have to look at the theoretic grounds on which Mr. Mill maintains these various positions. And first, Mr. Mill goes a long way with the believer in revelation in the admission of its *possibility*. On this point he is clear. As Nature affords independent evidence of the existence of an intelligent Creator, and also, to some extent, of His regard for the happiness of His creatures, no antecedent improbability attaches to the idea that He might give further proof of His concern for them 'by communicating to them some knowledge of Himself beyond what they were able to make out by their unassisted faculties, and some knowledge or precepts useful for guiding them through the difficulties of life.'[8] We would put this more strongly, and say, that granted a benevolent and wise Creator, there is a positive presumption in favour of such revelation. The next question which rises is as to the means by which a revelation, supposing one to be given, could be proved. Here Mill adopts the usual division into internal and external evidences, and discusses the two kinds separately. His view on the internal evidence is that it is not sufficient to prove a revelation, for the reason (urged also by Mr. Greg) that what the mind can recognize the excellence of, it may be capable also of discovering for itself – a very fallacious argument, on which, however, we need not dwell. Internal evidence, nevertheless, he thinks, though it cannot prove, may *disprove* a revelation, for if the moral character of an alleged revelation is bad, this alone is proof that it cannot have come from a good and wise Being. We might point out here that on Mr.

[7] *Three Essays*, p. 255.
[8] *Three Essays*, p. 215.

Mill's own principles this scarcely touches the question, seeing that, according to him, there is no absolute evidence that the Creator *is* a perfectly good and wise Being; and seeing, further, that the account he gives of the origin of our moral ideas does not warrant us in erecting them into a standard for the Supreme Being. The first of these points he himself recognizes, when he is led to argue that we ought not to be stumbled even by the difficulties and imperfections of Christianity – these furnishing 'no reason whatever,' he says, 'against its having come from a Being such as the course of Nature points to'[9] – a Being of limited attributes. This is an ingenious adaptation of Butler's reasoning, but it is very futile as respects the case in hand. It cannot be questioned that the God whom Christ reveals is not Mr. Mill's Deity of limited power and benevolence, but a God of infinite power, majesty, holiness, and love. Either, therefore, Mr. Mill's idea of Deity must be given up, or Christ's revelation must be rejected as untrue. On the whole, however, it is granted that Christianity, in its pure form, sufficiently satisfies moral tests to warrant in passing as a possibly true revelation.

Internal evidence being thus set aside, we are brought back practically to the position of the old Paley school, that the only thing which can positively certify or attest a revelation is the external evidence of

## MIRACLE

Here again Mr. Mill unquestionably renders an important service to Christianity in the clearness with which he has shown, in opposition to those who affirm the impossibility of miracles, that a miracle is no contradiction of the law of the uniformity of Nature in any sense in which that phrase can be used by science. The law in question affirms no more than that, given the same antecedents, the same consequences invariably follow. But a miracle is expressly the assertion of a new cause, and that, too, as Mr. Mill shows, if the evidence of Theism is admitted, of a *vera causa*. There is, therefore, no *a priori* ground for affirming the impossibility of a miracle; the only question relates to the evidence of its actually having been wrought. All the same, Mr. Mill does not feel at liberty to accept the Gospel miracles. His objections to them turn on

---

[9] *Three Essays*, p. 214.

the presumption against miracles derived from God's ordinary method of governing the universe; on the precariousness of the inference from the goodness of God, as a ground for believing that He will give a revelation; on the poor opinion he has of the value of the evidence for the miracles; and, finally, on the supposition that, even if faithfully reported, the works may be due to unknown natural causes. This last suggestion, it seems to us, may with great confidence be put aside, for few will doubt that if the works of Jesus in giving sight to the blind, healing the lepers, raising the dead really happened as recorded, they are not to be accounted for except as the effects of supernatural power. The other reasons, it may also be noticed, partly nullify each other. If, on its own merits, the evidence of the Gospel miracles is as poor as Mr. Mill alleges, there is no need of going into questions of antecedent presumption. If, on the other hand, that evidence is good, much weight cannot be attached to the negative presumption from the ordinary course of nature, in face of his own admission that miracles are possible, and that only by means of miracles can a supernatural revelation be adequately attested. His argument, in fact, amounts nearly to this: It is possible and reasonable that God should give mankind a revelation, but it is impossible for Him ever to prove that He has given one; as the only way He could do it is by miracles, and the presumption against miracles is always so great as to shake our confidence in their really having happened. We do not agree with Mill in basing the evidence for Christianity entirely on external miracles, yet, as we admit that miracles are an important branch of evidence, it is impossible for us to acquiesce in so self-stultifying a conclusion as the above. Assuming that it is God's will to give a real revelation to mankind, the presumption is in favour of miracles accompanying it, and the question resolves itself ultimately into one of evidence, whether, all things being taken into consideration, we can reasonably believe that the alleged miracles actually were wrought. On this point, it seems to us that Mr. Mill does anything but justice to the evidence for

### THE MIRACLES OF CHRIST

There are those with whom it might be necessary to conduct a lengthened argument on this subject, but Mr. Mill himself has laid the ground for a very brief and satisfactory reply.

When, for instance, he bids us remember that the original eye-witnesses were men of no standing or education, ready in their ignorance to believe anything they saw to be a miracle, &c., we are entitled to recall his own words in speaking of the Gospels: 'It is of no use to say that Christ as exhibited in the Gospels is not historical, and that we know not how much that is admirable has been superadded by the tradition of followers. . . . Who among His disciples, or among their proselytes, was capable of inventing the sayings ascribed to Jesus, or of imagining the life and character revealed in the Gospels? Certainly not the fishermen of Galilee.'[10] The fishermen did not invent these sayings of Christ, this portraiture of Christ, but *they transmitted them*; and the fact that they have done so with the perfection which Mr. Mill acknowledges is a testimony to their genuine sympathy with Christ, their rare power of appreciating His greatness, and their absolute fidelity as witnesses of His words and works. It was the same men who transmitted the words who transmitted also the narratives of the works; and their fitness to do the one is the evidence of their fitness to do the other. It is useless to ascribe the sayings to Christ while attempting to explain the miracles as assertions of a 'later tradition,' for more and more the criticism of the Gospels compels us to recognize that both narratives and discourses rest on undoubted Apostolic testimony. The miracles, moreover, are not 'insertions' in the sense of external appendages, which may be cut out, and leave the remainder of the narrative intact; they enter into the very web of the story, are bound up with Christ's most characteristic and indubitably original words, and form essential features in the *tout ensemble* of that portraiture of Christ on which Mill himself bestows such lavish praise. If the sayings could not be invented by the fishermen of Galilee, as little certainly could the miracles, which for the most part, bear precisely the same impress of simplicity, originality, dignity, and superiority to anything which credulous minds were likely to invent, as do the other acts and words of Christ.

There is only one thing more that need here be said. If Jesus Christ was what He supposed Himself to be, and this, says

---

[10] *Three Essays*, p. 253.

Mr. Mill, must always to the rational sceptic remain a possibility, He was

### MORE THAN MR. MILL ALLOWS

– more than mere man. We do not need to go to the Gospel of St. John in proof of this. We find it interwoven with every claim which Christ makes in the Synoptics as well. Did Mr. Mill, for example, ever ponder what was involved in an undoubtedly genuine part of Christ's claim – His claim to be the Judge of the world, the Arbiter of the everlasting destinies of mankind? Does this involve, or does it not, the possession of attributes higher than the human? Yet this is only a specimen of the manifold ways in which Christ, while on earth, arrogated supernatural greatness to Himself. Character and works here are of a piece. We need not reject the miracles, while allowing the supernatural claims to stand, for the one as well as the other points beyond the limits of the human. Christ did not come into the world merely to be a teacher and guide to virtue, as Mr. Mill in his rationalizing way supposes, but to be a Redeemer from sin; and it is through his weak hold on the idea of sin that Mr. Mill misses the clue to all the higher aspects of the Saviour's character and work. With all his mental and moral progress, this defect of his early training remained with him. We cannot wonder at it. The truer marvel is that he advanced so far.

The result of this survey, in relation to the truth of the Christian religion, is greatly to enhance our sense of the security of its defences. It is not unjust to say that Mr. Mill's adverse criticism of the claims of revelation presents little that is new or important, or likely to produce a permanent impression on the minds of present-day readers; while his counter theories of a limited Deity, and of the origin of evil in physical limitations, will receive no support in the temper of the age. What will live is the growing recognition which his writings manifest of the need and value of theistic and religious hopes; of the worth of the hope of immortality; of the legitimacy of the ideas of miracle and of revelation; above all, his glowing tribute to Him whose name he acknowledges with us to be above every name.

# [FROM] JOHN STUART MILL: A STUDY OF HIS PHILOSOPHY
## Charles Douglas

... When he comes to examine the natural order, Mill finds its relation to morality hard to make out. He sees 'no shadow of justice in the general arrangements of Nature.'[1] He maintains that nature is an incessant performance of acts which would be condemned as immoral if done by a human agent, and that it cannot be made a law or example for human conduct: 'nearly all the things which men are hanged or imprisoned for doing to one another, are nature's everyday performances.'[2] Nature is reckless, cruel, and destructive. The natural order is a source of misery no less than of happiness; and its distribution of pain and pleasure cannot be shown either to secure a balance of well-being, or to have any tendency to promote virtue: it 'is constructed with even less regard to the requirements of justice than to those of benevolence.'[3]

Nature, as it appears in human character, has no more authority for conduct than non-human nature has. 'Nearly every respectable attribute of humanity is the result not of instinct, but of a victory over instinct;'[4] and 'there is hardly a single point of excellence belonging to human character, which is not decidedly repugnant to the untutored feelings of human nature.' Even such rudiments of virtue as courage, cleanliness, self-control, and justice are all unnatural or artificial, in the sense of requiring for their development a discipline of natural inclinations. They are only established as the result of an effort:

---

[1] Ibid., p. 194.
[2] Essays on Religion, p. 28.
[3] Ibid., p. 37.
[4] Ibid., p. 46.

in so far as man is distinguished from nature, they are of human and not of natural origin.[5]

In this way, 'conformity to nature has no connection whatever with right and wrong;'[6] and the fact 'that a feeling is bestowed on us by Nature, does not necessarily legitimate all its promptings.'[7] Divine government is carried on, 'not by the mere indulgence of our natural tendencies, but by the regulation and control of them;'[8] and 'the duty of man is the same in respect to his own nature as in respect to the nature of all other things, namely, not to follow but to amend it.'[9] In fact, Mill's whole indictment of nature is meant to show that nature is not the source of moral law. When nature is taken to mean the whole system of things, including man, it is idle to enjoin conformity to natural laws or to give them 'moral' meaning; and when human efforts and ideals are excluded from nature, then nature ceases to be a reliable guide. 'While human action cannot help conforming to Nature in the one meaning of the term, the very aim and object of action is to alter and improve Nature in the other meaning.'[10]

The significance of Mill's criticism of nature appears in this conclusion. Moral good is relative to human needs, and it depends no less on human exertions. The demand which man makes upon nature returns upon himself. That limitation of the power of the divine beneficence, by which Mill expresses rather than explains the mysterious failure of nature, leaves something for man to do. Apart from man, nature realises no end, and is capable of no explanation. Mill's criticism thus proves itself to be double-edged. Even when it seems to weaken the authority of moral ideals by finding no ground for them in nature, it becomes at the same time, in Mill's hands, an additional necessity for the moral life. Man can expect nothing from nature on this theory. Nature is, at best, only the opportunity of goodness; and morality will not exist unless the effort

---

[5] Essays on Religion, pp. 46–53.

[6] Ibid., p. 62.

[7] Utilitarianism, p. 62.

[8] Examination of Hamilton, p. 171.

[9] Essays on Religion, p. 54.

[10] Essays on Religion, p. 19.

of men originates it. Nor is this all. Nature's failure to realise that divine end, which is manifest in the facts of the world as well as in man's spiritual life, leaves the burden of the world upon man himself. Only his effort can give to nature that meaning which he himself demands in it: only his obedience and faith can realise the divine purpose, and work out those ends in relation to which alone the world is intelligible. 'The earnest expectation of the creature waiteth for the manifestation of the sons of God:' the moral life is a divine necessity – a claim which the purpose revealed in things makes upon the character and personality of men. In this, as in other aspects of his philosophy, Mill betrays his profoundly ethical interest.[11]

On the other hand, this essentially religious conception of the moral life of man can hardly be reconciled with the individualistic Deism which is expressed in Mill's natural theology. It contains a view of man's relations, both to the natural world and to the Divine Spirit, which seems to count for nothing in the more official attempt to define those relations. In so far as human effort is the vehicle or instrument of the Divine Spirit, it constitutes a revelation of divine ends to which Mill gives little heed when he sets out explicitly to collect evidence for his theodicy; and, in so far as it is capable of redeeming the natural order from complete failure, it must belong to that order in such a way as to turn the edge of Mill's criticism, and make it impossible to convict nature of unspirituality.

Mill's assertion that the divine power is limited, and the indictment of nature on which that assertion is based, are made in forgetfulness of his own recognition of man's membership in the natural order. There is, indeed, nothing in that order, taken by itself, which can be called 'moral,' except by a figure of speech. Things must always be without moral significance, except in so far as they enter into experience, and become related to self-consciousness. Further, it may appear that the net result of nature, so far as experience has access to it, is pain; and this, if it be the case, condemns nature absolutely from a hedonistic point of view. It may appear, too, that moral failure, no less than virtue, has its roots in nature; and this would make it impossible to regard nature as a moral example, however far the natural pedigree of man's moralities might be

---

[11] Cf. Essays on Religion, pp. 37 ff., 256, &c.

traced back. But that very relation of man to nature, which makes it possible to criticise natural laws and facts as means to an end, renders the criticism of nature, taken in abstraction from human life, irrelevant and futile. In so far as nature can be criticised, it must include all the human facts; since it is the presence of man in nature that makes nature significant. But when the world is seen as the sphere and opportunity and potency of human life, with its ideal interests and its divine significance, things are no longer outside the divine purpose, so far as that purpose is open to human comprehension. It is true that our experience only gives effect, in an inadequate and partial way, even to our most limited ideas of good; and it can never be forgotten how little likely these ideas are to exhaust the demand that might be made upon things. But the inclusion of man in nature is fatal to that perverse cleavage of reality which makes the world independent of God.

Man himself, dependent on nature for his very life, and yet for himself, and first, and finally, neither machine, nor brute, but spirit, is the living refutation of all attempts to fix an absolute gulf between the natural order and the spiritual interests. So long as he lives by bread, and hungers still for every word that comes out of the mouth of God, so long will it be impossible to persuade him that nature is unspiritual; and it is because Mill's topic is human life, that the bonds of Deism cannot wholly restrain him from the attempt to interpret the natural world in terms of self-conscious reason.

# [FROM] THE ENGLISH UTILITARIANS
## Leslie Stephen

... Mill, we see, declared positivism to be reconcilable with theism. Comte himself, who declared atheism to be the most illogical form of theology, would have agreed that positivism does not disprove God's existence. But Comte would have said that an unverifiable hypothesis about an inconceivable being was simply idle or 'otiose.' Mill seems to treat the absence of negative proof as equivalent – not indeed to the presence of positive, but – to the existence of a probability worth entertaining. His theism, if so vague and problematical a doctrine can be called theism, is defended as neither self-contradictory nor inconsistent with fact. Now a theory which is self-contradictory is really no theory at all. Nor is a theory scientifically valuable simply because 'consistent' with facts. A theory must have some definite support in facts. It must at lowest be not only consistent with the known facts, but inconsistent with some otherwise imaginable facts. If it fits every conceivable state of things, it can throw light upon none. But this is obviously the case with Mill's theory. He makes way for a good being by an arbitrary division of nature into two sets of forces. He saves the benevolence by limiting the power of the deity; but then the limits are, by his own admission, utterly unknowable. A power, restrained by unknowable bounds, is a power from which nothing can be inferred. Whatever its attributes, we do not know whether they will affect any state of things. The goodness may be indefinitely frustrated. In fact, on Mill's showing, a power omnipotent but not benevolent, or an indefinite multitude of powers of varying attributes, or a good and a bad power eternally struggling, or, in short, any religious doctrine that has ever been held among men, would suit the facts. Mill's 'plurality of causes' might have suggested this difficulty. I see a corpse. The death may have been due to any one of an indefinite number of causes. What right have I to select one? I am in the same position when I regard the whole of nature as what Hume called a 'unique effect.' The four methods of induction become inapplicable, for there are no other universes and I have no compass to steer by in the region of the unverifiable.

What, then, can be the advantage of any belief where conflicting hypotheses must be all equally probable? The question is partly discussed in the second essay upon the utility of Religion. Here Mill takes up the old argument of 'Philip Beauchamp,' the 'only direct discussion' of the point with which he is acquainted,[1] and endeavours to state the case more fairly and in a less hostile spirit. His argument, however, is in general conformity with Bentham and Grote, and is very forcibly put. One point may be noticed. He virtually identifies 'religion' with a belief in 'the supernatural.'[2] He compares the efficacy of such beliefs with the efficacy of education (which, as he characteristically says, is 'almost boundless')[3] and of public opinion, and shows with 'Beauchamp' that when conflict occurs, these influences are stronger than those derived from supernatural sanctions. Now when we believe in a revelation it is intelligible to ask, What is the influence of a creed? It represents a new force influencing men's minds from without. But when the creed is supposed to be generated from antecedent beliefs, the argument must be altered by considering what are the true causes of the belief. How did it come to prevail? An admirer of Comte might have brought out more distinctly the fact that such beliefs mark an essential stage of progress, that what are now sporadic superstitions were once parts of a systematic religion and represented the germs of science. They were approximate hypotheses which had to be remodelled by extricating or dropping the 'supernatural' element. A full recognition of this would diminish the paradoxical appearance of the statement from which he starts, that 'a religion may be morally useful without being intellectually sustainable.' The truth surely is that we cannot separate the two elements of a creed. Doubtless there were no such beings as the Zeus or Apollo of popular belief; but polytheism may still have provided the only form in which certain truths could

---

[1] *Three Essays*, p. 76.

[2] *Ibid.* p. 100.

[3] *Ibid.* p. 82.

be presented; and was, as Comte would have said, a stage in the process from fetishism towards monotheism and positivism. A discussion of the utility of belief in the 'supernatural' without reference to the place of the supernatural in the whole system of belief must be necessarily inadequate. Mill admits this in substance, and argues that the moral truth may survive the superstitions in which it was bound up.[4] He goes on to argue, as Comte had argued, that the instincts which once found their sanction in the supernatural world might find their embodiment in the 'Religion of Humanity.'[5] This he holds to be not only entitled to the name of religion, but to be 'a better religion than any of those ordinarily called by that title.' It is disinterested and does not tend to cramp the intellect or degenerate into a worship of mere power. Mill says emphatically that the Bentham mode of considering religion as a supplement to police by providing 'sanctions' is inadequate; and that religion, like poetry, is valuable as suggesting higher ideals and gratifying the craving for knowledge of corresponding realities. To the selfish, supernatural religion offers heaven; and to the 'tender and grateful' it offers the love of God. He points out that it does not follow that we must 'travel beyond the boundaries of the world we inhabit' in order to obtain such consolation.[6] And the essay concludes by saying that, though the 'supernatural religions' have always the advantage of offering immortality, the value set upon immortality may diminish as life becomes higher and happier and annihilation may seem more desirable.[7]

Yet in the middle of this argument we have the defence of Manichæism as a possible creed,[8] and in the last essay we seem to reach the true account of his leanings to such a belief. He still, that is, requires a breathing-space for the imagination. 'Truth is the province of reason,' but 'in the regulation of the imagination literal truth of facts is not the only thing to be

---

[4] *Three Essays*, p. 97.
[5] Ibid. p. 111.
[6] Ibid. p. 104.
[7] *Three Essays*, p. 122.
[8] Ibid. p. 116.

considered.'[9] Reason must keep the fortress, but the 'imagination may safely follow its own end and do its best to make life pleasant and lovely inside the castle.' Thus, though we are only entitled to hope as to the government of the world and a life after death, the bare hope may have a beneficial effect. 'It makes life and human nature a far greater thing to the feelings, and gives greater strength and solemnity to all the sentiments which are awakened in us by our fellow-creatures and mankind at large.' Aspirations are no longer checked by the disastrous feeling of 'not worth while.' Religion, too, has set before us a 'Divine Person, as a standard of excellence and a model for imitation.'[10] The ideal, it is true, would remain, even if the person were held to be imaginary; and would not be encumbered by theological difficulties. Yet there is an advantage in the belief that a perfect being really exists and represents the ruler of the universe, which cannot be shared by the rationalist.[11] Hence as, after all, the truth of the belief is possible, it may be combined with the Religion of Humanity. That religion, 'with or without supernatural sanctions,' will be the religion of the future; but it will be strengthened by the feeling that we are 'helping God' and supplying 'co-operation' which 'he, not being omnipotent, really needs.'[12] Truly, Mill was nearly qualified for a place among the prophets.

Mill's arbitrary assumptions, like the metaphysical wiredrawings of Mansel, are rather unprofitable in themselves: few people will care to follow them in detail; and neither could boast of many converts. Believers soon became aware of the real scepticism of Mansel's position; and positivists saw that Mill left an opening for superstition. Both Mansel and Mill were troubled about the Religion of Nature. It is abundantly clear, as Mill might have foreseen, that such a theology as he contemplates could be of no real value. It depends essentially upon compromises and arbitrary distinctions. It is still within the sphere of science, though doomed to disappear as science advances, and from the first is inconsistent with the very aims which are proposed by theology. God is admittedly not omnip-

[9] *Ibid.* pp. 248–49.

[10] *Ibid.* p. 253.

[11] *Ibid.* p. 252.

[12] *Three Essays*, pp. 256–57.

otent, and his existence is no guarantee for morality or optimism. And hence there is an odd approximation between Mill and Mansel.

Mill observes[13] that the moral character of an alleged revelation cannot be of itself a proof of its divinity. The importance of the 'internal evidence' is therefore 'principally negative.' So says Mansel. 'The evidence derived from the internal character of a religion, whatever may be its value within its proper limits, is, as regards the divine origin of the religion, purely negative.'[14] Where is the difference? If the morality of a revelation be bad, Mill argues that the revelation must be at once rejected. Mansel thinks that although the morality be not clearly good, it may in some way represent a divine command. Immoral laws cannot be divine, says Mill, though a good law may be human. A law apparently bad, replies Mansel, may be divine, though, of course, the badness can only be apparent. Here, as elsewhere, the believer in the empirical character of morality appears to attribute most certainty to the moral judgment. The solutions differ accordingly. Mill supposes that God must be good, but reconciles this to facts by assuming that God is not all-powerful. Mansel will not give up the power, and to preserve the goodness has to assume a radical incapacity in the intellect – a necessity of believing where there is an impotence of conceiving. Mill, that is, is content with the empirical deity, who is necessarily limited; and Mansel keeps the deity of ontology but admits that he cannot be known. Mill's conception is purely arbitrary, though he keeps within the limits of conceivable experience; while Mansel preserves the language appropriate to the conception of absolute unity, and yet admits that it can mean nothing for us. 'Agnosticism' seems to be an easier and more rational alternative, if it means an open admission that we know nothing, when we can only save our appearance of knowledge by arbitrary assumptions or by the use of meaningless words. Of Mill's position it must be frankly admitted that his desire for a religious and even supernatural belief is a proof of dissatisfaction with his own position. He felt here, as elsewhere, that something was wanting in his philosophy. What that really was may partly appear by con-

---

[13] *Ibid.* p. 216.

[14] *Bampton Lectures*, p. 238.

sidering other contemporary solutions. Mansel represents a particular phase of thought which is already extinct, and views differing both from theirs and from Mill's had in practice a far wider influence than either.

The Utilitarian view naturally identifies a religious creed with a belief in certain historical statements of fact. If the facts be provable the religion is true; if disproved it is false. If there was such a being as Jehovah, it was desirable to worship him; and the creed would then be useful. If there was no such being, worship was folly. The test of the utility of a religion was, therefore, simply the truth or falsehood of its historical statements. If its gods were made by the fancy, not by the reason, the result is a condemnation of religion in general. That is simple and logical, and recognises an indisputable truth. So far as a religion makes false statements, they must be abandoned; and so far as its influence depends upon the falsity, it is pernicious.

A religion, however, represents more than can be estimated by this simple test. The poetical value of Homer is not destroyed by disproving the existence of the Pagan deisms, nor the value of the Hebrew Scriptures by disproving the existence of Jehovah. The facts alleged may be fabulous and absurd; but they are also symbols for setting forth views of the world and of conduct, and so giving emphatic utterance to important truths. The old religions were attempts of men, in early stages of thought, to embody ideals of conduct which may really have been of the highest value to mankind. They were essential, again, to the social bonds which have, in fact, determined the formation of society and facilitated the growth of sympathy and philanthropy. Therefore, if a religious creed be false when interpreted as a simple statement of fact, we have not exhausted its significance or even touched the really most important significance of the religion itself. Believers felt more or less clearly that such attacks as 'Philip Beauchamp' affected only externals, and left the need for religion unsatisfied. Only as the actual creed was pledged to maintain the truth of certain statements, which were daily becoming more incredible, the necessity appeared of finding some stronger position than the old Paley scheme, which virtually regarded religion as a mere statement of historical fact, or as a department of natural science. To trace the consequences would be to write a history of modern theology. I shall try only to indicate the relation to the Utilitarians of a few thinkers. Two main lines of thought were conspicuous in Mill's generation, and correspond to what Newman called 'liberalism' and 'dogmatism.'

# [FROM] THE PHILOSOPHY OF RELIGION IN ENGLAND AND AMERICA
## Alfred Caldecott

The nineteenth century gave us Mill: another Empiricist of Scottish blood. Like Hume, he was a man of wide literary culture, of cosmopolitan interest in affairs, keenly interested in political philosophy, and a master of style. A still further resemblance would no doubt have been found in his negative attitude to Theology, had we not had from Mill his three *Essays*. Like Hume's Dialogues, they were published after the author's death, although they had, in part at least, been in manuscript for years: but the effect was of a contrary kind. Hume's seems to have been reserved lest his many orthodox friends should be shocked, Mill's lest he should be charged by his philosophical associates with abandoning them for at least the rearguard of orthodoxy in Natural Theology. In his case the unexpected was the positive element which had grown into his views on the great question.

The interest of these Essays is due to their context, so to speak: to the eminent position in the history of culture in the nineteenth century won by their author. It was really a remarkable position. Heavily engaged in an important official capacity, home-educated, and living in a small but influential circle of literary and public men, he was so much a Master that in subject after subject as he issued his results they at once became text-books for study at the Universities of which he was not a member. In Political Economy, Logic, Politics, Ethics, the holders of the academic chairs had no chance against him in point of influence as teachers. Many Englishmen and Scotchmen of the generation now in authority in public affairs were brought up when Mill's influence was at its height, and the mark is still visible, but it has almost disappeared from the generation now rising. In Mill we see a fine British tradition taking its highest form: Empiricism and Individualism coming to bloom in Free Trade, and Liberalism, and Inductive Logic;

but now being submerged in the Darwinian and Hegelian broadening out of human thought.

Of these Essays, two on the Nature and Utility of Religion were written in the fifties: the last, *Theism*, about 1870, three years before his death. Taking them together, we find some things that his previous work leads up to, and others which cause surprise. The dissatisfaction with physical nature expressed in the first, and yet the retained trust in human nature, made an unstable position for one whose philosophy could only find a permanent substance behind physical nature, not in the soul of man. In the second Essay the dominance of logic and the precedence of *truth* as the final object of human search were retained, along with a growing recognition that it was not solely on this line that men sought for guidance in life or often found it. But there are protests against 'subornation of evidence' in favour of what men may desire to believe, and the admission of imagination to a place of legitimate influence in forming belief is hesitating and grudging.

The chief change that came was in the intellectual region: the force of what intellect could do and the scope for influence which it could rightly claim was regarded differently. Was Mill led to this by any glimpses of the insufficiency of the Empirical philosophy? It does not appear so. In this last Essay he reiterates his old maxims without any tendency to allow a foot of ground for Traditional Intellectualism or German Idealism. In Theism the Cosmological argument is still disallowed: on his theory of Causation we can get only antecedent events in a series, in which also a lower thing could quite well 'cause' a higher that came after it: all we can say is that the series seems to have commenced, but we can say no more. But here what is perhaps his strongest inconsistency asserts itself. He repeats his belief in one 'Substance,' which is permanent, – he even says 'eternal'; – namely, Matter and Force, as he calls it. This, he thinks, the physical sciences do really disclose, in spite of his reaffirmation of the sensational theory of knowledge. But this is all: no second Substance embarrasses him, none such appears behind the world of Consciousness. The Materialistic influence of his writings is, of course, due to this; for the general reader is sure to rise from them with an increased respect for that part of the universe which is based on a Substance, and a diminished respect for that in which all is only transitory and insubstantial. He might therefore fairly be pressed to mean that the Cosmological argument *is* effective; and that which it proves is that Matter is the basis, the source, the first antecedent, the cause; the substitute for what most men have called the Divine Being. But he does not press it to this point, and as he has no conception of a similarly substantial permanent Mind, he dismisses Cosmological proof altogether. Concerning the Ontological argument he naturally can have little to say: it is still one of the most egregious cases of the 'Fallacy of simple inspection': on his theory of what ideas are and what facts are, no one is concerned to dispute what he says. Of Transcendental proof he has nothing further to say – Hegel had been placed with Plato, and even with the Vedas, in the chapter on Fallacies in Mill's work on Logic, and Mill never saw reason for bringing him from out of that company of 'Mystics,' as he names them.

Neither the Moral argument nor that from Feeling receives admission as a primary factor. Feeling of dependence he thinks powerful, but it comes only after Intellectual action, not before it, and the Moral argument can only tell us about attributes, not about existence. The appeal to Consensus is disallowed: he will have no second-hand evidence.

But where the Essay raised some surprise was in his finding more cogency in the Design argument than he had ever found before. His survey of external Nature and of human history yields considerable evidence for design: not complete, and with some grave exceptions, but still, a preponderating probability: and this evidence is of 'a really scientific character,'[1] and deserves to have influence in the region of belief. And so he follows it up to the position of belief in a Creative mind. He foresees that the new doctrine of Natural selection may weaken the argument again by 'attenuating the evidence,' but he does not do more than simply state this.

Following our Type II. in thus establishing *existence* by an Intellectual argument, he then proceeds to consider what is to be learnt about the attributes. Infinity is quite disallowed, it is far beyond what can be proved. The Moral argument is then taken up: does it enable us to believe that the Creative mind is perfectly Good? He thinks not, if we try to think that it is also all-powerful. The imperfections of the world are set out

[1] P. 167.

in a passage as strong as that in Hume's Dialogues, and the inductive inference is taken to be conclusive against the combination of Might and Goodness. Inasmuch as the very nature of design implies 'contrivance,' as against opposing or resisting power, almightiness is given up: and on the other hand the abandonment of complete goodness is refused: of the alternatives therefore, it is Power which is acknowledged to be incomplete, limited, set over against another power which thwarts it. So we are back on the most ancient track of human thought: a power completely beneficent is behind the world, but it is neither sole creator nor sole governor of it. The duty of man is to take his place on the side of the beneficent Power in the perennial conflict between Good and Evil.

Such being the result of the inference from evidence, he so far repudiates Agnosticism. In a final chapter he steps out from Intellect into the field of Imagination: into the region of our moral and aesthetic life. He now is prepared to give candid recognition to the beneficent effect of allowing such considerations to influence our belief. As compared with the 'moral bribery' and 'subornation of the understanding' of Essay II., we have in III., 'Literal truth is not the only thing to be considered.' To retain beliefs because they elevate morals and inspire ideals has become to him even a mark of 'wisdom.'

He is very fair in disallowing many of the stock charges brought against the influence of Religion, but as he himself goes on to withdraw from its sphere much of what has been done in its name as really due to social opinion and ordinary morality, he feels no need for himself to go beyond a Religion of Humanity, even in the region of imagination and sentiment.

All that Theism can claim for this final deliverance is that Mill has consented to a partial removal of the case from the closed court of logical estimation of evidence, and that within even that court he has parted from Atheism and Agnosticism to the extent of seeing enough evidence for a Creative Mind. Against this must be set the ultimate limitation of Creative power: his reiteration that 'Matter and Force' is eternally in the background, and not Mind; and his own contentment, in the realm of Imagination and Feeling, with a world-view in which humanity is the highest object of regard, its welfare the highest goal of effort.

There are in these Essays some indications that the grave and sincere conscientiousness of Mill had its reward. In a sense he died young: there was within him a germ which his span of life did not suffice to mature. True, no other intellectual vision was clearly attained by him than his old logic gave. But the old Individualism was struggling with ampler views: in the eloquent passage on Authority in Essay II., as in those on Socialism in his later Economic writings, and the passages on social influence in Morals which glisten in his *Utilitarianism*, we see a growing recognition of the moral and imaginative sides of life: and prospects open out of more spacious fields into which his earnest and solid mind might have carried him had another period of mental activity been permitted him.

If between Mill and Hume there were strong likenesses, not least in their singular ability to rest intellectually on the narrowest ridge of philosophy which has ever satisfied British minds, there was also a difference. The gravity and pellucid sincerity of Mill was the mark of a nobler character than Hume's. The expression of his views in a Dialogue in which the most careful reader is mystified as to what belief the writer is recommending, if any at all, on so grave a subject as Religion was below Mill altogether: no man can speak of sophistries in connection with his name.